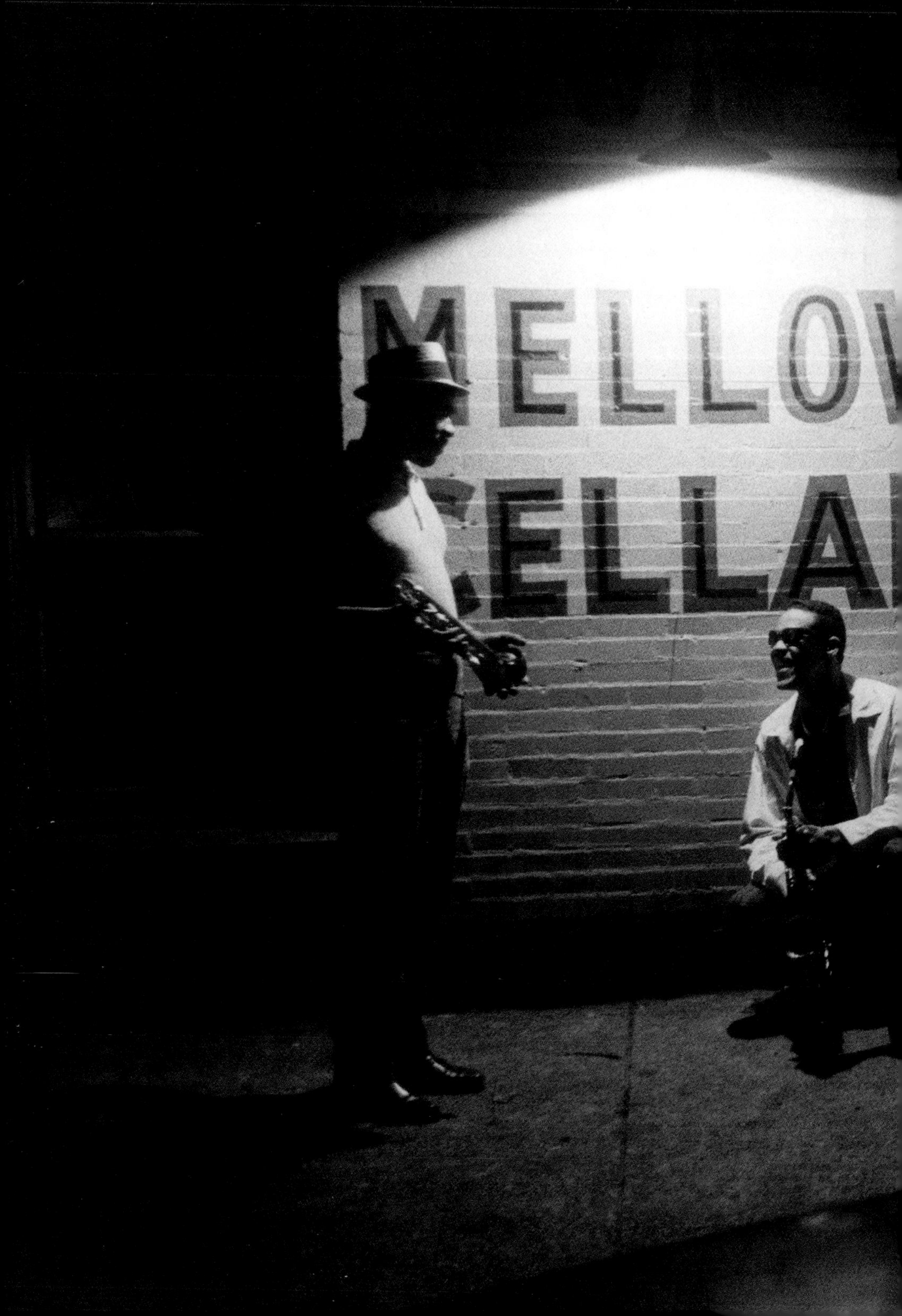
MELLO
ELLA

Joaquim Paulo
Ed. Julius Wiedemann

JAZZ COVERS

TASCHEN

CONTENTS

CTI
AC-30.018
STEREO

BOB CIANO

As art director during the busiest years of Creed Taylor's CTI, Kudu and Salvation labels, Bob Ciano helped to construct CTI's signature style, designing covers for an incredible roster of jazz legends. The label's lush and intricate recordings called for covers that could visually match the perfected sounds pressed on the vinyl. Today you can still recognize a CTI record cover from 20 yards away. From the simple, clean layouts and wonderful Pete Turner photos, to the high-gloss laminated finish, CTI's packaging looked more like a luxury gift presentation than a record sleeve. The cover designs do as much to capture CTI's time and place as do the recordings themselves. Bob Ciano's illustrious career as an art director has seen him shape the design and layout of many renowned publications such as *Life, The New York Times, Esquire, Travel + Leisure, Encyclopaedia Britannica, The Industry Standard, Forbes ASAP,* and *Opera News.*

Bob Ciano trug zu den besten Zeiten von Creed Taylors Labels CTI, Kudu und Salvation als Art Director dazu bei, den CTI-eigenen Stil zu schaffen, indem er die Cover für unzählige Jazzlegenden entwarf. Für die großartigen, aufwendigen Aufnahmen des Labels wurden Plattenhüllen kreiert, die perfekt zu dem auf Vinyl gepressten Sound passten. Noch heute kann man ein CTI-Cover aus zwanzig Metern Entfernung erkennen. Vom einfachen, klaren Layout und den wunderbaren Fotos von Pete Turner bis hin zu den Hochglanzcovern wirkten die Plattenhüllen von CTI wie Luxusartikel.

Die Coverentwürfe nahmen bei CTI genauso viel Zeit in Anspruch wie die Aufnahmen selbst. Bob Ciano hat in seiner glänzenden Karriere als Art Director das Design und Layout zahlreicher berühmter Publikationen wie *Life, The New York Times, Esquire, Travel + Leisure, Encyclopaedia Britannica, The Industry Standard, Forbes ASAP* und *Opera News* gestaltet.

Bob Ciano a été directeur artistique des labels CTI, Kudu et Salvation de Creed Taylor pendant leurs grandes années, et a contribué à la création du style caractéristique de CTI en concevant des pochettes pour une liste impressionnante de légendes du jazz. Les enregistrements somptueux et complexes du label exigeaient des pochettes dont la qualité visuelle correspondrait à la perfection des sons gravés sur le vinyle. Aujourd'hui, on peut encore reconnaître la pochette d'un disque CTI à vingt mètres de distance. Avec leur composition simple et claire, les merveilleuses photos de Pete Turner et leur finition glacée, les pochettes de CTI ressemblaient plus à la présentation d'un cadeau de luxe qu'à une pochette de disque. Le graphisme des pochettes est tout aussi important que les enregistrements eux-mêmes pour définir l'époque de CTI. Au cours de sa carrière illustre de directeur artistique, Bob Ciano a donné forme au graphisme et aux maquettes de nombreuses publications renommées, notamment *Life, The New York Times, Esquire, Travel + Leisure, Encyclopaedia Britannica, The Industry Standard, Forbes ASAP,* et *Opera News.*

DEODATO, *Deodato*, 1972, CTI (see page 162)

Can we talk a little about how you started working for CTI?

I officially became the art director in the early '70s. Before that I'd already done some covers for Columbia. I then did some freelance work for Creed [Taylor], and then he hired me. I stayed there for three years. It was a terrific job.

Are there any particularities to being a designer in the record business? Is it difficult?

It was difficult at Columbia because the artists had a lot of say on the covers. But with Creed they couldn't get involved at all. They were happy just to have covers at all. I could pretty much do what I wanted.

"Creed Taylor had very expensive tastes. You spent what you needed to spend to get the job done right."

This is a dream for any designer... to have total independence.

I used to show them what I was doing, but they were all so polite that they just said it was terrific. I wasn't used to that.

Were the musicians involved in the design process? Did they ever make any suggestions to you?

Hardly ever. I would show them things for them to react to, but very rarely did they come up with any visual suggestions.

When did you meet Creed Taylor?

He called me because I had been working with Pete Turner, the photographer. I was on a ladies magazine called *The Red Book*. They were looking for someone else to do the covers, and I had already done a few. Creed was expanding the office and needed a full-time art director. So he offered me the job.

Creed also had a reputation for not worrying too much about costs. Is this true?

He had very expensive tastes. You spent what you needed to spend to get the job done right. That's why the album covers were all foldout – and very well printed, much better printed than in most companies.

Did CTI have a marketing budget?

If they had a budget nobody knew what it was. I would tell him if something would be very expensive and I don't think he ever said no. The whole office was like that. The physical set up in the Rockefeller Center was beautifully designed offices with beautiful furniture. Everything had to be the best.

CTI had a very unique style and image, which was very modern for its time. Now the hip-hop generation is rediscovering labels like CTI with its image that you helped to create. This must be very flattering for you?

It's strange because in the last couple of years I've been called by people who collect CTI records and covers. And I know from friends that DJs are using them as well. When we were doing it we didn't have any idea of what was happening, we were just doing what we thought was right.

Can you describe the daily life at CTI?

Musicians were all around. People hung out in the art department because it was a big space. We would talk about forthcoming albums and maybe about what the titles would be. Then I would go out working with a small group of photographers and illustrators, trying to find images that might work as covers. I rarely heard the music in advance as I was trying to find images that were eye-catching. It was a small company and we had a very little promotional budget.

What would you do to make people stop and stare at a CTI record in a store?

The covers were used to promote the records in a big way. We used to print extra copies of just the cover and would send them out to stores who put them out on display. We used to give those out for free. Then we started selling the covers – just the image on the printed paper. I think they were sold for a dollar. A lot of people started collecting the covers.

You also designed covers for Creed's other labels like Kudu and Salvation?

Creed started Kudu and Salvation, which was a gospel label, while I was there. For Kudu we used a lot of illustration and different photographers. The covers were beautifully printed.

Was Kudu's image different from CTI's?

It had more of a lustred look. I set up a style which was distinctive. Each album was numbered, Kudu one, Kudu two, and so on.

How do you feel when you go to a record shop these days and see the CTI catalog on CD rather than vinyl?

Sad. They're too small. As a designer you can't make much of a statement on a CD package. There are very few CD packages that are really distinct. The only ones that come to my mind is the stuff that Radiohead does. But as far as the jazz catalog goes, it's very hard to do much on that size.

Can you remember the working process for designing an album cover? Let's take Prelude *by Deodato as an example.*

That's the one with the green cover! That had the 2001 theme on it, I remember. The process was pretty much the same for each one. Creed and I, along with some of the other people in the promotional department, would sit around just talking about the records that would be recorded that month.

There were usually several. I'd go out and start thinking about what images I could use, either by photographing something myself, or I'd go to a photographer I worked with regularly to see if they had any existing images that weren't being used. Then I would make up two or three versions for each cover... show them to Creed and he would make a decision, usually picking one or two from the group. I rarely had to go back and do a whole bunch more. From there I'd put it together for the printer. The only thing I'd have to wait for would be the titles for the different tracks, which weren't often decided until late.

Is there anything you miss most about working at CTI?

I miss the interaction with the musicians, and I miss hearing them as well. I'd often go to wherever they were playing in NY and listen to them. Not so much with covers in mind, but just to get a sense of what they were doing. Occasionally you work in a place where everyone is right and this was a place that was like that. That doesn't happen too often. Part of it was because Creed was very easy to work with.

Out of all the covers you designed, do you have any favorites?

I think that all the ones for Hubert [Laws] just happened. There's one called *Afro-Classic*. Then there was a Randy Weston cover (*Blue Moses*) with a big image of a man's face. We did it in different colors. I liked it a lot.

Can you pick out any recollections of other record label designers at that time?

Yes, there was a really wonderful group of covers done at Riverside. When I worked at Columbia Records, which was my first job in design, the art director who I worked for was Reid Miles. So I kind of had a good role model.

Wie sind Sie zu CTI gekommen?

Offiziell wurde ich Anfang der 70er Jahre Art Director. Vorher hatte ich schon einige Plattenhüllen für Columbia gestaltet. Anschließend habe ich freiberuflich für Creed [Taylor] gearbeitet, kurz darauf hat er mich dann eingestellt. Ich bin drei Jahre geblieben. Es war eine tolle Arbeit.

Gibt es irgendwelche Besonderheiten, wenn man als Designer im Plattengeschäft arbeitet? Ist es schwierig?

Bei Columbia war es schwierig, weil die Künstler bei den Covern viel mitreden konnten. Aber bei Creed konnten sie überhaupt nicht eingreifen. Sie waren froh, überhaupt Abbildungen auf den Plattenhüllen zu haben. Ich konnte so ziemlich machen, was ich wollte.

Das ist der Traum eines jeden Designers, vollkommene Unabhängigkeit zu haben.

Ich zeigte ihnen für gewöhnlich meine Entwürfe, aber sie waren so höflich, dass sie immer sagten, es sei toll. Das war ich nicht gewohnt.

Waren die Musiker bei der Erstellung der Entwürfe beteiligt? Gab es mal irgendwelche Vorschläge von ihnen?

Kaum. Ich zeigte ihnen hin und wieder etwas, damit sie etwas dazu sagen konnten, aber sie kamen selten mit Gestaltungsvorschlägen für die Plattenhüllen.

Wann haben Sie Creed Taylor zum ersten Mal getroffen?

Er rief mich an, weil ich mit dem Fotografen Pete Turner gearbeitet hatte. Ich war für die Frauenzeitschrift *The Red Book* tätig. Sie suchten jemand neues für die Gestaltung der Plattenhüllen, und ich hatte schon ein bisschen Erfahrung damit. Creed vergrößerte seine Firma und brauchte einen Art Director auf Vollzeitbasis. Da hat er mir die Stelle angeboten.

Creed war dafür bekannt, sich über Kosten keine großen Gedanken zu machen. Stimmt das?

Er hatte einen exklusiven Geschmack. Du hast das ausgegeben, was du ausgeben musstest, um deine Arbeit gut zu machen. Deswegen waren die Plattenhüllen alle ausklappbar, und beim Druck wurde eine sehr gute Qualität gewählt – besser als bei den meisten anderen Plattenfirmen.

Hatte CTI ein Marketingbudget?

Wenn sie ein Budget hatten, dann wusste keiner, wie hoch es war. Ich sagte ihm immer, wenn etwas sehr teuer werden würde, und ich glaube, er hat nie Nein gesagt. Das ganze Unternehmen war so. Die Büroräume im Rockefeller Center waren wunderschön designt und wunderbar eingerichtet. Alles musste vom Feinsten sein.

„Creed Taylor hatte einen exklusiven Geschmack. Du hast das ausgegeben, was du ausgeben musstest, um deine Arbeit gut zu machen."

CTI hatte einen einzigartigen Stil und ein unverwechselbares Image, beides für die damalige Zeit sehr modern. Jetzt entdeckt die Hip-Hop-Generation Labels wie CTI wieder – und sein Image, das Sie mitentwickelt haben. Das muss doch sehr schmeichelhaft für Sie sein.

Es ist merkwürdig, weil ich in den letzten Jahren von Leuten angerufen wurde, die CTI-Platten und Hüllen sammeln. Und von Freunden weiß ich, dass DJs sie auch verwenden. Als wir sie gemacht haben, hatten wir keine Ahnung, wie sich das auswirken würde, wir taten einfach, was wir für richtig hielten.

Wie sah der Alltag bei CTI aus?
Überall waren Musiker. Die Leute hingen alle im Art Department herum, weil dort viel Platz war. Wir sprachen immer über Alben, die in Kürze erscheinen sollten, und darüber, welchen Titel sie vielleicht bekommen würden. Dann stellte ich mir eine kleinen Gruppe von Fotografen und Illustratoren zusammen, und wir suchten Bilder, die man für die Cover nehmen könnte. Ich hörte mir die Musik selten vorher an, da die Bilder ein Blickfang werden sollten. Es war eine kleine Firma, und wir hatten nur ein sehr kleines Budget für die Promotion.

Was haben Sie gemacht, damit die Leute im Plattenladen auf ein CTI-Cover aufmerksam wurden und stehen blieben?
Die Plattenhüllen dienten dazu, den Verkauf der Platten in großem Maße zu fördern. Wir druckten zusätzliche Kopien der Plattencover und schickten sie an die Läden, die sie dann ins Schaufenster stellten. Diese Kopien gaben wir gratis heraus. Später verkauften wir die Plattenhüllen – einfach nur auf Papier gedruckte Bilder. Ich glaube, sie wurden für einen Dollar verkauft. Viele Leute fingen an, sie zu sammeln.

Haben Sie auch Cover für Kudu und Salvation, die anderen Labels von Creed, entworfen?
Als ich bei ihm arbeitete, gründete Creed Kudu und das Gospel-Label Salvation. Für Kudu verwendeten wir viele Illustrationen und arbeiteten mit verschiedenen Fotografen zusammen. Die Plattenhüllen waren wunderschön.

War das Image von Kudu anders als das von CTI?

Die Cover glänzten mehr. Ich kreierte einen unverwechselbaren Stil. Die Alben wurde durchnummeriert: Kudu one, Kudu two usw.

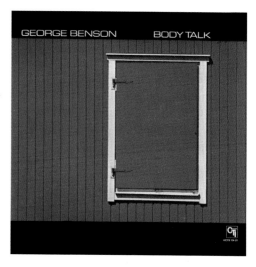

GEORGE BENSON, *Body Talk*, 1976, CTI
(see page 99)

Was empfinden Sie, wenn Sie heute in einem Plattenladen die CTI-Cover auf CD statt auf Vinyl sehen?
Das ist traurig. Sie sind viel zu klein. Als Designer kann man auf einer CD-Hülle keine große Aussage machen. Es gibt sehr wenige CD-Hüllen, die wirklich hervorstechen. Die einzigen, die mir einfallen, sind die von Radiohead. Aber was den Jazz angeht, ist es wirklich schwierig, in dieser Größe etwas Ordentliches zu gestalten.

Können Sie sich an den Arbeitsablauf für den Entwurf eines Albumcovers erinnern? Nehmen wir Prelude *von Deodato als Beispiel.*
Das ist das mit dem grünen Cover! Da war die Titelmusik von *2001: Odyssee im Weltraum* drauf. Der Ablauf war bei jeder Platte fast gleich. Creed und ich saßen für gewöhnlich mit ein paar anderen Leuten in der Promotionabteilung und redeten

darüber, welche Platten in diesem Monat aufgenommen wurden. Es waren meistens mehrere. Ich ging raus und fing an, darüber nachzudenken, welche Bilder ich verwenden könnte. Entweder fotografierte ich selber etwas oder ich ging zu einem Fotografen, mit dem ich regelmäßig zusammenarbeitete, um zu sehen, ob er irgendwelche Fotos hatte, die noch nicht verwendet worden waren. Dann gestaltete ich zwei oder drei Versionen von jedem Cover... ich zeigte sie Creed, und er traf eine Entscheidung. Dann bereitete ich alles für den Druck vor. Ich musste dann meistens noch auf die Titel für die verschiedenen Tracks warten, über die oft sehr spät entschieden wurde.

RANDY WESTON, *Blue Moses*, 1972, CTI
(see page 460)

Was vermissen Sie am meisten von der Arbeit bei CTI?
Ich vermisse die Interaktion mit den Musikern und sie zu hören. Immer, wenn einer von ihnen in New York spielte, ging ich hin, um sie zu hören. Nicht so sehr wegen der Cover, sondern um ein Gefühl dafür zu bekommen, was sie machen. Gelegentlich arbeitet man an einem Ort, wo sich jeder

am richtigen Platz fühlt – CTI war so ein Ort. Das erlebt man nicht so oft. Es lag auch mit daran, dass man mit Creed so gut zusammenarbeiten konnte.

Gibt es Favoriten unter Ihren eigenen Covern?
Ich glaube, das sind alle von Hubert [Laws]. Eins heißt *Afro-Classic*. Dann gab es ein Cover für Randy Weston (*Blue Moses*) mit einem riesigen Foto, das das Gesicht eines Mannes zeigt. Wir haben es in verschiedenen Farben herausgegeben. Ich mochte es sehr.

Erinnern Sie sich noch an andere Designer bei Plattenfirmen zu dieser Zeit?
Ja, bei Riverside wurden wirklich einige wunderbare Plattenhüllen gestaltet. Als ich den Job bei Columbia Records hatte, meine erste Stelle im Bereich Design, war Reid Miles Art Director, und ich habe für ihn gearbeitet. Ich hatte also ein gutes Vorbild.

Pouvez-vous nous expliquer un peu comment vous avez commencé à travailler pour CTI ?

Je suis devenu leur directeur artistique officiel au début des années 1970. Avant cela, j'avais déjà réalisé quelques pochettes pour Columbia. Par la suite, j'ai un peu travaillé en free-lance pour Creed [Taylor], puis il m'a engagé. J'y suis resté trois ans. C'était un boulot fabuleux.

Qu'y a-t-il de particulier lorsqu'on est graphiste dans le monde des disques ? Est-ce difficile ?

C'était difficile chez Columbia parce que les artistes avaient leur mot à dire sur les pochettes. Mais avec Creed ils n'étaient pas du tout consultés. Ils étaient déjà contents d'avoir des pochettes. Je pouvais faire pratiquement tout ce que je voulais.

L'indépendance totale ... c'est le rêve de tout graphiste.

Je leur montrais tout ce que je faisais, mais ils étaient tellement polis qu'ils disaient seulement que c'était super. Je n'étais pas habitué à ça.

Est-ce que les musiciens s'intéressaient au processus de création de la pochette ? Vous faisaient-ils des suggestions ?

Presque jamais. Je leur montrais des concepts pour obtenir leurs réactions, mais ils n'avaient que très rarement des suggestions à faire sur l'aspect visuel.

Quand avez-vous rencontré Creed Taylor ?

Il m'a appelé parce que j'avais travaillé avec Pete Turner, le photographe. J'étais sur un magazine féminin appelé *The Red Book*. Ils cherchaient quelqu'un d'autre pour faire les pochettes, et j'en avais déjà fait quelques-unes. Creed était en train d'agrandir son équipe et avait besoin d'un directeur artistique à plein temps. Il m'a donc proposé le poste.

Creed avait aussi la réputation de ne pas trop regarder à la dépense. C'est vrai ?

Il avait des goûts de luxe. C'était le résultat souhaité qui déterminait les dépenses. C'est pour cela que les pochettes des albums étaient toutes à volet et qu'elles étaient très bien imprimées, beaucoup mieux que ce que faisaient la plupart des autres maisons de disques.

Est-ce que CTI avait un budget marketing ?

S'ils avaient un budget, personne ne savait ce que c'était exactement. Lorsque je pensais que quelque chose allait coûter très cher je le lui disais, mais je ne crois pas qu'il ait jamais refusé. Les bureaux du Rockefeller Center étaient superbes, avec des meubles magnifiques. Il fallait que tout soit parfait.

« Creed Taylor avait des goûts de luxe. C'était le résultat souhaité qui déterminait les dépenses. »

CTI avait un style et une image tout à fait uniques, très modernes pour l'époque. Aujourd'hui la génération hip-hop redécouvre des labels comme CTI, avec cette image que vous avez contribué à créer. Cela doit être très flatteur pour vous, non ?

C'est étrange car, ces deux ou trois dernières années, j'ai reçu des appels de personnes qui collectionnent des disques et des pochettes de CTI. Et des amis m'ont dit que les DJs les utilisent aussi. Lorsque nous faisions tout cela nous n'avions pas du tout conscience de ce qui était en train de se passer, nous faisions simplement ce qui nous semblait être à faire.

Pouvez-vous décrire la vie quotidienne chez CTI ?

Il y avait des musiciens partout. Les gens se retrouvaient au service artistique, parce qu'il s'agissait d'un grand espace. On parlait des albums à venir, et parfois des titres. Je faisais des sorties avec un petit groupe de photographes et d'illustrateurs pour essayer de trouver des images qui pourraient devenir des couvertures. J'entendais rarement la musique à l'avance, et j'essayais de trouver des images qui retenaient l'attention. C'était une petite entreprise et notre budget promotionnel était très réduit.

HUBERT LAWS, *Morning Star*, 1972, CTI
(see page 278)

Que faisiez-vous pour que les gens s'arrêtent lorsqu'ils tombaient sur un disque CTI dans un magasin ?

Les couvertures avaient un rôle essentiel dans la promotion des disques. On imprimait des copies supplémentaires des pochettes et on les envoyait aux magasins pour qu'ils les mettent en vitrine. On les donnait gratuitement. Ensuite, on a commencé à vendre les couvertures. Juste

l'image imprimée sur du papier. Je crois qu'on les vendait pour un dollar. Beaucoup de gens ont commencé à collectionner les couvertures.

Avez-vous aussi créé des pochettes pour les autres labels de Creed, comme Kudu et Salvation ?

Creed a créé Kudu et Salvation, un label de gospel, à l'époque où je travaillais avec lui. Pour Kudu, nous avons utilisé beaucoup d'illustrations, et différents photographes. La qualité d'impression des couvertures était magnifique.

L'image de Kudu était-elle différente de celle de CTI ?

Kudu avait un look plus lustré. J'ai construit un style caractéristique. Chaque album était numéroté : Kudu un, Kudu deux, etc.

Que ressentez-vous lorsque vous entrez dans un magasin de disques aujourd'hui et que vous voyez les albums de CTI en CD plutôt qu'en vinyle ?

Ça me rend triste. Ils sont trop petits. En tant que graphiste, on ne peut pas vraiment faire passer grand-chose sur une surface aussi petite. Très peu de pochettes de CD se démarquent du lot. Les seules qui me viennent à l'esprit sont celles de Radiohead. Mais en ce qui concerne le jazz, on ne peut pas faire grand-chose sur ce format.

Vous rappelez-vous du processus de travail pour la création d'une couverture d'album ? Prenons Prelude *de Deodato, par exemple.*

C'est la couverture verte ! Je me souviens que cet album avait le thème *2001*. Le processus était très similaire à chaque fois. Creed et moi, ainsi que quelques autres du service promotion, nous parlions des disques qui allaient être enregistrés au cours du mois. Normalement, il y en avait plusieurs. Je sortais et je commençais à penser aux images que je pourrais utiliser, soit en photographiant quelque chose moi-même, soit en demandant à un photographe avec lequel je travaillais régulièrement s'il avait des images disponibles. Ensuite, je faisais deux ou trois versions de chaque couverture, je les montrais à Creed, et il prenait une décision. Généralement, il en choisissait une ou deux dans chaque groupe. Il était rare que je dusse reprendre tout depuis le début. Ensuite, je préparais le tout pour l'imprimeur. Mais il était inévitable d'attendre les titres des différents morceaux choisis très tard, le plus souvent.

Qu'est-ce qui vous manque le plus de votre travail chez CTI ?

L'interaction avec les musiciens. Ça me manque aussi de les entendre. J'allais souvent les écouter là où ils jouaient à New York. Pas tellement pour les couvertures, mais juste pour me rendre compte de ce qu'ils faisaient. Parfois, on travaille dans un endroit où tout le monde est parfaitement à sa place, et CTI était un endroit comme ça. Cela n'arrive pas souvent. En partie, c'était parce qu'il était très agréable de travailler avec Creed.

Parmi toutes les couvertures que vous avez créées, avez-vous vos préférées ?

Je pense que toutes celles réalisées pour Hubert [Laws] ont une vie propre. L'une d'elles s'appelle *Afro-Classic*. Et puis il y a une couverture pour Randy Weston *(Blue Moses)* avec une grande image, le visage d'un homme. Nous l'avons réalisée en plusieurs couleurs. Je l'aimais beaucoup.

Vous souvenez-vous d'autres créateurs de pochettes de disques de cette époque ?

Oui, Riverside avait des pochettes vraiment fantastiques. Lorsque je travaillais chez Columbia, dans mon premier poste de graphiste, le directeur artistique était Reid Miles. Alors on peut dire que j'ai eu un bon modèle.

FREDDIE HUBBARD, *Keep Your Soul Together*, 1973, CTI (see page 237)

FRED COHEN

Fred Cohen began a lifelong love of jazz when he heard Charles Mingus at the age of 12. For the last 25 years, Cohen has run New York's specialist Jazz Record Center. Tucked away in an eighth-floor loft located on West 26th Street, the Jazz Record Center is like a private club – it feels like you need to give a password to get in. This jazz haven is filled with thousands of LPs, CDs, pictures, videos and books, along with a two-man staff (including Cohen) who know practically every note on every record. Perhaps not the place to go for the latest Joshua Carter or Greg Osby, but if you're looking for an old Savoy, or some rare Blue Note then you're in heaven.

Für Fred Cohen begann die lebenslange Liebe zum Jazz, als er mit zwölf Jahren ein Stück von Charlie Mingus hörte. Seit 25 Jahren führt Cohen den Fachladen Jazz Record Center. Das Jazz Record Center in der 26th Street wirkt, versteckt auf einem Dachboden im achten Stock, wie ein privater Club, für den man ein Passwort braucht, um hineinzukommen. In diesem Jazzhimmel findet man Tausende LPs, CDs, Bilder, Videos und Bücher. Cohen und sein einziger Mitarbeiter kennen praktisch jede Note auf jeder einzelnen Platte. Hier ist vielleicht nicht der richtige Ort, um den neuesten Joshua Carter oder Greg Osby zu bekommen, aber wenn man einen alten Savoy oder seltene Blue-Note-Platten sucht, fühlt man sich hier wie im Himmel.

Fred Cohen tomba irrémédiablement amoureux du jazz à douze ans, lorsqu'il entendit Charles Mingus pour la première fois. Il dirige le Jazz Record Center à New York depuis vingt-cinq ans. Niché dans un loft au huitième étage d'un bâtiment de West 26th Street, le Jazz Record Center ressemble à un club privé, on a un peu l'impression de devoir montrer patte blanche pour entrer. Cette oasis du jazz est remplie de milliers de vinyles, de CD, de photos, de vidéos et de livres, et ses deux gardiens (en comptant Fred Cohen) connaissent pratiquement chaque note de chaque disque. Ce n'est peut-être pas le meilleur endroit pour trouver le dernier Joshua Carter ou Greg Osby, mais si vous voulez débusquer un vieux Savoy ou une édition rare de Blue Note, vous êtes au paradis.

DOLLAR BRAND, *Soweto*, 1965,
Chiaroscuro (see page 106)

Can you talk a little more about the Jazz Record Center and how it all started?

It started in 1983. It was a very small space then on the upper west side of Manhattan. Since there was no store in New York City that specialized in jazz at the time, my idea was to create one. At that time there were no CDs, 1983 was the year that the compact disc arrived on the market. So basically all I sold then was jazz books and LPs. Soon after that I started selling compact discs, videotapes, DVDs, posters, postcards, t-shirts... just about anything that's connected to jazz, except for instruments and instructional material.

"In the early '80s a lot of my customers traded their entire record collections for compact discs; now they've gone back and traded their CDs for records..."

Can you remember the first time you listened to a jazz record?

I remember exactly. As a matter of fact I went and bought the record, and I still have copies of it here. It's called *Modern Jazz Hall of Fame*, on a label called Design, and features tracks by a lot of different artists. The one track that caught my attention was a track by Charles Mingus called "Abstractions". It was the strangest music I'd ever heard, even though I'd been pretty much raised on classical music; this just captivated me. It's a combination of a classical string quartet and dissonance. I just couldn't take it out of my head; I had to get the record.

How do you buy records for the store?

They come from all sources. I buy someofthem brand new, as vinyl is still manufactured.

It's very curious that vinyl is still alive in the MP3 era.

I think that the impact of hip hop and turntable artists has a lot to do with that. It's a reminder that not long ago the only way to get music was on vinyl, and that vinyl still has a great, great sound. In the early '80s a lot of my customers traded their entire record collections for compact discs; now they've gone back and traded their CDs for records, but at a much greater expense, because it's so much more costly now to get the same records on vinyl.

Do you buy a lot of private collections?

Sure. A lot of people bring records into the store... bags of records... boxes of records. And then, of course, I go out and look at record collections when people call or write me.

As you said, the second-hand vinyl market can be very expensive, especially for jazz.

It can be a very inexpensive market as well. There are hundreds of thousands of records in beautiful condition that cost no more than eight dollars. Once you get into very collectable records that are in demand, then you are going to pay a lot for them, sometimes thousands of dollars.

Which label is in demand the most?

In the past 15 years, and maybe even longer, Blue Note has always been the label to collect.

What are the most expensive records that you sell?

The most expensive records that I sell are not necessarily Blue Note. There's a lot on Prestige. For example, Sonny Rollins' *Saxo-*

phone *Colossus*, or there's an album by the Tommy Flanagan Trio called *Overseas*. Lee Morgan and Hank Mobley records can sell for a minimum of a thousand dollars, or more. Certain Charlie Parker records on Dial can go from anywhere between five to ten thousand dollars. Also, a lot of avant-garde records are expensive... records by Albert Ayler or the Black Artists' Group. Some of these were very small productions that were on the cutting edge of the new music.

THE GIL EVANS ORCHESTRA, *Into The Hot*, 1961, Impulse! (see page 183)

The Internet has changed all of this. Now you can buy records on eBay.

The Internet has primarily changed the way that collectors have access to the music they are looking for. Before I had the store I used to do auction lists, even while I had the store. My auction lists would have a minimum of two thousand records. I'd have to type the lists out, which meant I would be sitting here for about two weeks doing absolutely nothing but typing. I'd then send them out to all the customers on my mailing list, and within a month they would

send back their bids. When they were bidding on a record they didn't know who else was bidding or how high the bid was. They would have to do blind bidding. That's a very different process from the Internet, where you can always see what somebody else is bidding, and at the very last minute put in a bid that outbids everybody else. So the whole psychology of auction bidding has very much changed since eBay.

Where do your clients come from? And who are the biggest collectors?

They come from everywhere. I still have a lot of mail-order clients, people I've never met from overseas, from Europe and Asia. And then I have regular customers that come in several times a year from England, France, Italy and Japan etc.

What's your explanation for this renewed interest in old jazz records? Earlier you referred to hip hop... Is it to do with the quality of the sound or a physical approach to vinyl?

There is some kind of romantic component to all of it. First of all, the size of the record allows for graphics, artwork and photography to be presented in a much more lively way than on a CD, which is so small that you almost don't pay any attention to the graphics. The second thing is that a lot of people never gave up on vinyl. Although they initially resisted the compact disc, eventually they realized that if they wanted to keep up with the music scene (a lot of music was not being issued on vinyl), they had at least to do both. They had to keep their records and they also had to get on compact discs. The fact that a lot of my customers invest in both areas (compact discs and vinyl) means that a lot of the recordings they are still looking for may not even be available on CD, so they have to look for vinyl.

Do you have a huge record collection?

No. Actually, my record collection stopped around 1989 when the room in my apartment where my records had been stored had to become my son's room. So, all of my records have been in storage for years. I haven't added anything to it since. But I don't need to have the collection... I've got the store.

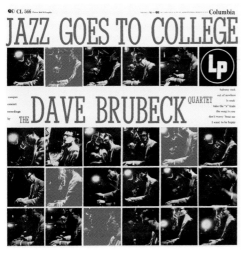

THE DAVE BRUBECK QUARTET, *Jazz Goes To College*, 1953, Columbia (see page 110)

Is there a record that you've always wanted but have never been able to find?

There are a couple of records that I've personally never seen. I know they exist because other people have them, but I've never seen them. One would be a Kenny Dorham record that was privately issued. Not many people know about it. It's a recording of a concert he gave about 40 years ago as a fundraiser. It was issued by a non-profit group on a very, very limited pressing. Even though it was done in New York, I've never seen a copy of the record.

How much would this record be worth?

Several thousand dollars. Another one I can think of would be a Chico Hamilton record with Eric Dolphy, called *That Hamilton Man*, on a label called Sesac. It's also a New York label but I've never actually held the 12-inch copy of the record.

What about records from other parts of the world, such as British or French jazz?

There are a lot of records that are so rare that no Americans have ever seen them. Very exotic records... English records on little labels like Nixa and Temple, featuring musicians from the heyday of British bebop, like Dizzy Reece, Tubby Hayes and Victor Feldman. Jazz is not just an American scene; there have been some wonderful, exceptional musicians from all around the world. René Thomas from France, Dollar Brand from South Africa. We could go on and on and on.

Erzählen Sie uns doch etwas über das Jazz Record Center und wie alles begonnen hat.
1983 fing alles an. Wir hatten zuerst einen ganz kleinen Raum an der Upper West Side von Manhattan. Da es zu dieser Zeit noch keinen Laden in New York City gab, der auf Jazz spezialisiert war, hatte ich die Idee, einen zu eröffnen. Zu der Zeit gab es noch keine CDs, erst 1983 wurden ja die ersten Compact Discs auf den Markt gebracht. Daher verkaufte ich hauptsächlich Jazzbücher und -platten. Aber schon bald begann ich, CDs, Videos, DVDs, Poster, Postkarten, T-Shirts etc. in mein Sortiment aufzunehmen – eigentlich alles, was mit Jazz zu tun hat, außer Instrumente und Lehrmaterial.

„In den frühen 80ern tauschte eine ganze Reihe meiner Kunden ihre komplette Schallplattensammlung gegen CDs ein. Jetzt machen sie es umgekehrt und tauschen ihre CDs gegen Schallplatten ein…"

Erinnern Sie sich noch an die erste Jazz-Platte, die Sie gehört haben?
Ich erinnere mich ganz genau. Ich habe mir die Platte dann auch tatsächlich gekauft – ich besitze immer noch einige Kopien davon. Das Album heißt *Modern Jazz Hall of Fame*, ist bei dem Label Design erschienen und enthält Stücke von verschiedenen Künstlern. Ein Stück fesselte mich ganz besonders: Es war „Abstractions" von

Charles Mingus. Das war die seltsamste Musik, die ich jemals gehört hatte. Das Stück kombiniert den Klang eines klassischen Streichquartetts mit Dissonanzen. Ich bekam es nicht aus dem Kopf und musste die Platte unbedingt haben.

Wie und wo kaufen Sie Ihre Platten für den Laden ein?
Ich beziehe sie von überall her. Einige Alben – sofern sie auf Vinyl veröffentlicht werden – sind frisch gepresst.

Es ist wirklich merkwürdig, dass es im Zeitalter der MP3 immer noch Vinyl gibt.
Ich glaube, das liegt auch am Einfluss von Hip-Hop-Künstlern und DJs. Vor nicht allzu langer Zeit war Musik nur auf Vinyl erhältlich, und es hat einfach immer noch einen großartigen Klang. In den frühen 80ern tauschte eine ganze Reihe meiner Kunden ihre komplette Schallplattensammlung gegen CDs ein. Jetzt machen sie es umgekehrt und tauschen ihre CDs gegen Schallplatten ein – aber mit erheblich weniger Gewinn, denn mittlerweile sind Vinylplatten viel teurer geworden.

Kaufen Sie viele Privatsammlungen auf?
Sicher. Ziemlich viele Leute bringen ihre Platten in den Laden … Taschen voller Platten … Kisten voller Platten. Und dann fahre ich natürlich herum und schaue mir Plattensammlungen an, wenn mich Leute anrufen oder mir schreiben.

Second-Hand-Vinylplatten können also sehr teuer sein, vor allem im Jazzbereich.
Man kann sie aber auch sehr günstig bekommen. Es gibt Hunderttausende Platten in wundervollem Zustand, die nicht mehr als acht Dollar kosten. Für gefragte Sammlerstücke bezahlt manch einer sehr viel, manchmal Tausende von Dollar.

Welches Label ist am gefragtesten?
Während der letzten 15 Jahre oder länger war Blue Note immer das Sammlerlabel.

Welches sind die teuersten Platten in Ihrem Angebot?
Die teuersten Platten sind nicht unbedingt die von Blue Note. Es gibt beispielsweise einiges von Prestige. Zum Beispiel Sonny Rollins' *Saxophone Colossus* oder das Album *Overseas* des Tommy Flanagan Trio. Platten von Lee Morgan und Hank Mobley erzielen mindestens Tausend Dollar oder mehr. Einige Charlie-Parker-Alben von Dial gehen für fünf- bis zehntausend Dollar über den Tisch. Außerdem gibt es einige teure Avantgarde-Platten ... Platten von Albert Ayler oder der Black Artists' Group. Einige davon waren Vorreiter der Neuen Musik und sind nur in geringer Auflage gepresst worden.

Durch das Internet ist alles anders geworden. Man kann jetzt Platten bei eBay kaufen.
Das Internet hat vor allem eines verändert: Sammler haben nun ganz andere Möglichkeiten, an die Musik zu kommen, die sie suchen. Bevor ich den Laden hatte, habe ich Auktionslisten geschrieben – damit habe ich auch noch nach der Eröffnung weitergemacht. Auf meinen Auktionslisten standen mindestens 2000 Alben. Ich musste die Listen abtippen, das heißt, ich saß hier manchmal zwei Wochen lang und machte nichts außer Tippen. Dann schickte ich die Listen an alle Kunden in meiner Kartei, und innerhalb eines Monats mussten sie mir dann ihre Gebote schicken. Wenn sie auf die Platten boten, wussten sie nicht, wer außer ihnen mitbot oder wie hoch die anderen Gebote waren. Sie mussten ihre Gebote blind abgeben. Das war damals ganz anders als heute im Internet: Da sieht man immer, was die anderen bieten, und kann in der letzten Sekunde ein Gebot abgeben, das alle anderen übertrifft. Durch eBay ist das

Verhalten bei Auktionen komplett anders geworden.

Woher kommen Ihre Kunden?
Wer sind die größten Sammler?
Sie kommen aus der ganzen Welt. Ich habe immer noch eine ganze Menge Versandkunden – Leute, die ich nie getroffen habe und die von Übersee, aus Europa und Asien, stammen. Dann habe ich noch einige Stammkunden, die einige Male pro Jahr aus England, Frankreich, Italien, Japan etc. hierher kommen.

Was, glauben Sie, ist der Grund für dieses wieder auflebende Interesse an alten Jazz-platten? Eben haben Sie von Hip Hop gesprochen... Hat es mit der Klangqualität zu tun oder mit der äußeren, physischen Gestalt von Vinylplatten?
Das alles hat eine romantische Komponente. Erst einmal erlaubt die Größe der Schallplatten im Vergleich zu CDs eine viel lebendigere Gestaltung, was die Grafik, Illustrationen und Fotografie betrifft; eine CD ist so klein, dass meistens nicht einmal viel Wert auf die grafische Gestaltung gelegt wird. Der zweite Grund ist, dass sehr viele Leute nie Abschied vom Vinyl genommen haben. Auch wenn sie anfangs CDs ablehnten, mussten sie schließlich akzeptieren, dass sie, wenn sie den Anschluss in der Musikszene nicht verlieren wollten (sehr viel Musik wurde nicht auf Vinyl veröffentlicht), beide Wege gehen mussten. Die Tatsache, dass viele meiner Kunden in beide Medien investieren (CDs und Vinyl) rührt auch daher, dass eine große Anzahl von Aufnahmen, nach denen sie suchen, gar nicht auf CD erschienen, sondern nur auf Vinyl erhältlich sind.

Haben Sie eine große Plattensammlung?
Nein. In der Tat habe ich 1989 aufgehört zu sammeln. Das war das Jahr, in dem mein Sohn das Zimmer bekam, in dem ich

meine Platten aufbewahrte. Daher ist meine Sammlung seit Jahren eingelagert. Ich habe seitdem nichts mehr hinzugefügt. Aber ich brauche auch gar keine Sammlung. Ich habe ja den Laden.

Gibt es ein Album, das Sie schon immer haben wollten, aber bis jetzt noch nicht gefunden haben?
Es gibt ein paar Platten, die ich nie gesehen habe. Eine davon ist ein Kenny Dorham-Album, eine Privatveröffentlichung. Nur wenige Leute wissen überhaupt davon. Es ist die Aufnahme eines Konzertes, das er vor etwa 40 Jahren als Wohltätigkeitsveranstaltung gab. Das Album wurde von einer gemeinnützigen Vereinigung in einer sehr kleinen Auflage gepresst. Obwohl sie in New York erschienen ist, habe ich nie ein Exemplar der Platte gesehen.

CHARLES MINGUS, *Changes One*, 1974, Atlantic (see page 306)

Wie viel wird diese Aufnahme wohl wert sein?
Einige Tausend Dollar. Eine andere, die mir einfällt, ist eine bei einem Label namens Sesac erschienene Chico-Hamilton-Aufnahme mit Eric Dolphy: *That Hamilton*

Man. Das ist auch ein New Yorker Label, aber ich habe noch nie die 12-Inch-Kopie in den Händen gehalten.

Was ist mit Platten aus anderen Teilen der Welt, zum Beispiel mit britischem oder französischem Jazz?
Es gibt eine ganze Reihe von Alben, die so selten sind, dass kein Amerikaner sie jemals gesehen hat. Sehr seltene Platten ... Englische Aufnahmen bei kleinen Labels wie Nixa und Temple, mit Musikern aus der Blütezeit des britischen Bebop, zum Beispiel Dizzy Reece, Tubby Hayes und Victor Feldman. Jazz ist keine rein amerikanische Szene. Es gab einige wunderbare außergewöhnliche Musiker aus der ganzen Welt. René Thomas aus Frankreich, Dollar Brand aus Südafrika. Ich könnte noch einige mehr aufzählen.

Pouvez-vous parler un peu du Jazz Record Center et de sa création ?

Tout a commencé en 1983. C'était alors un tout petit espace dans le quartier de l'Upper West Side de Manhattan. Comme à l'époque il n'y avait pas de magasin spécialisé dans le jazz à New York, j'ai eu l'idée d'en créer un. Il n'y avait pas encore vraiment de CD, ils sont arrivés sur le marché cette même année. Je vendais donc essentiellement des livres sur le jazz et des vinyles. Peu après, j'ai commencé à vendre des CD, des cassettes vidéo, des DVD, des posters, des cartes postales, des t-shirts ...tout ce qui avait un rapport avec le jazz, sauf des instruments ou du matériel pédagogique.

« Au début des années 1980, beaucoup de mes clients ont échangé toute leur collection de vinyles contre des CD. Aujourd'hui ils font l'inverse et échangent leurs CD contre des vinyles... »

Vous rappelez-vous de la première fois que vous avez écouté un disque de jazz ?

Je m'en souviens parfaitement. En fait, j'ai acheté le disque et j'en ai encore des copies ici. Il s'intitule *Modern Jazz Hall of Fame*, sorti sous le label Design, et contient des morceaux de plusieurs musiciens. Celui qui avait attiré mon attention était un morceau de Charles Mingus, « Abstractions ». C'était la musique la plus étrange que j'avais jamais entendue. J'avais été élevé à la musique classique, mais j'étais captivé. C'est une combinaison de quatuor de cordes classique et de dissonance. Je n'arrivais pas à me sortir le morceau de la tête, il fallait que je mette la main sur ce disque.

Comment achetez-vous vos disques pour le magasin ?

Aucune source n'est néligée. Je les achète parfois tout neufs, puisque les vinyles sont encore édités.

C'est très bizarre que le vinyle soit encore d'actualité à l'époque du MP3.

Je pense que l'impact du hip-hop et des virtuoses de la platine y est pour beaucoup. Cela nous rappelle qu'à une époque pas si lointaine le vinyle était le seul support disponible, et qu'il a toujours eu un très très bon son. Au début des années 1980, beaucoup de mes clients ont échangé toute leur collection de vinyles contre des CD. Aujourd'hui, ils font l'inverse et échangent leurs CD contre des vinyles, mais à un coût bien plus élevé, parce que se procurer les mêmes disques sur vinyle est bien plus cher maintenant.

Achetez-vous beaucoup de collections privées ?

Oui. Beaucoup de gens apportent des disques au magasin ... des sacs, des cartons remplis de disques. Et bien sûr, je vais jeter un coup d'œil aux collections de disques lorsqu'on m'appelle ou qu'on m'écrit.

Comme vous l'avez dit, les vinyles d'occasion peuvent être très chers, particulièrement dans le jazz.

Ils peuvent aussi être très bon marché. Il y a des centaines de milliers de disques en très bonnes conditions qui ne coûtent pas plus de huit dollars. Mais si vous vous intéressez à des pièces de collection, à des disques très demandés, alors le prix monte en flèche et atteint parfois plusieurs milliers de dollars.

Quel est le label le plus demandé ?

Depuis quinze ans, ou peut-être même pluslongtemps, c'est Blue Note qui a toujours été le label des collectionneurs.

Quels sont les disques les plus chers que vous ayez en magasin ?

Les disques les plus chers que je vends ne sont pas nécessairement de Blue Note. Il y en a beaucoup qui viennent de chez Prestige. Par exemple, *Saxophone Colossus* de Sonny Rollins, ou bien *Overseas* du Tommy Flanagan Trio. Les disques de Lee Morgan et de Hank Mobley peuvent se vendre pour mille dollars ou plus. Certains albums de Charlie Parker sortis chez Dial peuvent coûter de cinq à dix mille dollars. Beaucoup de disques d'avant-garde sont également chers... Ceux d'Albert Ayler ou du Black Artists' Group par exemple. Certains avaient été édités en quantité très limitée.

Internet a changé tout ça. Aujourd'hui, on peut acheter des disques sur eBay.

Internet a avant tout changé la façon dont les collectionneurs ont accès à la musique qu'ils cherchent. Avant d'avoir le magasin, je faisais des listes de vente aux enchères, et même après. C'étaient des listes d'au moins deux mille disques. Il fallait que je les tape, ce qui veut dire que je pouvais rester assis à taper pendant deux semaines sans faire absolument rien d'autre. Puis je les envoyais à tous les clients de ma liste de distribution, et ils avaient un mois pour m'envoyer leurs offres de prix. Lorsqu'ils faisaient une enchère sur un disque, ils ne savaient pas qui d'autre le voulait, ni quel prix avait été proposé. Ils devaient enchérir à l'aveugle. C'est très différent sur Internet, parce qu'on peut toujours voir les prix que les autres proposent, et on peut faire une offre gagnante à la dernière seconde. Toute la psychologie des enchères a donc beaucoup changé depuis eBay.

D'où viennent vos clients ? Et qui sont les plus gros collectionneurs ?

Ils viennent de partout. J'ai encore beaucoup de clients qui commandent par correspondance et que je n'ai jamais vus, en Europe et en Asie. Et puis j'ai des clients réguliers qui viennent plusieurs fois par an d'Angleterre, de France, d'Italie et du Japon, etc.

LEE MORGAN, *The Rumproller*, 1965, Blue Note (see page 320)

Comment expliquez-vous ce regain d'intérêt pour les vieux disques de jazz ? Tout à l'heure vous parliez du hip-hop...Est-ce que cela tient à la qualité du son, ou bien à la sensation physique du vinyle ?

Il y a une certaine composante romantique. Tout d'abord, la taille des disques permet de présenter le graphisme, les illustrations et les photos d'une manière bien plus attrayante que sur les CD, qui sont tellement petits qu'on ne fait pratiquement pas attention aux éléments graphiques. Ensuite, il y a beaucoup de gens qui n'ont jamais abandonné le vinyle. Au début ils rejetaient les CD, puis ils ont compris que s'ils voulaient continuer de suivre l'actualité musicale (beaucoup d'albums n'étaient jamais gravés sur vinyle), ils devaient au moins acheter les deux. Ils devaient garder leurs vinyles et aussi acheter des CD. Le fait qu'une grande partie de mes clients investissent dans les deux (CD et vinyle) signifie que beaucoup des enregistrements qu'ils recherchent peuvent ne pas exister sur CD, et qu'ils doivent donc prendre des vinyles.

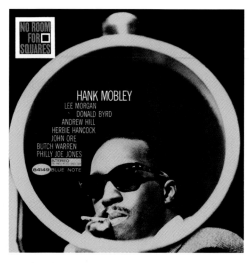

HANK MOBLEY, *No Room For Squares*, 1963, Blue Note (see page 311)

Avez-vous une grande collection de disques ?
Non. En fait, ma collection de disques s'arrête en 1989, lorsque la pièce qui me servait à l'entreposer est devenue la chambre de mon fils. Tous mes disques sont en garde-meuble depuis des années. Je n'ai rien ajouté à ma collection depuis. Mais je n'ai pas besoin d'avoir une collection…J'ai le magasin.

Y a-t-il un disque que vous avez toujours voulu posséder mais que vous n'avez jamais pu trouver ?
Il y a deux ou trois disques que je n'ai jamais vus de mes yeux. Je sais qu'ils existent parce que d'autres les ont vus, mais

pas moi. Par exemple un disque de Kenny Dorham, une édition privée. Peu de gens en connaissent l'existence. Il s'agit de l'enregistrement d'un concert qu'il a donné il y a quarante ans pour un gala de charité. C'est une association à but non lucratif qui l'a gravé, en édition très, très limitée. Ça s'est passé à New York, mais je n'ai jamais vu d'exemplaire de ce disque.

Combien peut-il valoir ?
Plusieurs milliers de dollars. Il y a aussi *That Hamilton Man*, sorti chez Sesac, de Chico Hamilton avec Eric Dolphy. Là encore, c'est un label new-yorkais, mais je n'en ai jamais vu de mes yeux un exemplaire en 45 tours.

Et les disques d'autres régions du monde, par exemple le jazz britannique ou français ?
Il y a beaucoup de disques qui sont si rares qu'aucun Américain ne les a vus. Des disques très exotiques…Les disques anglais de petits labels comme Nixa et Temple, avec des musiciens de la grande époque du be-bop britannique comme Dizzy Reece, Tubby Hayes et Victor Feldman. Le jazz n'est pas confiné aux États-Unis, il y a eu des musiciens exceptionnels et magnifiques dans le monde entier. René Thomas en France, Dollar Brand en Afrique du Sud. On pourrait continuer comme ça des heures et des heures.

SONNY ROLLINS, *Saxophone Colossus*, 1956, Prestige (see page 369)

STEREO

PRESTIGE

SONNY ROLLINS SAXOPHONE COLOSSUS

herbie hancock

man-child

MICHAEL CUSCUNA

Michael Cuscuna has worked tirelessly to keep the music of countless jazz legends alive. He was a key figure in the jazz reissue boom of the '80s and '90s. In 1983, Cuscuna and Charlie Lourie founded Mosaic, a label dedicated to reissuing high quality luxury limited-edition box sets of complete sessions. After gaining some popularity as an underground DJ in Philadelphia and later in New York, he was hired as a staff producer at Atlantic Records in 1972, where he worked with jazz icons like Dave Brubeck and the Art Ensemble of Chicago. Shortly thereafter Cuscuna went freelance, putting together new albums for nearly every major record label, yet he continued to search for unreleased and neglected music. Cuscuna was also involved in the Freedom and Novus labels with Steve Backer in the late '70s. From 1975-81 he developed an impressive program in which he unearthed scores of important sessions for Blue Note.

Michael Cuscuna hat unermüdlich gearbeitet, um die Musik unzähliger Jazz-legenden am Leben zu erhalten. Er war maßgeblich am Boom der Jazzneuauflagen in den 1980er und 1990er Jahren beteiligt. 1983 gründete er zusammen mit Charlie Lourie Mosaic, ein Label, das vollständige Sessions in hervorragend ausgestatteten Box-Sets als Limited Edition neu herausbrachte. Er erlangte in Philadelphia und später in New York einen gewissen Erfolg als DJ in der alternativen Szene und wurde 1972 bei Atlantic Records als Produzent eingestellt. Dort arbeitete er mit Jazz-Ikonen

wie Dave Brubeck und dem Art Ensemble of Chicago zusammen. Kurz darauf machte Cuscuna sich selbstständig und stellte für fast jede große Plattenfirma Alben zusammen. Zu dieser Zeit begann er bereits, nach unveröffentlichter und unbekannter Musik zu suchen. Ende der 1970er Jahre arbeitete er bei den Labels Freedom und Novus mit Steve Backer zusammen. 1975-81 initiierte er ein faszinierendes Projekt, in dem er alte Filmmusik ausgrub, die in bedeutenden Sessions bei Blue Note entstanden ist.

Michael Cuscuna a travaillé sans relâche pour faire vivre la musique d'une multitude de légendes du jazz. Il a joué un rôle essentiel dans le boom des rééditions de disques de jazz dans les années 1980-90. En 1983, il créa Mosaic avec Charlie Lourie. C'est un label spécialisé dans les rééditions en série limitée et en coffrets de luxe. Il gagna une certaine popularité en tant que DJ alternatif à Philadelphie et plus tard, à New York, il fut engagé comme producteur chez Atlantic Records en 1972, où il travailla avec des icônes du jazz comme Dave Brubeck et le groupe Art Ensemble of Chicago. Peu après, il se lança en indépendant et monta de nouveaux albums pour presque toutes les grandes maisons de disques, mais poursuivit sa recherche de musique inédite et méconnue. Il collabora également avec les labels Freedom et Novus vers la fin des années 1970, avec Steve Backer. De 1975 à 1981, il développa un programme impressionnant au sein duquel il mit au jour une multitude d'enregistrements très importants pour Blue Note.

HERBIE HANCOCK, *Man-Child*, 1975, CBS (see page 220)

One of your earliest jazz memories was going to Birdland. Can you remember the atmosphere at the time?

Birdland was in midtown Manhattan, while most of the clubs were down in Greenwich Village. It was the last left-over from 52nd Street. It was right on Broadway, in a very touristic part of town. You'd go downstairs, buy an admission ticket, and then you'd go down another flight of stairs and [Charlie] Parker would be there, abusing everybody that came in... he was very rude. Then you'd go down another flight of stairs and there was the club. It was a very large open club, with a bandstand at the back, next to the kitchen doors. It was very comfortable and looked more like a night club than a jazz club. So you got a lot of night clubbers and lot of jazz club fans too.

"I think the real hard jazz fan likes to collect... likes packaging, and likes liner notes. Even as I listen I don't miss the vinyl sound, I miss the LP jacket, the cover."

When Bebop appeared, it took jazz away from the dance floors and it was no longer popular music. That had a major impact on jazz music as a whole.

That's true, but it didn't stop, it was just less popular. When Blue Note and Prestige started recording and putting out 12-inch records by people like Art Blakey, Jimmy Smith, Jack MacDuff, Gene Ammons – people that have a very soulful approach – they started to reach a lot of people.

Bob Weinstock from Prestige was as much responsible for bringing jazz back into popularity as were the musicians themselves.

At that time, in the '60s, several clubs in New York closed and a lot of musicians went to play in Europe. Playing is a part of survival in jazz.

During the '60s there were a lot of economic problems. There were always clubs in New York, but not as many as before, and the possibilities for employment became less and less. Not just in New York, but around the country. We had a lot of great clubs in Detroit, Chicago, Washington DC, and cities where there were riots in the summers, civil rights or student riots. That put a lot of clubs out of business. People started to become afraid to go to a black neighborhood, if they weren't black, I know... of course, sometimes even if they were black. So the possibilities for employment in the United States in general were shrinking during that time. Also FM radio became the way to listen to music. Before that it was just AM, and mostly Top 40 stuff. By the late '60s a lot of Rock 'n' Roll groups started to make a different kind of album. It was more like what they now call the 'rock concept album'; not just pop singles, but more stretched out, interesting music. That took a lot of audience away from jazz. As a result a lot of musicians like Hank Mobley, Philly Joe Johnson, Lionel Hampton, and Dexter Gordon went to Europe. They got a lot more work and lot more respect over there. In '60s America, if you were black, you still felt like a nigger in a way. Some of these guys went over to Europe to visit and just fell in love with it because they were just treated with respect. So we lost a lot of people to Europe for quite a while.

In the '70s the fusion scene was the reaction to all these transformations. It was a way to get a bigger audience.
Yeah.

And it also started a whole new process by the bigger labels. In short, the fusion scene was big business.
It was big business at the time. All the fusion musicians were originally jazz musicians: Herbie Hancock, Billy Cobham, Randy and Michael Brecker. They founded a new industry. They would play in a rock auditorium and they would play concerts instead of clubs. Miles Davis did the same thing. It didn't really change his music to fusion, he had a funk kind of thing going, but they all got kind of sick of playing in clubs for little money and found ways to play concerts and make a better living and sell more records.

The critics hated the fusion scene, didn't they?
It was very strong. The older critics, I think. But, you know, one of the best records made in the '70s – and this isn't so much fusion but more of a commercial re-cord – was *Mr. Magic* by Grover Washington Jr. Just listen to the arrangements by Bob James, the rhythms that Ralph MacDonald laid down, and Grover's playing which is beautiful. At the time Leonard Feather probably hated that. But that is a great record. It stood the test of time. Lots of those things have stood the test of time. When something is new a lot of the more established critics react violently to it.

Acoustic jazz almost died at that time.
It didn't almost die. A lot was going on, only there were fewer opportunities to record, because there were no independent labels left. They all got bought by major labels. And the major labels were all inter-ested in fusion.

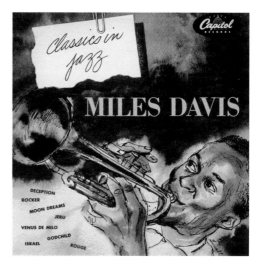

MILES DAVIS, *Classics In Jazz*, 1949, Capitol (see page 158)

Why is it that so many original jazz record-ings are now resurfacing as reissues?
Reissues are the best way to support a re-cord company. When I started at Blue Note in 1985, we did about 30 or 40 reissues in that year, and those made money. Whereas the music that we were recording took a lot longer to make any profit. So reissues were supporting the creation of new music.

This is one of your passions, isn't it? Rediscovering this wealth of hidden material and making it available.
Yeah. When I started to produce records in the early '70s I got to know a lot of the guys who were on Blue Note, and during breaks at recording sessions they talked about things like, "Remember that Lee Morgan record that never came out?" So I started to take notes of musician's memories of sessions. I figured that some of those sessions weren't released because the music didn't work, but I also realized that there had to be some great stuff in there too. And this was at the time when Lee Morgan had just died. A few years later we lost Grant

Green and Hank Jones, so many great musicians. So that became one of my passions, to get into the Blue Note vault, because the people that were running it at the time weren't interested in jazz at all, they were just interested in making hits. I really felt that this was one of the most important catalogs in the world, and we just had to do our best to preserve it.

JIMMY SMITH, *Midnight Special*, 1961, Blue Note

When did you set up Mosaic Music?
I started Mosaic before we started with Blue Note because EMI was not interested in doing any jazz at the time. I approached them about reissuing Blue Note recordings and they said, "No, maybe in about two or three years, but not right now." So, my partner Charlie Lourie and I started Mosaic as a reaction to that. There was very little jazz in 1982 because the music business was in a bad economic climate and people weren't even bothering to keep jazz in print, let alone reissues or recording new material. So I started Mosaic to sort of fill that gap, and to let a lot of the Blue Note legacy out.

Mosaic records are very luxurious and expensive, especially in today's market, so that must have been a very adventurous enterprise?
It would have been impossible to do if you were distributing it to stores, so being mostly mail-order only was the only way we could do it to make sense economically.

What's the future of jazz?
I have no idea. As Thelonious Monk once said, "It's going everywhere, all the time, and never stops."

Do you think music as a physical object, i.e., vinyl or CD, will disappear in the coming years?
No, I think the real hard jazz fan likes to collect... likes packaging, and likes liner notes. Even as I listen I don't miss the vinyl sound, I miss the LP jacket, the cover. You are able to read the liner notes. CD booklets are made for people under 25 years old. I have to use magnifying glasses to read the goddamn things.

If you had to choose just one record in your life, what would it be?
Just one? I think it would have to be John Coltrane – *Live at the Village Vanguard*.

Eine ihrer frühesten Jazzerfahrungen ist Birdland. Erinnern Sie sich an die Atmosphäre damals?

Birdland lag in Midtown Manhattan, wohingegen die meisten Clubs unten in Greenwich Village angesiedelt waren. Es war einer der letzten Clubs der 52nd Street und lag genau am Broadway in einem touristischen Teil der Stadt. Man ging runter und kaufte eine Eintrittskarte, dann ging man noch einen Treppenabsatz hinunter und dort stand [Charlie] Parker und beschimpfte jeden, der reinkam ... er war sehr unhöflich. Man ging einen weiteren Treppenabsatz nach unten und landete im Club. Es war ein sehr großer offener Club mit einem Podest für die Band am Ende des Raumes neben den Küchentüren. Es war sehr gemütlich und sah eher aus wie ein Nachtclub als ein Jazzclub. Deshalb kamen sowohl viele Nachtclubbesucher als auch zahlreiche Jazzclubbesucher hierher.

„Ich glaube der echte Jazzfan sammelt gerne ... er interessiert sich für die Hüllen und die Begleittexte. Selbst ich vermisse, wenn ich Musik höre, nicht den Vinylklang, sondern die Hülle, das Cover."

Als der Bebop aufkam, verdrängte er den Jazz von den Tanzflächen, der dann an Beliebtheit verlor. Das hatte großen Einfluss auf den gesamten Jazz.

Das stimmt, aber Jazz verschwand nicht, er war nur nicht mehr so beliebt. Als Blue Note und Prestige begannen, Aufnahmen als 12-Inch-Platten zu veröffentlichen, von Leuten wie Art Blakey, Jimmy Smith, Jack MacDuff und Gene Ammons – also von Leuten, die sehr soulige Musik machten –, haben sie damit ein großes Publikum erreicht. Bob Weinstock von Prestige sorgte genauso wie die Jazzmusiker für ein Comeback des Jazz.

Damals, in den Sechzigern, schlossen mehrere Clubs in New York, und viele Musiker gingen nach Europa, um dort zu spielen. Live zu spielen, ist ein wesentlicher Teil des Jazz.

In den 60ern hatten viele wirtschaftliche Probleme. Es gab zwar immer noch Clubs in New York, aber nicht mehr so viele wie vorher, und man hatte immer weniger Möglichkeiten für Engagements. Nicht nur in New York war es so, sondern im ganzen Land. Es gab viele tolle Clubs in Detroit, Chicago, Washington DC und Städten, in denen in den Sommern Aufstände von Bürgerrechtlern oder der Studentenbewegung stattfanden. Dadurch mussten viele Clubs schließen. Die Leute hatten Angst, in die Viertel der Schwarzen zu gehen, wenn sie nicht selbst schwarz waren ... manchmal ging es den Schwarzen selbst natürlich genauso. Daher gab es in den USA im Allgemeinen weniger Arbeit zu dieser Zeit. Man begann auch, über FM-Radio Musik zu hören. Vorher gab es nur AM, und man hörte meistens nur die Top 40. Ende der 60er begannen viele Rock'n'Roll-Bands, andere Alben zu machen. Es ging mehr in Richtung dessen, was man heute als ‚Konzeptalbum' bezeichnet; nicht nur Popsingles, sondern längere Stücke, interessantere Musik. Dadurch wandten sich viele Hörer vom Jazz ab. Und viele Musiker wie Hank Mobley, Philly Joe Johnson, Lionel Hampton und Dexter Gordon gingen daraufhin nach Europa. Sie konnten dort besser arbeiten und erfuhren mehr Beachtung. In den 60ern fühlte man sich als Schwarzer in den USA immer noch diskriminiert. Einige reisten ursprünglich nur zu Besuch nach Europa und waren dann total begeistert, einfach weil sie respektiert wurden. Deshalb verließen eine Zeit lang eine Menge Leute die USA.

Die Fusionszene war in den Siebzigern eine Reaktion auf all diese Veränderungen. Es war eine Möglichkeit, ein größeres Publikum zu gewinnen.
Ja, genau.

Damit begann auch eine völlig neue Ära für die großen Plattenfirmen. Kurz gesagt, die Fusionszene war ein großes Geschäft.
Es war damals ein ziemlich großes Geschäft. Alle Fusionmusiker kamen ursprünglich vom Jazz: Herbie Hancock, Billy Cobham, Randy und Michael Brecker. Sie begründeten einen neuen Zweig innerhalb der Musikindustrie. Sie spielten in Rockauditorien und gaben richtige Konzerte, statt in Clubs zu spielen. Miles Davis machte das Gleiche. Seine Musik änderte sich nicht, sie war eher funkiger. Alle hatten es satt, in Clubs für wenig Geld zu spielen, und sie fanden Möglichkeiten, Konzerte zu geben und mehr Platten zu verkaufen, um besser von der Musik leben zu können.

Die Kritiker mochten die Fusionszene nicht, oder?
Die Ablehnung war ziemlich groß, vor allem bei den älteren Kritikern, glaube ich. Aber wissen Sie, eine der besten Platten aus den Siebzigern – es ist eigentlich nicht Fusion, sondern eher eine kommerzielle Platte – war *Mr. Magic* von Grover Washington Jr. Hören Sie sich einmal die Arrangements von Bob James an – mit den Rhythmen, die Ralph MacDonald darunter gelegt hat, und Grovers wunderschönem Saxofonspiel. Damals verabscheute Leonard Feather diese

Musik wahrscheinlich. Aber es war eine großartige Platte, und sie ist es immer noch. Viele dieser Platten sind zeitlos geworden. Etablierte Kritiker reagieren oft heftig auf neue Entwicklungen.

Der akustische Jazz ist damals fast verschwunden.
Nein, er ist nicht verschwunden. Es gab ihn noch, man hatte nur weniger Möglichkeiten für Plattenaufnahmen, weil es keine Independent-Labels mehr gab. Sie wurden alle von den großen Plattenfirmen aufgekauft. Und die großen Plattenfirmen waren alle nur noch an Fusion interessiert.

Weshalb werden so viele Erstausgaben von Jazzaufnahmen jetzt wieder neu aufgelegt?
Neuauflagen bilden die beste Möglichkeit, Plattenfirmen zu finanzieren. Als ich 1985 bei Blue Note angefangen habe, brachten wir in dem Jahr etwa 30 oder 40 Wiederveröffentlichungen heraus und verdienten Geld damit. Dagegen brauchte die Musik, die wir aufnahmen, viel länger, um Gewinn einzubringen. Die Neuauflagen finanzierten also die neue Musik.

Es ist eine Ihrer Leidenschaften, verstecktes Material aufzuspüren und verfügbar zu machen, nicht wahr?
Oh ja. Als ich Anfang der 1970er begann, Platten zu produzieren, lernte ich viele Leute kennen, die bei Blue Note waren, und in den Pausen zwischen den Aufnahmesessions sagten sie Sachen wie „Erinnert ihr euch an die Platte von Lee Morgan, die nie veröffentlicht wurde?" So begann ich, mir Notizen zu den Session-Erinnerungen der Musiker zu machen. Ich fand heraus, dass manche dieser Sessions nicht veröffentlicht worden waren, weil die Musik nicht funktionierte, aber ich hatte auch das Gefühl, dass darin auch etwas Großartiges stecken musste. Das war zu der Zeit, als Lee Morgan gerade gestorben war. Einige Jahre später

starben Grant Green und Hank Jones, so viele großartige Musiker. So wurde es meine Leidenschaft, Zugang zu dem Keller von Blue Note zu bekommen. Die Leute, die damals Blue Note leiteten, waren an Jazz überhaupt nicht interessiert, sie waren nur daran interessiert, Hits zu produzieren. Ich spürte wirklich, dass diese Aufnahmen zu den bedeutendsten der Welt gehören und wir alles daran setzen müssen, sie zu erhalten.

Wann haben Sie Mosaic Music gegründet?
Ich gründete Mosaic, bevor ich bei Blue Note anfing, weil EMI damals überhaupt nicht an Jazz interessiert war. Ich habe sie wegen Neuauflagen von Blue-Note-Aufnahmen angesprochen, und sie haben gesagt: „Nein, vielleicht in zwei oder drei Jahren, aber jetzt nicht". Als Reaktion darauf habe ich mit Charlie Lourie als Partner Mosaic gegründet. 1982 lag die Jazzszene fast brach, weil es der Musikindustrie wirtschaftlich schlecht ging. Die Leute waren nicht einmal daran interessiert, den aktuellen Jazzkatalog zu pflegen, geschweige denn, Neuauflagen oder neue Aufnahmen herauszubringen. Deshalb habe ich Mosaic gegründet, um sozusagen die Lücke zu schließen und soviel wie möglich von dem Blue-Note-Erbe herauszubringen.

Die Platten von Mosaic sind aufwendig gestaltet und teuer, besonders für den heutigen Markt. War das riskant?
Plattenverkauf über Läden wäre unmöglich gewesen. Nur im Versand ist das wirtschaftlich sinnvoll.

Wie sieht die Zukunft des Jazz aus?
Keine Ahnung. Thelonious Monk meinte mal: „Er existiert immer weiter, entwickelt sich in alle Richtungen und ist nicht aufzuhalten".

Glauben Sie, dass es Musik auf den klassischen Tonträgern wie Vinyl oder CD in Zukunft nicht mehr geben wird?
Nein, ich glaube der echte Jazzfan sammelt gerne ... er interessiert sich für die Hüllen und die Begleittexte. Selbst ich vermisse, wenn ich Musik höre, nicht den Vinylklang, sondern die Hülle, das Cover.

GRANT GREEN, *Iron City!*, 1967, Cobblestone (see page 209)

Man kann dort die Begleittexte lesen. CD-Booklets sind für Leute unter 25 gemacht. Ich brauche eine Lupe, um die verdammten Dinger zu lesen.

Welche Platte würden Sie auf eine einsame Insel mitnehmen?
Ich glaube, es wäre John Coltrane – *Live at the Village Vanguard*.

L'un de vos souvenirs les plus anciens liés au jazz est Birdland. Vous souvenez-vous de l'atmosphère de l'époque ?

Birdland se trouvait dans le centre de Manhattan, alors que la plupart des clubs se concentraient dans le Greenwich Village. C'était le dernier club qui restait de 52nd Street. Il se trouvait juste à côté de Broadway, dans un quartier très touristique. Il fallait descendre, acheter un ticket et descendre un autre escalier. [Charlie] Parker était là, et il malmenait tous ceux qui entraient...il était très grossier. Ensuite, on descendait encore un autre escalier, et on se retrouvait dans le club. C'était un club ouvert et très grand, avec une scène au fond, près des cuisines. C'était très confortable et ça avait plus l'air d'une boîte de nuit que d'un club de jazz. Le public était donc composé d'amateurs de jazz, mais aussi de gens qui aimaient aller en boîte.

« Je pense que les vrais amateurs de jazz aiment collectionner. Ils aiment les pochettes et les notes d'accompagnement. Lorsque j'écoute un CD, ce qui me manque ce n'est pas le son du vinyle, mais plutôt la pochette. »

Lorsque le be-bop est apparu, le jazz a disparu des pistes de danse et n'était plus une musique populaire. Cela a eu un grand impact sur le jazz en général.

C'est vrai, mais le jazz n'a pas disparu, il était juste moins populaire. Lorsque Blue Note et Prestige ont commencé à enregistrer des 30 cm de gens comme Art Blakey, Jimmy Smith, Jack MacDuff, Gene Ammons – des gens qui étaient très proches de la soul, ils ont commencé à atteindre un public très vaste. Bob Weinstock, de Prestige, a autant contribué au retour du jazz que les musiciens eux-mêmes.

À cette époque, dans les années 1960, plusieurs clubs new-yorkais ont fermé et beaucoup de musiciens sont partis en Europe. Dans le jazz, il est important de jouer pour survivre.

Il y avait beaucoup de problèmes économiques dans les années 1960. Il y avait toujours des clubs à New York, mais pas autant qu'avant, et il y avait de moins en moins de travail. Pas seulement à New York, mais dans tout le pays. Nous avions beaucoup de grands clubs à Detroit, Chicago, Washington DC et des villes où il y avait des émeutes en été, des émeutes à propos des droits civils et des émeutes d'étudiants. Cela a mis de nombreux clubs sur la paille. Les gens ont commencé à avoir peur d'aller dans les quartiers noirs, s'ils n'étaient pas noirs, je sais...bien sûr, parfois même s'ils étaient noirs. Les chances de trouver de l'emploi aux États-Unis en général se réduisaient à l'époque. Et puis, les gens adoptèrent la radio FM pour écouter leur musique. Avant, il n'y avait que la radio AM, et surtout le Top 40. Vers la fin des années 1960, beaucoup de groupes de rock commencèrent à faire des albums différents. Ça ressemblait plus à ce qu'on appelle maintenant les «albums-concepts». Pas seulement des singles de pop, mais une musique plus approfondie et plus intéressante. Cela a détourné une bonne partie du public du jazz. C'est pour cela que beaucoup de musiciens comme Hank Mobley, Philly Joe Johnson, Lionel Hampton et Dexter Gordon sont partis en Europe. Ils y trouvaient beaucoup plus de travail et de respect. Aux États-Unis, dans les années 1960, si vous étiez noir, vous vous sentiez encore comme un nègre, d'une certaine façon.Certains sont partis en Europe pour visiter, et sont restés parce qu'on les traitait avec respect. Nous avons donc perdu beaucoup de gens pendant un bon bout de temps.

Dans les années 1970, la fusion était la réaction à toutes ces transformations. C'était une manière de toucher un public plus vaste.
Oui.

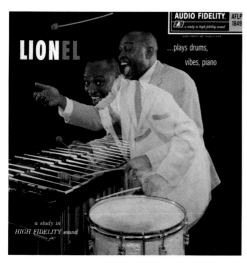

LIONEL HAMPTON, *Lionel Plays Drums, Vibes, Piano*, 1958, Audio Fidelity

Et cela a aussi enclenché tout un nouveau mouvement chez les grandes maisons de disques. En d'autres termes, la fusion brassait beaucoup d'argent.
Oui, à l'époque. Tous les musiciens de fusion étaient des musiciens de jazz au départ. Herbie Hancock, Billy Cobham, Randy et Michael Brecker. Ils ont créé un nouveau secteur. Ils jouaient dans des salles de rock, et ils faisaient des concerts plutôt que d'aller jouer dans des clubs. Miles Davis a fait la même chose. Il ne s'est pas vraiment mis

à faire de la fusion, il était plutôt dans le funk, mais tous se sont lassés de jouer pour trois sous dans les clubs et ont trouvé le moyen de faire des concerts, de mieux gagner leur vie et de vendre plus de disques.

Les critiques détestaient la fusion, n'est-ce pas?
C'était quelque chose de très fort. Surtout les critiques de la vieille génération, je crois. Mais vous savez, l'un des meilleurs disques des années 1970 (et il ne s'agit pas tant de fusion, plutôt de musique commerciale) était *Mr. Magic* de Grover Washington Jr. Écoutez les arrangements de Bob James, les rythmes de Ralph MacDonald et le jeu magnifique de Grover. À l'époque, Leonard Feather détestait probablement. Mais c'est un disque superbe. Il a bien résisté au passage du temps. Une grande partie de cette musique a résisté au passage du temps. Lorsque quelque chose de nouveau apparaît, les critiques vétérans réagissent souvent violemment.

Le jazz acoustique a pratiquement disparu à cette époque.
Non, il n'a pas pratiquement disparu. Il y avait beaucoup d'activité, mais il y avait moins d'occasions d'enregistrer, parce qu'il ne restait plus de labels indépendants. Ils avaient tous été rachetés par de grandes maisons de disques. Et elles s'intéressaient toutes à la fusion.

Pourquoi autant d'enregistrements de jazz originaux sont-ils réédités aujourd'hui?
Les rééditions sont la meilleure façon de financer une maison de disques. Lorsque j'ai commencé chez Blue Note en 1985, nous avons fait entre 30 et 40 rééditions cette même année, et elles ont rapporté beaucoup d'argent. Alors que la musique qu'on enregistrait mettait beaucoup plus de temps à devenir rentable. Les rééditions finançaient la création.

C'est l'une de vos passions, n'est-ce pas ? Redécouvrir ces trésors cachés et les remettre sur le marché.

Oui. Lorsque j'ai commencé à produire des disques au début des années 1970, j'ai rencontré beaucoup des gens qui étaient chez Blue Note, et lors des pauses des séances d'enregistrement ils parlaient de choses du genre : « Tu te souviens de cet album de Lee Morgan qui n'est jamais sorti ? » Alors, j'ai commencé à prendre des notes sur les souvenirs que les musiciens avaient des séances. Je me suis rendu compte que certaines n'avaient jamais été gravées parce que la musique ne fonctionnait pas, mais j'ai aussi réalisé qu'il y avait de très bonnes choses. Cela se passait juste après le décès de Lee Morgan. Quelques années plus tard, nous avons perdu Grant Green et Hank Jones, et beaucoup de grands musiciens. Fouiller les archives de Blue Note est donc devenu l'une de mes passions, parce que les dirigeants de l'époque ne s'intéressaient pas du tout au jazz, ils voulaient juste faire des tubes. Je trouvais vraiment que c'était l'un des catalogues les plus importants du monde, et que nous devions faire tout notre possible pour le préserver.

Pourquoi avez-vous créé Mosaic Music ?

J'ai lancé Mosaic Music avant de commencer avec Blue Note, parce qu'EMI ne souhaitait pas faire de jazz à l'époque. Je leur avais proposé de rééditer des disques de Blue Note, et ils avaient répondu : « Non, peut-être dans deux ou trois ans, mais pas maintenant. » J'ai donc créé Mosaic avec mon partenaire Charlie Lourie, en réaction à cette réponse. Il y avait très peu de jazz en 1982 parce que le secteur de la musique souffrait d'un mauvais climat économique et que les gens se fichaient pas mal qu'il y ait des disques de jazz dans les bacs, et encore moins de faire des rééditions ou d'enregistrer des nouveautés. Mosaic était donc censé combler cette lacune, et propo-

ser au public une partie de l'héritage de Blue Note.

Les disques de Mosaic sont très luxueux, et très chers, surtout pour le marché actuel. Cela a dû être une entreprise très risquée.

Cela aurait été impossible à distribuer en magasin. Ils se vendent principalement par correspondance. C'était le seul moyen de s'y retrouver financièrement.

Quel est l'avenir du jazz ?

Je n'en ai aucune idée. Thelonious Monk a dit un jour : « Ça va partout, tout le temps, et ça ne s'arrête jamais. »

Pensez-vous que la musique en tant qu'objet physique, par exemple le vinyle ou le CD, disparaîtra dans quelques années ?

Non, je pense que les vrais amateurs de jazz aiment collectionner. Ils aiment les pochettes et les notes d'accompagnement. Lorsque j'écoute un CD, ce qui me manque ce n'est pas le son du vinyle, mais plutôt la pochette. Là, on peut lire les notes. Les livrets des CD sont faits pour les moins de 25 ans. Il me faut une loupe pour lire ces satanés machins.

Si vous n'aviez droit qu'à un seul disque, lequel choisiriez-vous ?

Seulement un ? Je pense que ce serait John Coltrane – *Live at the Village Vanguard.*

JOHN COLTRANE, *Live At The Village Vanguard Again!*, 1966, Impulse!

coltrane
live at the village vanguard again!

i!
impulse!
A-9124

MOTION LEE KONITZ

RUDY VAN GELDER

Rudy Van Gelder is one of the most important sound engineers in the history of recorded music. Between 1953 and 1967 he was responsible for nearly every session on the Blue Note label, from Miles Davis to Thelonious Monk. In addition, his prolific output also extended to such significant jazz labels as Prestige, Impulse!, Verve and CTI. Rudy Van Gelder started out as an amateur radio operator and recording enthusiast. However, around 1952 the inevitable seemed to happen, through friend and saxophonist Gil Mellé, Van Gelder had a fortuitous introduction to Alfred Lion, founder and producer of Blue Note Records. Thus began a long and illustrious career. In 1959 Van Gelder moved to a larger studio in Englewood Cliffs. It was here that John Coltrane recorded his magnum opus *A Love Supreme* for Impulse! Records in 1964. Later it would play host to a diverse spectrum of recordings, including a popular series of studio albums for CTI Records in the '70s.

Rudy Van Gelder gilt als einer der bedeutendsten Toningenieure in der Geschichte der Musik. Zwischen 1953 und 1967 war Van Gelder für fast jede Session des Labels Blue Note – von Miles Davis bis Thelonious Monk – verantwortlich. Zusätzlich war er für andere bedeutende Jazz-Label wie Prestige, Impulse!, Verve und CTI tätig. Rudy Van Gelder übte sich schon früh in der Kunst der Tontechnik, als Amateur-Radiofunker und bei Musikaufnahmen. Im Jahr 1952 allerdings schien das Unmögliche wahr zu werden: Sein Freund, der Saxofonist Gil Mellé, stellte Van Gelder zufällig Alfred Lion vor, dem Gründer und Produzenten von Blue Note Records. Damit begann eine lange und schillernde Musikkarriere. 1959 zog Van Gelder in ein größeres Studio in Englewood Cliffs um. Genau dort nahm John Coltrane 1964 sein Opus Magnum *A Love Supreme* für Impulse! Records auf. Später war das Studio Ort unzähliger Aufnahmen, so zum Beispiel auch für berühmte Studioalbum-Serien für CTI Records in den 1970ern.

Rudy Van Gelder est l'un des ingénieurs du son les plus importants de l'histoire de la musique enregistrée. Il a participé à presque toutes les séances de Blue Note entre 1953 et 1967, de Miles Davis à Thelonious Monk. D'autres grands labels de jazz comme Prestige, Impulse!, Verve et CTI ont également bénéficié de ses services. Il débuta dans la radio amateur et se passionna pour l'enregistrement. Mais l'inévitable se produisit en 1952 quand, grâce à son ami le saxophoniste Gil Mellé, il rencontra Alfred Lion, le créateur et producteur de Blue Note Records. C'est alors que commença une carrière longue et illustre. En 1959, il prit un studio plus grand à Englewood Cliffs. C'est là que John Coltrane enregistra en 1964 son œuvre maîtresse *A Love Supreme* pour Impulse! Records. Ce studio allait être le témoin de nombreux enregistrements très variés, notamment une série très populaire d'albums réalisés pour CTI Records dans les années 1970.

LEE KONITZ, *Motion*, 1961, Verve (see page 268)

How did you get involved in the recording business?

It happened a long time ago. As a child I used to listen to radio and became an amateur (ham) radio operator. Right after that I was interested in jazz music – the two things.

When you first started, how much recording equipment was available?

Available to me? Nothing, I constructed my own and put all the electronics together. There were recording machines, but they were home disc recorders.

You are the first "sound engineer" to be credited on an album sleeve. That was quite an achievement.

That was a piano record by Lennie Tristano. He was fascinated by the whole dubbing process – being able to play something and record over it. And so we made a record where I did that, and he was so grateful to me for doing the technical work that he put my name on it. That was first time.

"When Alfred Lion came into the studio I knew what the finished product was that he wanted to sell and he made sure I could do that."

Your output was very prolific. You recorded sessions for Blue Note, Prestige and Savoy. How did you manage your time?

It was impossible... everybody would just call up and say, "I need this done on a certain date." So what I used to do I would allocate a particular day in the week for a particular client. They would call me only on those days. Prestige took advantage of that. I also recorded for a classical company called Vox Records and would reserve two days for mastering for them...and then Blue Note, that was always Friday. That's how I did it.

How did you come to meet Alfred Lion?

I recorded a nice small band led by Gil Mellé. Alfred listened to the record and got interested in it. This was in the days of 10-inch LPs. At that time Alfred was working in New York, and he was using a studio by the name of WOR, which is a radio station in New York City and they also did commercial recording. So, he went to the engineer he was using and said, "I want to do a record of this band, and I want it to sound like this." The engineer listened to it and said, "I can't do that, you'd better go to the guy who did it." And so he did. He came out to see me in New Jersey and asked me. I said, "Sure, let's do it." I never went any place else after that.

And that was the beginning of an incredible relationship. What was the working atmosphere like in the Blue Note sessions? How did Alfred Lion work?

He was very organized. When he came into the studio I knew what the finished product was that he wanted to sell and he made sure I could do that.

Did Blue Note have a particular influence on your development as an engineer?

Sure. Alfred, in particular, and Francis Wolff too. They very much influenced my thinking about recording. Their attitudes and feelings, the way they looked at the music.

How did the invention of stereo change your approach to recording jazz?

As I said before, I was also working for a classical company. The jazz people had no interest in stereo. They were happy with mono, with their one speaker. The musicians too, they couldn't care less about stereo. But there was the influence of the classical people on me, they wanted stereo, it was a big deal for them. It's understandable because there were always big orchestras where the stereo was exciting to hear. I influenced Alfred to switch over to stereo, but even then he didn't want to leave mono. So we used to end up doing two tapes, recording one in mono and one in stereo. He (Alfred) never cared about stereo. A lot of jazz people still don't.

A completely different approach to your work with Creed Taylor at CTI?

By that time stereo was acceptable. [Creed] took the excitement of recording to a whole new level. He used bigger orchestras, he'd get the people he wanted and was very focused on a perception basis. He focused all his attention on making that thing as good as he possibly could, and whatever it took. That's the way he worked.

What about this whole catalog of reissues that you are involved in, the Rudy Van Gelder (RVG) editions? Working with the stereo and mono tapes, how did you decide which format to use for the new master?

A lot of the time it depends on whether the tapes are available or not. Some mono tapes have disappeared, some have survived. The tapes that I would like to get are not available any more. The tapes that I do get are a representation of mishandling over the years, not by anyone particularly. The people I work for today want stereo, they are not interested in mono any more. I read a recent review online where they compare the mono masters I did with an SACD of the same music and there was a big discussion about it. It was interesting.

How did Blue Note come to ask you to re-record and remaster your own tapes?

That idea came from Mr Hitoshi Namekata, who is from the Japanese arm of Blue Note. I've now made somewhere between 200 or 300 albums on this series. At least 250, and beyond, I think?

Michael Cuscuna says it took you three days to decide whether to do them or not. Why did it take you so long? It was an incredible opportunity.

It was such a huge job. It's a time consuming process, I couldn't do anything else for a while, nothing but that.

What did it feel like to listen back to all those original tapes?

Technically speaking, I was going through all my old problems again. There they were in front of me again. The positive side was listening to the music in a way that I've never heard it before, because when I did all those sessions in the past, I was trying to make sure that it recorded properly with the limited equipment we had at that time. I had all the people out there in the studio, and he [John Coltrane] was making all those records with his quartets and big groups, you know... I never really heard that music. And now I could sit back and listen. It was astounding to hear it properly as a producer.

It is truly fantastic. It sounds so modern, like you recorded it today.

When I heard it on the radio I commented, "It sounds just like it was made two weeks ago."

Wie verlief Ihr Einstieg ins Musikgeschäft?
Oh, das ist sehr lange her. Als Kind hörte ich viel Radio und übte mich bald als Amateur-Radiofunker. Kurz darauf lernte ich die Jazzmusik kennen. Das waren die beiden wichtigsten Faktoren.

Über welche Ausstattung verfügten Sie, als Sie damit anfingen?
Ausstattung? Ich? Ich brauchte gar nichts. Ich baute mir alles selbst und bastelte mir die Elektronik dazu. Es gab zwar schon professionelle Aufnahmegeräte, aber ein Heim-Plattenrecorder tat es auch.

„Wenn Alfred Lion ins Studio kam, wusste ich bereits genau, wie das Endprodukt aussehen sollte, das er verkaufen wollte, und er vergewisserte sich, dass ich das auch genau so hinbekam."

Sie sind der erste Toningenieur, der namentlich auf einem Plattencover erwähnt wurde. Das war eine Errungenschaft, nicht wahr?
Es handelte sich dabei um eine Klavieraufnahme von Lennie Tristano. Tristano war so fasziniert von der Methode des Nachvertonens, er konnte es einfach nicht glauben, dass man zwei Tonspuren übereinander legen konnte. Also machten wir eine Platte, auf der ich genau das tat. Er war mir so dankbar dafür, dass ich die gesamte technische Arbeit übernommen habe, dass er

meinen Namen aufs Cover drucken ließ. Das war das erste Mal.

Ihre Karriere verlief unglaublich produktiv. Sie nahmen Platten für Blue Note, Prestige und Savoy auf. Wie bekamen Sie das zeitlich unter einen Hut?
Das war wirklich unmöglich ... Ich bekam ständig Aufträge, ohne gefragt zu werden, ob ich Zeit dafür hatte. Um dieses Problem zu lösen, reservierte ich jeden Tag der Woche für einen anderen Kunden. Sie durften mich nur an diesen Tagen anrufen. Prestige profitierte davon. Ich arbeitete ja noch für ein Klassik-Label namens Vox Records, für das ich zwei Tage in der Woche reservierte. Blue Note lag immer auf einem Freitag. So habe ich es geschafft.

Wie lernten Sie Alfred Lion kennen?
Ich machte Aufnahmen für eine kleine, aber gute, von Gil Mellé geleitete Band. Alfred hörte sich die Platte an und begann, sich dafür zu interessieren. Das war noch zu Zeiten der 10-Inch-LPs. Damals ließ Alfred seine Aufnahmen noch in New York in einem Studio namens WOR machen. WOR war ein Radiosender in New York City, der auch kommerziell arbeitete. Also ging er zu dem Toningenieur, mit dem er normalerweise zusammenarbeitete, und sagte zu ihm: „Ich brauche eine Aufnahme von dieser Band, und ich möchte, dass es genau so klingt." Der Tonmeister hörte es sich an und antwortete: „So etwas kann ich nicht, es ist besser, wenn du zu dem Typen gehst, der die Aufnahmen gemacht hat." Genau das tat er dann auch. Er fuhr raus nach New Jersey, um mich zu fragen, ob ich für ihn arbeiten will. Ich antwortete: „Klar, wir können gleich anfangen." Und ich ging nie wieder woandershin.

Und das war der Beginn einer langen, fruchtbaren Zusammenarbeit. Wie war die Atmosphäre in einer Blue-Note-Session?

Wie ließ es sich mit Alfred Lion arbeiten?
Er arbeitete sehr organisiert. Wenn er ins Studio kam, wusste ich bereits genau, wie das Endprodukt aussehen sollte, das er verkaufen wollte, und er vergewisserte sich, dass ich das auch genau so hinbekam.

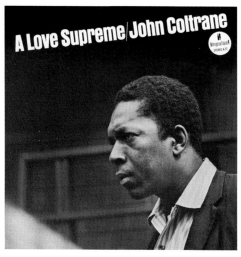

JOHN COLTRANE, *A Love Supreme*, 1964, Impulse! (see page 134)

Beeinflusste Blue Note Ihre Arbeit als Toningenieur?
Ja, sicher. Alfred besonders, aber auch Francis Wolff. Vor allem auf meine Aufnahmemethoden übten sie einen starken Einfluss aus. Sie hatten eine ganz besondere Einstellung zur Musik.

Inwiefern veränderte die Erfindung der Stereotechnik Ihre Arbeitsmethode bei den Jazzaufnahmen?
Wie ich ja bereits erzählte, arbeitete ich für eine Plattenfirma, die klassische Musik herausbrachte. Die Jazzleute hatten überhaupt kein Interesse an der Stereotechnik. Sie waren glücklich mit ihren Mono-Aufnahmen und ihrem einen Lautsprecher. Bei den Musikern war es ähnlich, sie interessierten sich ebenso wenig für Aufnahmen in Stereoqualität. Aber die Leute aus der Klassiksparte hatten einen enormen Einfluss auf mich. Sie bestanden auf der Zweikanaltechnik. Das ist nachvollziehbar, denn man spielte ja immer mit großen Orchestern, bei denen der Stereoklang richtig gut wirkte. Ich überredete Alfred, auf Stereo zu wechseln, aber nicht einmal dann wollte er ganz auf seine Monoaufnahmen verzichten. Also nahmen wir jedesmal zwei Bänder auf, eines in Mono und eines in Stereo. Er (Alfred) machte sich nie etwas aus den Stereoaufnahmen. Viele Jazz-Leute sind immer noch so eingestellt.

Die Zusammenarbeit mit Creed Taylor bei CTI war komplett anders, nicht wahr?
Zu dieser Zeit war das Zweikanalton-System schon viel verbreiteter. [Creed] ließ sich darauf ein, die Aufnahmen auf einer völlig neuen Ebene stattfinden zu lassen. Er setzte größere Orchester ein und suchte sich genau die Leute, die er brauchte – für ihn lag der Fokus vor allem auf der Wahrnehmung, auf den Sinneseindrücken. Sein wichtigstes Ziel war es, die bestmögliche Qualität zu erreichen, egal wie viel Arbeit damit zusammenhing.

Wie gingen Sie bei der RVG (Rudy Van Gelder)-Edition vor, der Wiederveröffentlichungsreihe, an der Sie mitarbeiteten? Sie hatten ja sowohl Stereo- als auch Mono-Aufnahmen zur Verfügung. Welches Format verwendeten Sie für die Neuaufnahmen?
Es hing vor allem davon ab, ob die Tonbänder noch auffindbar waren oder nicht. Über die Jahre hatten sie öfter ihre Besitzer gewechselt. Einige Mono-Tonbänder waren verschwunden, andere waren noch da. Aber ausgerechnet die Tonbänder, die ich gerne gehabt hätte, waren nicht mehr vorhanden – und die noch erhaltenen waren häufig durch ungeeignete Aufbewahrung und Handhabung beschädigt worden. Heute mache ich nur noch Stereoaufnahmen,

niemand interessiert sich mehr für Mono. Kürzlich las ich ein interessantes Interview, in dem man meine Mono-Aufnahmen eines Stückes mit einer SACD-Aufnahme der gleichen Musik verglich – es gab eine heiße Diskussion darum.

Wie kam es dazu, dass Blue Note auf Sie zukam und Sie darum bat, Ihre eigenen Tonbänder neu aufzunehmen und wiederzuveröffentlichen?
Das Ganze war eine Idee von Hitoshi Namekata, der bei Blue Note in Japan arbeitet. Bis jetzt habe ich bereits 200 oder 300 Alben in dieser Serie fertig gestellt.

LENNIE TRISTANO, *Descent into the Maelstrom*, 1978, Inner City

Michael Cuscuna berichtete davon, dass Sie ganze drei Jahre brauchten, um die Entscheidung zu treffen, ob Sie bei dem Projekt mitmachen oder nicht. Warum dauerte es so lange? Es war doch eine einmalige Gelegenheit.
Ja, aber es war so ein riesiges und zeitaufwendiges Projekt! Während ich daran arbeitete, gab es Phasen, in denen ich für nichts anderes Zeit hatte.

Wie fühlte es sich an, nach so langer Zeit die Originalaufnahmen noch einmal zu hören?
Vom technischen Standpunkt aus stand ich noch einmal vor genau den gleichen Problemen wie damals. Der positive Aspekt war, dass ich die Musik nun noch einmal mit ganz anderen Ohren hörte. Damals bei den Aufnahmen musste ich mich voll darauf konzentrieren, dass ich mit meinen begrenzten Mitteln das bestmögliche Ergebnis erzielte. Die Künstler kamen zu mir ins Studio, und er (John Coltrane) wollte Aufnahmen mit Quartetten und auch größeren Bands machen... Ich hörte die Musik damals nicht wirklich, verstehen Sie? Und jetzt kann ich mich zurücklehnen und einfach nur zuhören.

Die Qualität ist allerdings auch hervorragend. Es klingt so modern, als hätten Sie es gerade erst aufgenommen.
Ja, genau! Als ich es im Radio hörte, war mein erster Gedanke: „Der Sound ist so gut, dass man denken könnte, die Aufnahmen seien erst vor zwei Wochen entstanden."

Comment avez-vous commencé dans l'enregistrement ?

C'était il y a longtemps. Enfant, j'écoutais la radio et j'ai fait de la radio amateur. Tout de suite après, je me suis intéressé au jazz. Les deux choses.

Lorsque vous avez commencé, de quel équipement d'enregistrement disposiez-vous ?

Ce dont je disposais ? De rien. J'ai construit mon propre équipement, j'ai assemblé toute l'électronique moi-même. Il y avait des appareils enregistreurs, mais c'était pour faire des disques à usage domestique.

> **« Lorsqu' Alfred Lion arrivait au studio je savais quel produit fini il voulait vendre, et il vérifiait que je pouvais le faire. »**

Vous êtes le premier ingénieur du son à avoir été cité sur la couverture d'un album. C'était un grand honneur.

C'était sur un disque de piano de Lennie Tristano. Il était fasciné par le fait que l'on pouvait faire jouer une bande et enregistrer par-dessus. Alors nous avons fait un disque dans lequel j'utilise cette technique, et il m'était tellement reconnaissant pour le travail technique qu'il a mis mon nom dessus. C'était une première.

Vous avez été très prolifique. Vous avez enregistré des séances pour Blue Note, Prestige et Savoy. Comment faisiez-vous pour gérer votre temps ?

C'était impossible…Tout le monde appelait et disait : « J'ai besoin de ça pour telle date. » Alors ce que je faisais, c'est que j'affectais à chaque client certains jours de la semaine. Ils ne pouvaient m'appeler que lorsque c'était leur jour. Prestige en a profité. Je travaillais aussi pour une maison de disques classiques, Vox Records, et je leur réservais deux jours pour le mastering. Et pour Blue Note, c'était toujours le vendredi. C'est comme ça que je faisais.

Comment avez-vous rencontré Alfred Lion ?

J'avais enregistré un bon petit groupe dirigé par Gil Mellé. Alfred a écouté l'enregistrement, et ça l'a intéressé. C'était à l'époque des 33 tours de 25 cm. Alfred travaillait à New York, et il utilisait un studio qui s'appelait WOR, une station de radio new-yorkaise qui faisait aussi des enregistrements commerciaux. Il est allé voir l'ingénieur du son avec qui il travaillait et il lui a dit : « Je veux faire un disque avec ce groupe, et je veux le même son. » L'ingénieur a écouté et a répondu : « Je ne peux pas faire ça, il vaudrait mieux aller voir le type qui l'a fait. » Alors il est venu me voir dans le New Jersey et m'a demandé de le faire. J'ai dit : « Bien sûr, allons-y. » Et je suis resté.

Et ce fut le début d'une relation incroyable. Comment était l'atmosphère de travail lors des séances de Blue Note ? Comment travaillait Alfred Lion ?

Il était très organisé. Lorsqu'il arrivait au studio, je savais quel produit fini il voulait vendre, et il vérifiait que je pouvais le faire.

Est-ce que Blue Note a eu une influence particulière sur votre évolution en tant qu'ingénieur du son ?

Oui. Alfred en particulier, et Francis Wolff aussi.

Comment l'invention de la stéréo a-t-elle modifié votre approche de l'enregistrement du jazz ?

Comme je l'ai dit plus tôt, je travaillais aussi dans la musique classique. Dans le jazz, le public ne s'intéressait pas à la stéréo. Les gens étaient contents en mono, avec un seul haut-parleur. Les musiciens aussi. Ils se fichaient pas mal de la stéréo. Mais les gens qui faisaient du classique m'ont influencé. Ils voulaient la stéréo, c'était important pour eux. C'est compréhensible, parce qu'il y avait toujours de grands orchestres qui donnaient un résultat très intéressant en stéréo. J'ai persuadé Alfred de passer à la stéréo, mais il n'a jamais voulu abandonner la mono. Alors on finissait souvent par faire deux bandes, l'une en mono et l'autre en stéréo. Il (Alfred) ne s'est jamais intéressé à la mono. Dans le jazz, beaucoup ne s'y intéressent toujours pas.

C'était une approche totalement différente, par rapport à votre travail avec Creed Taylor chez CTI.
À cette époque, la stéréo était devenue acceptable. [Creed] rendait le processus d'enregistrement absolument passionnant. Il utilisait des orchestres plus grands, il obtenait les gens qu'il voulait et il était très attentif à la perception. Il voulait faire les choses aussi bien que possible, et il concentrait toute son attention sur cet objectif.

Et pour tout ce catalogue de rééditions, RVG (Rudy Van Gelder) Editions ? Comment avez-vous choisi entre les bandes mono et stéréo pour le nouveau master ?
Souvent, cela dépend de si les bandes sont disponibles ou non. Elles ont changé de mains au cours des années. Certaines bandes mono ont disparu, d'autres ont survécu. Les bandes que j'aimerais obtenir ne sont plus disponibles. Celles que j'arrive à obtenir ont mal vieilli et ont été maltraitées, par personne en particulier. Les gens pour lesquels je travaille aujourd'hui veulent de la stéréo, ils ne s'intéressent plus à la mono. Récemment, j'ai lu une critique sur Internet où ils comparaient les masters en mono que j'avais faits avec un SACD de la même musique, il y avait un grand débat autour de ce thème. C'était intéressant.

Comment se fait-il que Blue Note vous ait demandé de réenregistrer et de remastériser vos propres bandes ?
Cette idée est venue de M. Hitoshi Namekata, qui fait partie de la branche japonaise de Blue Note. J'ai déjà fait entre 200 et 300 albums de cette série. Au moins 250, et plus, je crois ?

Michael Cuscuna dit que vous avez mis trois jours pour décider si vous alliez le faire. Pourquoi si longtemps ? C'était une opportunité magnifique.
C'était un travail tellement énorme. Le processus demande beaucoup de temps, je n'ai rien pu faire d'autre pendant un certain temps.

Qu'est-ce que cela vous a inspiré, de réécouter toutes ces bandes originales ?
En ce qui concerne la technique, je revivais tous mes vieux problèmes. Le côté positif, c'était d'écouter la musique d'une toute nouvelle façon, parce qu'en travaillant sur toutes ces séances à l'époque j'essayais de m'assurer que l'enregistrement était correct avec l'équipement limité dont nous disposions. Tout le monde était dans le studio et il (John Coltrane) faisait tous ces disques avec des quartettes ou de grands groupes. Vous savez...je n'avais jamais vraiment écouté cette musique. Et là je pouvais me détendre et écouter. C'était stupéfiant de pouvoir l'écouter véritablement, en tant que producteur.

Le résultat est vraiment fantastique. Le son est si moderne, on dirait que vous l'avez enregistré hier.
Lorsque je l'ai entendu à la radio, j'ai dit : «On dirait que ça date d'il y a deux semaines.»

DIZZY GILLESPIE, *Cornucopia*, 1969, United Artists

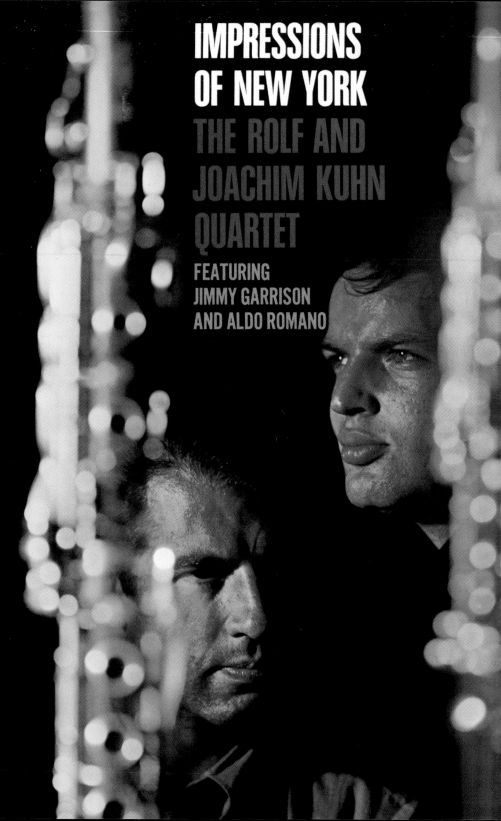

IMPRESSIONS OF NEW YORK

THE ROLF AND JOACHIM KUHN QUARTET

FEATURING
JIMMY GARRISON
AND ALDO ROMANO

ASHLEY KAHN

Ashley Kahn is an American music historian, journalist and producer. As well as being Music Editor at VH1, Kahn is a primary contributor to the *Rolling Stone Jazz & Blues Album Guide*. He writes for *The New York Times*, *Rolling Stone*, *Down Beat*, *JazzTimes* and *Mojo*. His most critically acclaimed books have been on two seminal jazz albums, *Kind Of Blue: The Making of the Miles Davis Masterpiece* and *A Love Supreme: The Story of John Coltrane's Signature Album*. In his most recent book, *The House That Trane Built: The Story of Impulse! Records*, Kahn examines the history of one of the most groundbreaking record labels in the jazz genre.

Ashley Kahn, amerikanischer Musikhistoriker, Journalist und Produzent, ist als Musikredakteur bei VH1 tätig. Außerdem wirkte er maßgeblich bei der Entstehung des *Rolling Stone Jazz & Blues Album Guide* mit. Er schreibt für *The New York Times*, *Rolling Stone*, *Down Beat*, *JazzTimes* und *Mojo*. Von der Kritik mit Beifall aufgenommen wurden insbesondere seine Bücher über zwei bedeutende Jazzalben: *Kind of Blue – Die Entstehung eines Meisterwerks* und *A Love Supreme – John Coltranes legendäres Album*. In seinem aktuellsten Buch *Impulse! Das Label, das Coltrane erschuf* erkundet Kahn die Geschichte eines der einflussreichsten und innovativsten Plattenlabels der Jazzmusik.

Ashley Kahn est historien de la musique américaine, journaliste et producteur. Il est rédacteur musical chez VH1, et est l'un des principaux coauteurs du *Rolling Stone Jazz & Blues Album Guide*. Il écrit pour le *New York Times*, *Rolling Stone*, *Down Beat*, *JazzTimes* et *Mojo*. Ses deux livres les plus applaudis par la critique avaient pour sujet deux grands albums de jazz, *Kind Of Blue : The Making of the Miles Davis Masterpiece* et *A Love Supreme : The Story of John Coltrane's Signature Album*. Dans son dernier livre, *The House That Trane Built : The Story of Impulse! Records*, il examine l'histoire de l'une des maisons de disques les plus révolutionnaires du jazz.

THE ROLF AND JOACHIM KÜHN QUARTET, *Impressions Of New York*, 1967, Impulse!

Kind of Blue was your first book about jazz. What was the driving force behind it?

I came up with the idea on the 40th anniversary of the album's release. *Kind of Blue* was released in August 1959 and to mark the occasion I proposed an article to *The New York Times*. I was given 1,000 words to describe why this album is still so important. The article appeared on a Sunday and the next Monday morning I got a call from a book agent asking if I could make a book out of this idea. Remember that back in 1999 books on music, especially on jazz, were usually biographies or essays about a music scene. No one had thought of focusing on one detail – one album. I had to come up with the idea of how this would come together. I went back to the book agent and said, "Yes, I can do this."

"I held it in my hands and said, 'Oh my God, it just feels like quality, it looks like quality.' It was the package that made me buy that album."

That must have required a huge amount of investigation? Did you have access to the record label archives?

They brought the tape out of the archives for me. All tapes are kept in an underground storage facility in New York called Iron Mountain. And they gave me the honor of setting up a studio where I could go and sit for a whole day. As the tape is so fragile they only play it when they really have to, so I could only get the engineer to play it one time. I wrote down everything I heard, including all the studio conversations, and all that became part of the book. I also had access to all the paper archives, including

the correspondence that producer Teo Macero had. So yes, I was very lucky and had access to some very special things. I also worked on a radio station here in New York that has unpublished interviews with Bill Evans where he talked about *Kind of Blue*.

This must have been an emotional experience?

Of course! It was one of those albums that opened up a whole new world of music for me. Before *Kind of Blue* I was just a Rock 'n' Roll guy who thought the only valuable music that was made happened after Woodstock – and it had to be Rock 'n' Roll.

From listening to the original session tape, did you manage to pick up on Miles' mood? What kind of tone did he set for the musicians?

He was a really happy guy. He was comfortable in the studio. He had one of the best bands in the business and was only in his early 30s, so he had sort of made it. He was just about to get married to someone he was deeply in love with, Frances Taylor, the dancer. He was joking with the producer and the other band members, and was very happy with the results – but he was very focused on the music. He was taking the job very seriously, especially on a difficult tune like "Flamenco Sketches", which is not in a normal jazz structure. He paid very close attention to what Paul Chambers was doing because the bass' role on that tune is very important. He had this ability of finding the right way of giving small suggestions to musicians that would make them go through the tune and make the music come together. He realized that Paul was closing his eyes to focus and concentrate on the music. He said to Paul, "Don't close your eyes, watch Bill's hands." The tune is divided into five different tonal sections and watching Bill Evans' left hand would help him know when these tonal sections were coming up. He made really small suggestions and – boom – the next take is what we know from the record.

How spontaneous was the playing in the recording sessions?
It had to be very spontaneous. And that's exactly what Miles wanted to get. He wanted to get that first time feel, not something well practiced, but that spark of creativity that happens on a first take.

Did Kind of Blue *create a revolution in jazz?*
It was a very quiet revolution. Bebop was the explosion. You still kept the structure but you started to bend it in a sort of way that allowed geniuses and virtuosi like Charlie Parker and Thelonious Monk to play around with these structures. But structures didn't change. The jazz vocabulary stayed pretty much the same. It was just like people were speaking in a more creative and faster way. That was the genius of bebop. I've interviewed many people who were there when jazz fusion started to happen, like Keith Jarrett, Chick Corea and Herbie Hancock, among others. We talked about how the genius of *Kind of Blue* and what Miles was doing with modal jazz influenced them.

What was the relationship like between Miles Davis and John Coltrane?
It was a five-and-a-half-year relationship. Later John Coltrane would always refer to Miles as "the teacher". Early on, Coltrane saw himself as a musician but not as an innovator, or someone who came up with a sound or had an approach to songs, tunes, etc., in such a way that he couldn't even compete with other top players in the field. So when Miles Davis first hired him, Coltrane was waiting for direction. Miles started to kick him in the butt by saying, "No, you figure out your sound in what we are doing now. You figure out what sounds best.

You are a professional musician. That's what I'm paying you for." John Coltrane had never been treated that way. That five-year period (with a year off for advance study with Thelonious Monk) was the sort of push that John Coltrane needed. He left to form his own band in 1960. This probably wouldn't have been possible without going through that period of learning and experiencing the freedom that he was offered in Miles' band.

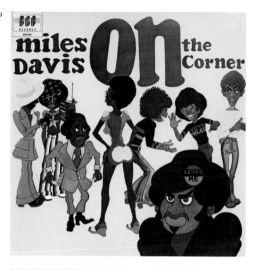

MILES DAVIS, *On the Corner*, 1972, CBS (see page 155)

Was John Coltrane aware that he was ahead of his time?
Oh yeah. He was very conscious of that. He was moving so fast along his pathway that he was afraid of leaving listeners behind. And that's what really happened if you look at where he went after *A Love Supreme*. When he started using a new drummer, Rashid Ali, there was not a regular beat or a regular pulse in his music. Throughout the history of music it's very difficult to find anyone, in any style, that changed as fast as he did from 1957 to 1967, except maybe The Beatles.

KEITH JARRETT, *Life Between the Exit Signs,*
1967, Vortex

*Did you have access to the original tapes while
researching your book,* A Love Supreme*?*
There are no original tapes left. Sadly, it
seems the record company threw them away
in the '70s when they were clearing out to
make more space. I did hear some session
tapes from the next day or, at least, the first
part of it. Coltrane is much like Miles. He's
very quiet in the studio – doesn't say much.
A lot of music comes from that spontaneous
energy. But what made it different from
Kind of Blue is that a lot of tunes had been
worked out on the stages of various night
clubs from September 1964. Part two of
A Love Supreme's four-part suite is called
"Resolution" and is taken from a live recording made in Philadelphia. I managed to get
hold of everything else: interviews with the
musicians, photographs from the studio session, etc. The doors were very much open for
me, and I had the record company's support.
Creed Taylor was a very valuable resource.

*It's fantastic the way Creed Taylor combined
jazz with more popular approaches.*

What Creed Taylor started was this very
valuable idea of raising the level of jazz in
the LP marketplace. What happened was
that in the 1950s the only music that would
be packaged in gatefold covers was classical
music. This was expensive and raised the
record's price. Nobody thought a jazz audience
would be willing to spend extra money for
this kind of stuff. Of course, none of the
packaging would mean anything if the music
wasn't fantastic as well. And he had the
highest production standards in the studios.

*Are there any designers from the jazz world
that you really admire?*
Between Bob Ciano and Reid Miles of Blue
Note, the only other guy is Robert Flynn
from Viceroy. He did so many of the Impulse! covers. I really love a lot of the photographs for the Atlantic covers taken by Lee
Friedlander. I will never forget when I saw
Charles Mingus' Impulse! album *Mingus
Mingus Mingus Mingus Mingus* in a record
store. I held it in my hands and said, "Oh
my God, it just feels like quality, it looks
like quality." It was the package that made
me buy that album. Buying an LP simply
because of the cover's quality was something
I was willing to do at the age of 16.

*Would you say the emotional approach to
vinyl is completely different compared to CD?*
Of course! The level of involvement... you're
involved in reading it, you're involved in
looking at it, you're involved in feeling it. In
my Impulse! book I talk about how people
even used record covers for other purposes,
like cleaning marijuana. They could name
the best album by the number of seeds left
inside. Back in the '60s and '70s the involvement with the music was much more of
a social event. The LP cover was like a door-
way into the music.

Kind of Blue *war Ihr erstes Buch über Jazz. Was war der Auslöser dafür, dass Sie dieses Buch verfassten?*
Die Idee hatte ich 1999, als das Album 40 Jahre alt wurde. *Kind of Blue* wurde im August 1959 veröffentlicht, und um dieses bedeutungsvolle Ereignis zu würdigen, schlug ich der *New York Times* vor, einen Artikel darüber zu verfassen. Ich sollte in 1000 Wörtern beschreiben, warum dieses Album so wichtig ist. Der Artikel erschien an einem Sonntag, und am Montagmorgen darauf bekam ich einen Anruf von einem Verlagsagenten, der mir anbot, aus dieser Idee ein Buch zu machen. Man muss dabei bedenken, dass zu dieser Zeit Musikbücher, vor allem im Jazzbereich, normalerweise Biografien waren, oder Essays, die eine bestimmte Musikszene behandelten. Bis dahin hatte noch niemand daran gedacht, sich auf ein ganz bestimmtes Detail zu konzentrieren: auf ein einziges Album. Ich musste mich erst einmal mit der Idee vertraut machen und eine Weile überlegen, wie sie umgesetzt werden könnte. Und irgendwann sagte ich dem Agenten „Ok, ich werde das Buch schreiben".

Sie müssen sehr lange und gründlich recherchiert haben. Hatten Sie Zugriff auf die Archive der Plattenfirma?
Ich bekam die Tonbänder mit Aufnahmen aus dem Archiv. Die werden in einem unterirdischen Lager in New York aufbewahrt, das man „Iron Mountain" nennt. Außerdem bekam ich ein eigenes Arbeitszimmer. Da die Tonbänder mittlerweile extrem empfindlich sind, werden sie nur abgespielt, wenn es unbedingt sein muss – ich durfte die Aufnahmen darum nur einmal hören. Ich schrieb alles auf, was ich hörte, sogar die Unterhaltungen im Studio. Die wurden dann auch ein wichtiger Teil des Buches. Außerdem hatte ich Zugang zum gesamten Papierarchiv und damit zur Korrespondenz des Produzenten Teo Macero. Ich war wirklich dankbar für dieses wertvolle Material. Außerdem erhielt ich von einem New Yorker Radiosender unveröffentlichte Interviews, in denen Bill Evans über *Kind of Blue* spricht.

Das muss ein bewegendes Erlebnis gewesen sein.
Oh ja! *Kind of Blue* hat mir einen völlig neuen Einblick in die Welt der Musik verschafft. Vorher war ich ein nur Rock'n'Roll-Fan, der dachte, die Musik sei mit Woodstock erfunden worden – ich akzeptierte bloß Rock'n'Roll.

> **„Ich hielt es in den Händen und sagte: ‚Wahnsinn, das fühlt sich an wie Qualität und es sieht aus wie Qualität'. Es war wirklich das Cover, das mich davon überzeugte, die LP zu kaufen."**

Konnten Sie anhand der Originalaufnahmen erkennen, wie Miles drauf war? Wie ging er mit den Musikern um?
Er war ein ziemlich fröhlicher und freundlicher Typ. Na ja, er spielte ja auch mit einer der besten Bands überhaupt – und das mit Anfang dreißig! Er hatte es also geschafft. Bald wollte er die Tänzerin Frances Taylor heiraten, die er sehr liebte. Miles scherzte mit dem Produzenten und den Bandmitgliedern und war mit den Ergebnissen sehr zufrieden, aber er konzentrierte sich trotzdem ausschließlich auf die Musik. Vor allem bei schwierigen Stücken war er sehr genau – zum Beispiel bei „Flamenco Sketches", einem Stück, das keine normale Jazzstruktur hat. Weil hier der Bass ausge-

sprochen wichtig ist, achtete er sehr stark auf Paul Chambers. Davis hatte eine besondere Fähigkeit: Er gab bestimmte Tipps und Anregungen, damit die Musiker ihre Musik wirklich fühlen und verstehen konnten. Er sah, dass Paul sich mit geschlossenen Augen ganz und gar auf die Musik konzentrierte, und meinte: „Paul, lass die Augen offen und schau auf Bills Hände." Das Stück ist in fünf Abschnitte aufgeteilt, und indem Paul Bill Evans' linke Hand beobachtete, konnte er feststellen, wann welcher Abschnitt begann. Nur eine kleine, wirkungsvolle Bemerkung, und das Ergebnis kennen wir ja von der Platte.

Wie spontan spielten die Musiker während der Aufnahmesessions?
Spontaneität spielte eine große Rolle. Miles wollte es so. Er wollte dieses Gefühl des ersten Spielens einfangen, nicht etwas, das die Musiker schon in- und auswendig kannten, sondern diese prickelnde Kreativität, die nur bei der ersten Aufnahme spürbar ist.

Kann man bei Kind of Blue *von einer Revolution im Jazz sprechen?*
Es war eine sehr ruhige Revolution. Bebop hingegen war eine Explosion. Man behielt zwar die Struktur, aber verbog sie gewissermaßen, sodass solche Genies und Virtuosen wie Charlie Parker und Thelonious Monk damit herumspielen konnten. Aber die Struktur wurde nicht verändert, auch das Jazz-Vokabular kaum. Man redete jetzt nur viel schneller und auf eine originellere Weise. Das war das Besondere am Bebop. Ich interviewte zahlreiche Leute, die aktiv waren, als man mit Fusion-Jazz anfing – darunter zum Beispiel Keith Jarrett, Chick Corea und Herbie Hancock. Wir sprachen über den Einfluss von *Kind of Blue*, und vor allem darüber, welche Wirkung Miles' Art, mit Modal-Jazz umzugehen, auf sie hatte.

Wie war die Beziehung zwischen Miles Davis und John Coltrane?
Die Beziehung dauerte fünfeinhalb Jahre. Fortan bezeichnete John Coltrane Miles stets als „Lehrer". Früher sah Coltrane sich selbst als Musiker, aber nicht als Erneuerer oder als jemanden, der Sounds erfinden oder Songs bzw. Melodien kreieren konnte. Er fand sogar, er könne es mit anderen Top-Musikern nicht aufnehmen. Also wartete Coltrane beim ersten Zusammenspiel mit Miles Davis auf Anweisungen. Miles aber sagte: „Nein, du musst selbst herausfinden, welchen Teil du hier zu spielen hast und was der beste Sound ist. Du bist Profimusiker. Genau dafür bezahle ich dich." Noch nie war John Coltrane so behandelt worden. In diesen fünf Jahren (mit einem Jahr Pause, in dem er, um seine Technik zu verbessern, mit Thelonious Monk spielte) bekam John Coltrane genau den Antrieb, den er brauchte. Er beendete seine Zusammenarbeit mit Davis 1960, um seine eigene Band zu gründen. Das hätte er wahrscheinlich ohne die Phase in Miles' Band, in der er so viel lernen und experimentieren konnte, nicht geschafft.

War sich John Coltrane bewusst, dass er seiner Zeit voraus war?
Oh ja, ganz sicher. Er bewegte sich so schnell voran, dass er Angst hatte, manche seiner Hörer hinter sich zu lassen. Und genau das geschah auch – man denke nur daran, welche Richtung er nach *A Love Supreme* einschlug. Nachdem Einstieg Rashid Alis als Schlagzeuger war kein regelmäßiger Beat oder Takt mehr in seiner Musik wahrzunehmen. Er war sich dessen sehr bewusst, aber änderte nichts daran. In der ganzen Musikgeschichte, egal in welcher Musikrichtung, findet man kaum einen, der seine Richtung so schnell wechselte wie Coltrane von 1957 bis 1967, außer vielleicht die Beatles.

Hatten Sie Zugriff auf die Originaltonbän-der, als Sie für Ihr Buch A Love Supreme *recherchierten?*

Es gibt keine Originaltonbänder mehr. Anscheinend hat die Plattenfirma sie in den 1970ern weggeworfen, als aufgeräumt wur-de, um mehr Platz zu schaffen. Ich habe einige Session-Tonbänder vom nächsten Tag gehört - oder zumindest einen Teil davon. Coltrane hat sehr viel Ähnlichkeit mit Miles. Im Studio ist er sehr ruhig und eher schweigsam. Ein großer Teil seiner Musik ist aus seiner spontanen Energie heraus ent-standen. Aber es gibt einen wichtigen Unter-schied zu *Kind of Blue*: Einige Songs wurden bereits im September 1964 auf der Bühne verschiedener Clubs erarbeitet. Der zweite Teil der vierteiligen Suite auf *A Love Supreme* heißt „Resolution" und stammt von einer Liveaufnahme in Philadelphia. Ich habe es geschafft, alles Mögliche aufzutrei-ben, unter anderem Interviews mit den Mu-sikern, Fotos von den Studio-Sessions usw. Alle Türen standen mir offen und ich hatte die volle Unterstützung der Plattenfirma. Creed Taylor war mir eine wichtige Hilfe.

Es ist großartig, wie Creed Taylor Jazz und Popmusik miteinander kombiniert hat.

Creed Taylor war einer der Ersten, die die wunderbare Idee hatten, den Jazz aus seiner Nische auf dem Musikmarkt herauszulo-cken. In den 1950ern war ausschließlich klassische Musik im aufwendigen Gatefold-Cover erhältlich. Diese Art von Plattenhülle war teuer und steigerte den Preis. Niemand dachte, dass Jazzhörer bereit wären, Geld für solche Extras auszugeben. Natürlich hatte es nur Sinn, ein solches Cover zu ver-wenden, wenn die darin enthaltene Musik genauso gut war. Und bei Taylor galten, was die Produktion betraf, die höchsten Maßstäbe.

Gibt es Designer in der Jazzwelt, die Sie bewundern?

Außer Bob Ciano und Reid Miles von Blue Note gibt es nur noch Robert Flynn von Viceroy. Er hat eine ganze Reihe der Impulse!-Plattenhüllen gestaltet. Ich liebe viele der Fotografien von Lee Friedlander, die auf Atlantic-LPs abgebildet sind. Ich werde nie den Moment vergessen, in dem ich Charles Mingus' Impulse!-Album *Min-gus Mingus Mingus Mingus Mingus* in einem Plattenladen entdeckte. Ich hielt es in den Händen und sagte: „Wahnsinn, das fühlt sich an wie Qualität und es sieht aus wie Qualität". Es war wirklich das Cover, das mich davon überzeugte, die LP zu kaufen. Eine Platte zu kaufen, nur weil ich das Cover gut fand, das war eines der vielen seltsamen Dinge, die ich mit 16 tat.

Würden Sie sagen, dass der Umgang mit Vinyl auf einer anderen gefühlsmäßigen Ebene stattfindet als bei CDs?

Oh, ja, natürlich! Man geht mit Vinylplat-ten ganz anders um… Emotional ist man mehr drin, wenn man Texte liest, Bilder betrachtet und die Musik fühlt. In meinem Buch über Impulse! steht, für was manche die Plattenhüllen verwendet haben, um z.B. bei den getrockneten Marihuanablüten die Samen von den Blättern zu trennen. Sie erkannten das beste Album an der Anzahl der Samen, die darin zurückblieben. In den 1960ern und 1970ern war die Beschäfti-gung mit Musik noch viel mehr ein soziales Ereignis. Das Plattencover war wie eine Tür zur Welt der Musik.

Kind of Blue *était votre premier livre sur le jazz. Quelle était votre motivation ?*

J'ai eu l'idée pour le 40e anniversaire de la sortie de l'album. *Kind of Blue* est sorti en août 1959, et pour marquer l'occasion j'ai proposé un article au *New York Times*. Je devais expliquer en 1000 mots pourquoi cet album est encore si important. L'article est paru un dimanche, et le lundi matin j'ai reçu un appel d'un agent littéraire qui m'a demandé si je pouvais transformer cette idée en livre. N'oubliez pas qu'en 1999, les livres sur la musique, et particulièrement sur le jazz, étaient généralement des biographies ou des essais sur un domaine musical. Personne n'avait pensé à analyser un détail particulier, en l'occurrence un album. Je devais trouver une idée pour monter ce projet. J'ai rappelé l'agent littéraire et je lui ai dit : « D'accord, je vais le faire. »

« Je l'ai pris dans les mains et j'ai dit : ‹ Oh mon Dieu, ça respire la qualité. › C'est la pochette qui m'a fait acheter l'album. »

Il a sans doute fallu faire beaucoup de recherches. Avez-vous eu accès aux archives de la maison de disques ?

Ils m'ont sorti la bande des archives. Toutes les bandes sont entreposées à New York, dans des archives souterraines appelées Iron Mountain. Et ils m'ont fait l'honneur de mettre un studio à ma disposition toute une journée. Comme la bande est extrêmement fragile, ils ne la font jouer que lorsque c'est vraiment nécessaire, et l'ingénieur du son ne me l'a passée qu'une seule fois. J'ai noté tout ce que j'entendais, et même toutes les conversations du studio, et tout cela se retrouve dans le livre. J'ai aussi eu accès à toutes les archives sur papier, jusqu'à la correspondance du producteur Teo Macero. Donc oui, j'ai eu beaucoup de chance et j'ai eu accès à des documents exceptionnels. J'ai aussi travaillé sur une station de radio ici, à New York, qui avait des entretiens inédits avec Bill Evans où il parlait de *Kind of Blue*.

Cela a dû être une expérience très émouvante.

Bien sûr ! C'est l'un des albums qui m'ont ouvert tout un monde musical. Avant *Kind of Blue*, je n'étais qu'un amateur de rock qui pensait que la seule musique valable avait été enregistrée après Woodstock.

En écoutant la bande originale de la séance d'enregistrement, avez-vous pu capter l'humeur de Miles Davis ? Quel ton donnait-il aux musiciens ?

C'était vraiment un type enjoué. Il était très à l'aise dans le studio. Il avait l'un des meilleurs groupes et il n'avait qu'une trentaine d'années, on peut dire qu'il avait réussi. Il était sur le point de se marier avec la danseuse Frances Taylor, dont il était très amoureux. Il blaguait avec le producteur et les autres membres du groupe, et il était très content du résultat, mais il était très concentré sur la musique. Il prenait le boulot très au sérieux, surtout pour les morceaux difficiles comme « Flamenco Sketches », qui n'a pas une structure normale pour du jazz. Il faisait très attention à ce que faisait Paul Chambers, parce que pour ce morceau la contrebasse joue un rôle très important. Il savait faire de petites suggestions aux musiciens de façon à les guider tout au long du morceau et à ce que l'ensemble soit cohérent. Il s'est rendu compte que Paul fermait les yeux pour se concentrer sur la musique. Il lui a dit : « Ne ferme pas les yeux, regarde les mains de Bill ». Le morceau est divisé en cinq sections tonales, et la main gauche de Bill l'aiderait à prévoir les passages entre sections. Il donnait de tout petits conseils et, boum, la prise suivante était celle retenue pour l'album.

Lors des séances d'enregistrement, le jeu des musiciens était-il spontané ?
Il fallait que ce soit très spontané. Et c'est exactement ce que Miles voulait obtenir. Il voulait une impression de première fois, pas quelque chose de bien répété, mais cette étincelle de créativité qui jaillit lors de la première prise.

Est-ce que Kind of Blue *a révolutionné le jazz ?*
C'était une révolution très calme. C'est le be-bop qui a été une explosion. On gardait la structure, mais on commençait à la tordre de façon à ce que des génies et des virtuoses comme Charlie Parker et Thelonious Monk puissent jouer avec. Mais les structures ne changeaient pas. Le vocabulaire du jazz restait plus ou moins le même. C'était comme si les gens s'étaient mis à parler plus vite, et avec plus de créativité. C'était cela, le génie du be-bop. J'ai interviewé beaucoup de gens qui ont assisté à la naissance du jazz fusion, comme Keith Jarrett, Chick Corea et Herbie Hancock, entre autres. Nous avons parlé de l'influence que le génie de *Kind of Blue* et le travail de Miles sur le jazz modal ont eue sur eux.

Quel genre de relation avaient Miles Davis et John Coltrane ?
C'est une relation qui a duré cinq ans et demi. Ensuite, John Coltrane a toujours appelé Miles «le professeur». Au début, Coltrane se considérait comme un musicien, mais pas comme un innovateur, ni comme quelqu'un qui pourrait inventer son propre son ou avoir une approche personnelle des chansons ou des morceaux qui lui permettrait de se mesurer aux meilleurs. Lorsque Miles l'a embauché, Coltrane attendait des instructions. Miles a commencé à lui botter les fesses et à lui dire: «Non, débrouille-toi pour trouver ton propre son dans ce que nous sommes en train de faire. C'est à toi de décider ce qui sonnera le mieux. Tu es un musicien professionnel. C'est pour ça que je te paie.» John Coltrane n'avait jamais été traité de cette façon. Ces cinq années (avec une année de parenthèse pour des études très poussées avec Thelonious Monk) ont été exactement le coup de pouce qu'il lui fallait. Il est parti en 1960 pour former son groupe. Cela n'aurait sans doute pas été possible s'il n'était pas d'abord passé par cette période d'apprentissage et d'expérimentation de la liberté que le groupe de Miles lui a donnée.

Est-ce que John Coltrane était conscient d'être en avance sur son temps ?
Oh oui. Il le savait très bien. Il avançait si vite qu'il avait peur de perdre son auditoire. Et c'est bien ce qui s'est passé, si l'on regarde où il est allé après *A Love Supreme*. Lorsqu'il a commencé à travailler avec un nouveau batteur, Rashid Ali, sa musique n'avait plus de rythme ou de pouls régulier. Il le savait très bien, mais il n'a pas arrêté. Dans toute l'histoire de la musique, il est très difficile de trouver qui que ce soit, dans quelque style que ce soit, qui ait changé aussi vite qu'il l'a fait de 1957 à 1967, à part peut-être les Beatles.

Avez-vous eu accès aux bandes originales lorsque vous faisiez les recherches pour votre livre A Love Supreme *?*
Les bandes originales n'existent plus. Malheureusement, il semble que la maison de disques les ait jetées dans les années 1970, alors qu'elle faisait le ménage pour gagner de l'espace. J'ai pu écouter quelques bandes de la première partie de la séance du lendemain. Coltrane ressemble beaucoup à Miles. Il est très calme en studio, il ne parle pas beaucoup. Une grande partie de la musique vient de cette énergie spontanée. Mais ce

qui a différencié cet album de *Kind of Blue*, c'est que beaucoup de ses morceaux avaient été travaillés sur scène dans plusieurs clubs à partir de septembre 1964. La deuxième partie de la suite en quatre parties de *A Love Supreme* s'appelle «Resolution» et vient d'un enregistrement en direct fait à Philadelphie. J'ai réussi à retrouver tout le reste : les entretiens avec les musiciens, les photographies de la séance d'enregistrement, etc. La maison de disques me soutenait et m'a ouvert toutes les portes. Creed Taylor m'a été d'une grande aide.

Creed Taylor a combiné le jazz avec des approches plus populaires d'une façon vraiment fantastique.

Creed Taylor a lancé la grande idée d'élever le niveau du jazz sur le marché des 33 tours. Ce qui s'est passé, c'est que dans les années 1950 les pochettes à volet étaient réservées à la musique classique. Elles étaient chères et augmentaient le prix du disque. Personne ne pensait que les amateurs de jazz seraient prêts à dépenser plus pour ce genre de choses. Bien sûr, la pochette ne valait rien si la musique n'était pas aussi fantastique. Et il avait les critères de production les plus élevés.

Y a-t-il des graphistes du monde du jazz que vous admirez particulièrement ?

Entre Bob Ciano et Reid Miles de Blue Note, le seul autre est Robert Flynn de Viceroy. Il a créé une multitude de pochettes pour Impulse !. J'aime beaucoup les photographies de Lee Friedlander sur les pochettes d'Atlantic. Je n'oublierai jamais le moment où j'ai vu l'album de Charles Mingus sorti chez Impulse !, *Mingus Mingus Mingus Mingus Mingus*, dans un magasin de disques. Je l'ai pris dans les mains et j'ai dit : «Oh mon Dieu, ça respire la qualité.» C'est la pochette qui m'a fait acheter l'album. Acheter un 33 tours rien que pour la qualité de la pochette, c'est quelque chose que j'étais prêt à faire quand j'avais 16 ans.

Diriez-vous que l'approche émotionnelle du vinyle est complètement différente de celle du CD ?

Bien sûr ! Cela tient au niveau d'investissement personnel que l'on ressent quand on le lit, quand on le regarde et quand on le touche. Dans mon livre *Impulse !* j'explique que les gens utilisaient même les pochettes de disques pour d'autres choses, par exemple pour trier la marijuana. Ils pouvaient désigner le meilleur album en fonction du nombre de graines qui étaient restées à l'intérieur. Dans les années 1960 et 1970, la musique était bien plus qu'un événement social. La couverture du 33 tours était une sorte de passage qui menait directement dans la musique.

EARL HINES, *Once Upon A Time*, 1966, Impulse!
(see page 230)

Once Upon a Time in the days of the

Great Society, the citizens of Fun City were subjected to many and various hardships. After sources of light and power had wholly failed them, and they had been cast into Stygian Darkness, they were next deprived of their normal means of transport. Some trode long miles to their places of Labor through streets choked with the chariots and carts of farmers, shepherds and peasants from all the countryside around. Others meditated in lonely chambers on ways to improve the lot of their harassed fellow-men.

One such, with much faith in the healing power of Music, had a vision of bringing together so noble a company of musicians that the minds of the citizens could not but be lifted up out of the Slough of Despond.

It happened that there was within the city a Consort of Players whose leader and certain others were many leagues away, beyond communication. The Visionary decided to summon the most famous of those who remained to make plans for a Musical Celebration, and he sent messengers running through the streets to the houses of John Cornelius Hodges and Lawrence Brown. These twain came in due course to the appointed meeting place.

Now at that time the Fatha, Earl Hines, a great player of the piano, had come to the East, and him they had known for many years, and him they forthwith chose to head their company. There was also, within the northern boundaries of the city, an associate of yesterday, a formidable beater of hides, one Sonny Greer, and they sent word that he should come to them with all dispatch, bringing his tambours large and small.

(continued on back cover)

CREED TAYLOR

Creed Taylor was one of the most influential personalities in the history of jazz. He began his musical career as a trumpet player, but soon got into the business end of music with Bethlehem Records, where he worked as Head of A&R. After moving to ABC-Paramount, he founded the Impulse! label in 1960. He wasn't there long, though he signed John Coltrane to the label. Creed's next job was with Verve records where he was very successful. Next, Taylor moved to A&M where he worked with Wes Montgomery and a young George Benson, bringing both artists to a wider audience by utilizing string arrangements and popular songs of the day. In 1970 he founded CTI where he balanced commercial success with artistic achievement. The label had an aura of sophistication due in part to its trademark arrangements, solid group of house artists, and distinctive cover designs and photography by Pete Turner.

Creed Taylor gilt als eine der einflussreichsten Persönlichkeiten der Jazzgeschichte. Den Zutritt zur Musikwelt verschaffte ihm sein Trompetenspiel – seine Karriere nahm jedoch bald eine andere Richtung: Er stieg bei Bethlehem Records ins Musikgeschäft ein, wo er als Leiter der Artists and Repertoire (A&R)-Abteilung arbeitete. Nach einem Zwischenstopp bei ABC-Paramount gründete Taylor 1960 das Label Impulse! – obwohl er nicht lange dabei blieb, schaffte er es, John Coltrane bei Impulse! unter Vertrag zu nehmen. Verve Records bildete die nächste Station seiner erfolgreichen Karriere. Danach wechselte er zu A&M, wo er mit Wes Montgomery und dem jungen George Benson zusammenarbeitete. In den 1970er Jahren gründete Taylor CTI. Dort gelang es ihm, kommerziellen Erfolg mit künstlerischen Höchstleistungen zu kombinieren. CTI baute sich durch seine unverkennbaren Arrangements, eine Gruppe fest angestellter Musiker, besondere Coverdesigns und die Mitarbeit des Fotografen Pete Turner einen Ruf als besonders exklusives Label auf.

Creed Taylor a été l'un des personnages les plus influents de l'histoire du jazz. Il commença sa carrière dans la musique comme trompettiste, mais entra bientôt dans la partie commerciale chez Bethlehem Records, où il fut directeur du développement artistique. Puis il partit chez ABC-Paramount et fonda le label Impulse! en 1960. Il n'y resta pas longtemps, mais y engagea John Coltrane. Il poursuivit sa carrière chez Verve, avec beaucoup de succès. Il partit ensuite chez A&M où il travailla avec Wes Montgomery et un jeune George Benson. Il créa CTI en 1970 et y trouva un équilibre entre le succès commercial et artistique. Le label avait une aura de sophistication due en partie à ses orchestrations caractéristiques, à son groupe solide d'artistes maison et aux pochettes originales du photographe Pete Turner.

HANK CRAWFORD, *Help Me Make It Through The Night*, 1972, Kudu

Bethlehem was the first label you worked for. How did you get this job, and what recollections do you have of that time?

It was sort of like being on a Nobel list. A Swiss fellow by the name of Gustav Wildi started the label. I just happened to be at the right place at the right time. I said, "I can produce records that will sell!" I don't quite know how I did it, but I got Charlie Mingus, Stan Getz, Hank Jones, Billy Taylor – all the jazz greats that were available. They had a run with Norman Granz's JATP (Jazz at the Philharmonic). Norman was very successful in recording and promoting jam sessions in front of an audience. That was what actually got me interested in the first place, though it was a bit too chaotic for my taste. Then I started listening to Blue Note records. The sound was great, although I felt they had too many bass and drum solos, which were excessively long. I thought it would be quite easy for me to go to New York and find some way to produce records with more melody and shorter improvizations.

> **"I wasn't trying to do something that I thought would have instant market success. I was involved in something I liked, and I believed in it."**

And then from Bethlehem you switched to Impulse!?

Actually it was ABC-Paramount. After about three years I started the Impulse! label. It was still at the same place within ABC.

The record company logo was very distinct: "The New Wave of Jazz!"

The inverted exclamation mark! Peter Turner did some of the major covers for Impulse! Why did I start Impulse!? Because the whole environment at ABC-Paramount was geared towards producing "bobby soxer" pop acts like Danny and the Juniors. I never really liked popular music, or at least not that kind.

Impulse! had a very strong marketing image with the logo, the record sleeves...

And the laminated, gatefold covers with extensive liner notes. Meanwhile, I was recording at Rudy Van Gelder's. There were five releases to begin with: Oliver Nelson's *The Blues and the Abstract Truth*; *Genius + Soul = Jazz* [Ray Charles]; Quincy Jones' *The Quintessence*; Jay Jay Johnson [and Kai Winding]: *The Great Kai & J.J.*; and Gil Evans' *Out of the Cool*.

You had people like John Coltrane recording for Impulse!

I only produced one record with Coltrane on Impulse! That was very well organized because Eric Dolphy was the arranger, and a much disciplined musician. He came to the studio with the arrangements and did exactly what he wanted. He talked with Coltrane about the form he thought the music should take in the studio and went right on it... and quickly.

You are a close friend to the musicians. Did you get to know John Coltrane well?

I didn't know him that well. We were friendly. He didn't hang out with anybody at night.

You've always worked with incredible arrangers, such as Claus Ogerman and Don Sebesky. The arranger is a key person in the recording process, isn't he?

Sure, they paint the picture. Don Sebesky and I worked on so many albums together. It was like an invisible, unheard criticism that shaped those sessions.

JEREMY STEIG, *Firefly*, 1977, CTI (see page 415)

The West Coast scene was totally different from the sound produced in New York.

Yes it was. It also had a lot to do with the players at that point. But when I think about it I don't find a different sound unless I label it. New York has a heartbeat that California doesn't. We have Harlem and the black churches. New York was more of a hotbed of soul players. We had – "Meet me uptown on 12th street." California had – "Meet me at Redondo beach in the sunshine", and everything was lovely – but the streets were orange juice. I don't know about the geographic validity, or where it really comes from historically. It's not that there weren't any churches in California, but the whole culture there was quite different from New York. Then there was the issue of transportation. We couldn't just fly back and forth that easily. When somebody from California came to New York to record it was an event, and vice versa.

You then moved from Impulse! to Verve Records and went in a completely new direction. Why did you do that?

It's very simple. Norman Granz sold Verve to MGM and MGM didn't have anybody to manage Verve. MGM was across the street from the ABC-Paramount building, so there was an easy communication. We made a friendly agreement. I didn't mind because it was such a challenge.

You then created an incredible phenomenon by mixing jazz with bossa nova. It was completely revolutionary at the time. How did it happen?

Charlie Byrd, the guitar player, went on a tour of Brazil. There he ran into António Carlos Jobim, who gave Charlie a bunch of songs. He brought them back to Washington and then called me up and said, "I've got these really, really interesting songs. Do you think we can record them?" I said, "Sure, why not?" I just liked the music. In Washington I called a sound engineer I knew and he brought his equipment over to a black church. Stan Getz was a phenomenal musical genius. He'd hear a song once and do one take. Suddenly we would have a record.

How about your relationship with the musical genius, António Carlos Jobim?

We hung out. I liked Jobim. He was a beautiful person. I called him António, not Tom. I could never bring myself to call him that. Anyway, as soon as the record started getting airplay on AM radio at the time, in the United States, it took off in the pop charts. But the board of MGM was absolutely against it. We would have called it jazz samba, because you can't simply call it samba. After that it was possible to do all kinds of things without labeling it as jazz – because jazz had become a commercial commodity. The real worldwide cue was "The Girl from Ipanema", which happened about three years later. The Brazilians had started to move out to New York. It was like a constant carnival. 46th street was like Little Brazil in those days.

What was the appeal of Brazilian music?
Up to that point everybody thought that Brazilian music was Carmen Miranda with bananas in her hair. Jobim changed all that. He took away the comical image that, ironically, MGM had placed on the American audience. Jobim wrote some nice music and sold a lot of records in Brazil. It created a positive effect. The Brazilian government began to like it so much they even changed the name of Rio's international airport. It's now called António Carlos Jobim International Airport.

Then from Verve you switched to CTI, another completely different project?
It was A&M Records to start with. Not really a completely different project. The business was wider, maybe.

Do you remember the first title you recorded for CTI?
I think it was Wes Montgomery's *A Day in the Life*, which was also a Pete Turner album cover – with the cigarettes in the ashtray...

CTI had an incredible operation; from the arrangements and production to the photos on the record sleeves. The concerts were also amazing. Once again you were working with Rudy Van Gelder. You made a great impact in the market.
I very much liked what I was doing. I wasn't trying to do something that I thought would have instant market success. I was involved in something I liked, and I believed in it.

Why do you think people at the time thought that jazz was dead – because of the emergence of fusion?

No, that was before fusion. *Down Beat* was always cheerleading jazz, and meanwhile pop was out there making a lot of money. But now the jazz players were beginning to have paradise incomes, because the audience was growing.

Do you think the arrival of fusion killed jazz?
What is fusion? The very word means a blending of elements. So it depends on who is fusing the fusion. It was the labels and the press that tagged various records or concerts as fusion, because the players that were there were successful in stretching the music into some different idiom, that's all. You can't generalize that way.

Eumir Deodato also did a lot of arrangements for CTI.
I can only say the obvious, and the obvious is that he had a concept that is absolute genius. The energy he put in. What he was doing gave the thing real vitality. He was also a very warm and intelligent person. He "felt" the music, whether it was a Brazilian sound, rock or whatever. He wasn't confined to any particular way of doing things.

What advice would you give to a young person wanting to start producing jazz records?
He or she has to make up his or her own mind. I don't know... It's a gut feeling and a passion that I had and have. I'm not comfortable in trying to articulate technical advice to someone who wants to get involved.

Bethlehem war das erste Label, bei dem Sie arbeiteten. Wie gelangten Sie an diesen Job? Erinnern Sie sich noch an diese Zeit?

Ich hatte einfach nur ein Riesenglück. Gustav Wildi, ein Schweizer Freund und Kollege, gründete das Label. Ich überzeugte ihn mit dem Spruch: „Ich kann Platten produzieren, die sich verkaufen!" Ich weiß wirklich nicht, wie ich das geschafft habe, aber ich holte alle Jazzgrößen an Bord: Charlie Mingus, Stan Getz, Hank Jones und Billy Taylor. Die Künstler hatten einen Auftritt mit Norman Granz' JATP (Jazz at the Philharmonic) und Normans erfolgreiche Strategie, live gespielte Jam Sessions aufzunehmen und zu verkaufen, interessierte mich, auch wenn es für meinen Geschmack etwas zu chaotisch war. Ich hörte mir dann Blue-Note-Platten an. Großartiger Sound, aber in den Stücken gab es zu viele lange Bass- und Schlagzeug-Soli. Ich dachte mir, es wäre kein Problem, in New York Platten zu produzieren, die melodiösere und vor allem kürzere improvisierte Stücke enthielten.

Von Betlehem wechselten Sie dann direkt zu Impulse!?

Nein, erst noch zu ABC-Paramount. Drei Jahre später gründete ich dann Impulse!. Der Geschäftssitz befand sich im gleichen Gebäude wie der von ABC.

Das Logo der Plattenfirma war etwas Neues, Besonderes: „The New Wave of Jazz!" hieß das Leitmotiv.

Das umgekehrte Ausrufezeichen wurde zum Markenzeichen. Peter Turner gestaltete einige der besten Impulse!-Cover. Warum ich das Label gegründet habe? Weil alles bei ABC-Paramount darauf ausgerichtet war, Teenie-Pop herauszubringen, so etwas wie Danny and the Juniors. Popmusik hat mir nie gut gefallen, zumindest nicht solche.

Das Marketing bei Impulse! funktionierte gut – das Logo und die Plattenhüllen hatten einen hohen Wiedererkennungswert.

Genauso die schicken Gatefold-Cover, die ausführliche Begleittexte enthielten. Die ersten Platten nahm ich in Rudy Van Gelders Studio auf. Vier Stück sollten zu Beginn herauskommen: Oliver Nelsons *The Blues and the Abstract Truth; Genius + Soul = Jazz* (Ray Charles); Quincy Jones' *The Quintessence*; Jay Jay Johnsons [und Kai Windings] *The Great Kai & J.J.* und Gil Evans' *Out of the Cool.*

> „Ich versuchte nicht irgendetwas zu produzieren, nur um einen kommerziellen Erfolg zu landen. Ich beschäftigte mich mit etwas, das ich mochte und an das ich glaubte."

Sie gewannen solche Größen wie John Coltrane dafür, ihre Platten bei Impulse! herauszubringen.

Ich produzierte mit Coltrane bei Impulse! nur eine Platte. Die Organisation war perfekt, denn Eric Dolphy, der Arrangeur, entpuppte sich als ein ausgesprochen disziplinierter Musiker. Er kam ins Studio, hatte seine Arrangements bereits vorbereitet und verfolgte genau das, was er vorhatte. Er sprach mit Coltrane ab, welche Formen seine Musik annehmen sollte, und begann sofort mit der Arbeit.

Sie waren mit Ihren Musikern häufig eng befreundet. Haben Sie John Coltrane näher kennen gelernt?

So gut kannte ich ihn nicht. Wir waren nett zueinander, mehr nicht. Er ging abends nicht mit den anderen aus.

Sie arbeiteten stets mit den besten Arrangeuren zusammen, so etwa mit Claus Ogermann und Don Sebesky. Der Arrangeur ist die Schüsselfigur im Aufnahmeprozess, nicht wahr?

Natürlich, der Arrangeur sorgt für das Grundgerüst. Don Sebesky und ich produzierten eine ganze Reihe Platten zusammen. Während dieser Sessions war sein kritischer Blick stets gegenwärtig.

Die West-Coast-Szene unterschied sich komplett vom New Yorker Sound.

Genau. Das hatte vor allem mit den Musikern zu tun. Aber die Unterschiede fallen mir erst auf, wenn ich sie benennen kann. New York tickte einfach ganz anders als Kalifornien. Hier gibt es Harlem und die schwarzen Kirchengemeinden. New York war so etwas wie eine Soul-Brutstätte. In Kalifornien gab es auch Kirchen, aber trotzdem war die Kultur in New York einfach ganz anders. Wegen der großen Entfernung konnte man auch nicht einfach so hin- und herfliegen.

Nach Impulse! fingen Sie bei Verve Records an und schlugen damit eine komplett neue Richtung ein. Warum haben Sie so gehandelt?

Das ist ganz einfach. Norman Granz verkaufte Verve an MGM – und MGM suchte jemanden, der Verve managen könnte. MGM lag genau gegenüber vom ABC-Paramount-Gebäude, daher gab es einen regen Informationsaustausch. Wir einigten uns auf freundschaftlicher Basis. Aber das machte mir nichts aus, denn die Herausforderung reizte mich.

Sie erfanden eine neue Musikrichtung, indem Sie Jazz mit Bossa Nova mixten. Zu dieser Zeit war das so etwas wie eine Revolution. Wie kam es dazu?

Der Gitarrist Charlie Byrd ging in Brasilien auf Tournee. Dort lernte er António Carlos Jobim kennen, der Charlie mit einer Menge Songs versorgte. Er rief mich an und meinte, wir sollten diese Stücke aufnehmen. Die Musik gefiel mir ziemlich gut. In Washington ließ ich einen befreundeten Tontechniker seine Ausrüstung zu uns bringen. Stan Getz war ein Musikgenie. Er hörte sich einen Song ein einziges Mal an und machte nur eine Aufnahme. Und auf einmal hatten wir ein ganzes Album zusammen.

Erzählen Sie uns ein bisschen von Ihrer Freundschaft mit dem Genie António Carlos Jobim?

Wir verbrachten viel Zeit miteinander. Ich mochte Jobim sehr gerne, denn er war ein wunderbarer Mensch. Das Album landete sofort, nachdem es in den USA im Radio gelaufen war, in den Pop-Charts. Den Leuten von MGM allerdings gefiel es gar nicht. Wir nannten diese Musikrichtung Jazz-Samba, denn einfach nur Samba war es ja nicht. Danach konnte man alles mögliche machen, ohne es gleich als Jazz zu bezeichnen - Jazzmusik war zu einer Massenware geworden. Drei Jahre später kam „The Girl from Ipanema" auf dem Markt, das zu einem weltweiten Hit wurde. Zu dieser Zeit begannen die Brasilianer, nach New York einzuwandern. Es kam einem vor wie ein ständiger Karneval: Die 46ste Straße war ein „Little Brazil"

Was war so anziehend an der brasilianischen Musik?

Bis dahin dachte jeder, die brasilianische Musik bestünde aus Carmen Miranda und ihrer Bananenfrisur. Jobim änderte das komplett. Er nahm dem Ganzen das komische Image, für das ironischerweise –

zumindest auf dem amerikanischen Markt – MGM verantwortlich war. Jobim schrieb einfach gute Musik, und er verkaufte in Brasilien eine Menge Platten. Das hatte sehr positive Auswirkungen. Die brasilianische Regierung mochte die Musik so gerne, dass sie sogar den internationalen Flughafen umbenannten: Er heißt jetzt „Aeroporto Internacional do Rio de Janeiro/Galeão – António Carlos Jobim".

Anschließend nahmen Sie erneut ein komplett anderes Projekt in Angriff – sie wechselten von Verve zu CTI.
Dazwischen lag noch die Zeit bei A&M Records. Aber so einen riesigen Unterschied gab es gar nicht, außer vielleicht, dass die Firma viel größer war.

Erinnern Sie sich an den ersten Titel, den Sie für CTI aufnahmen?
Ich glaube, das war Wes Montgomerys *A Day in the Life*, dessen Cover Pete Turner gestaltet hatte – das mit den Zigaretten im Aschenbecher...

Die Qualität bei CTI war beeindruckend, angefangen bei den Arrangements und der Produktion bis hin zu den Fotografien auf den Plattenhüllen. Auch die Konzerte waren außergewöhnlich. Und wieder arbeiteten Sie mit Rudy Van Gelder zusammen. Sie hatten einen großen Einfluss auf den Markt.
Ich liebte einfach, was ich tat. Ich versuchte nicht irgendetwas zu produzieren, nur um einen kommerziellen Erfolg zu landen. Ich beschäftigte mich mit etwas, das ich mochte und an das ich glaubte.

Warum glauben Sie, dass man in dieser Zeit behauptete, der Jazz sei tot – lag das an den Fusion-Stilen, von denen die Musikszene überschwemmt wurde?
Nein, das fing schon vorher an. Bei *Down Beat* war immer schon Jazz Thema,

während mit Popmusik stets viel Geld gemacht wurde. Aber dann hörten immer mehr Jazz, und Jazzmusiker wurden plötzlich gut bezahlt.

Glauben Sie, dass Fusion den Jazz vernichtet hat?
Was ist eigentlich Fusion? Das Wort bedeutet Verschmelzung, Zusammenschluss. Also kommt es darauf an, wer die Musik miteinander verschmilzt. Die Labels und die Presse bezeichneten bestimmte Platten oder Konzerte schon als Fusion, wenn sich die Musik einfach nur irgendwie anders anhörte. Aber man kann das alles nicht so verallgemeinern.

Eumir Deodato arbeitete auch als Arrangeur bei CTI.
Ich weiß nur das, was offensichtlich war, und offensichtlich ist, dass sein Konzept einfach genial war. Er legte so viel Energie in seine Arbeit. Egal was er tat, er verlieh allem eine gewisse Dynamik. Außerdem war er eine sehr warmherzige und intelligente Person. Er fühlte die Musik, egal ob es sich um brasilianische Klänge, Rock oder etwas anderes handelte. Er war stets offen für neue Einflüsse und Arbeitsmethoden.

Welchen Ratschlag würden Sie jungen Menschen geben, die heutzutage anfangen wollen Jazzplatten zu produzieren?
Dass sie ihre ganz eigenen Entscheidungen treffen müssen. Ich weiß nicht... Ich hatte immer einen guten Instinkt, gepaart mit meiner Hingabe zur Musik. Da ist es schwierig irgendeinen technischen Ratschlag zu erteilen.

Bethlehem est le premier label pour lequel vous avez travaillé. Comment avez-vous décroché le poste, et quels souvenirs avez-vous de cette époque ?

C'était un peu comme être pressenti pour un prix Nobel. C'est un Suisse du nom de Gustav Wildi qui a créé le label. Il se trouve simplement que j'étais au bon endroit au bon moment. J'ai dit : « Je peux produire des disques qui se vendront bien. » Je ne sais pas vraiment comment j'ai fait, mais j'ai obtenu Charlie Mingus, Stan Getz, Hank Jones, Billy Taylor – tous les grands du jazz qui étaient disponibles. Ils ont fait un concert JATP (Jazz at the Philharmonic) avec Norman Granz. Norman savait y faire pour enregistrer et promouvoir des jam-sessions en public. C'est cela qui m'avait intéressé au début, même si je trouvais tout ça un peu trop chaotique. Puis j'ai commencé à écouter des disques de Blue Note. Le son était excellent, mais je trouvais qu'ils avaient trop de solos de contrebasse et de batterie, et qu'ils duraient trop longtemps. Je pensais que je n'aurais pas trop de mal à aller à New York et à trouver un moyen de produire des disques avec plus de mélodie et des improvisations plus courtes.

Puis, de Bethlehem, vous êtes parti chez Impulse ! ?

En fait, c'était chez ABC-Paramount. Après environ trois ans, j'ai créé le label Impulse !. C'était toujours au même endroit, au sein d'ABC.

Le logo était très reconnaissable : « The New Wave of Jazz ! »

Le point d'exclamation inversé ! Peter Turner a créé certaines des meilleures pochettes d'Impulse !. Pourquoi ai-je créé ce label ? Parce que chez ABC-Paramount, tout était orienté pour produire des ados bien dans les tendances commerciales du moment, comme Danny and the Juniors. Je n'ai jamais vraiment apprécié la musique populaire, ou en tout cas pas de ce genre.

> « Je n'essayais pas de faire quelque chose qui aurait un succès commercial immédiat. Je m'engageais dans quelque chose que j'aimais, et dans lequel je croyais. »

Impulse ! avait une image marketing très forte, avec le logo, les pochettes…

Et les pochettes à volet en papier laminé, avec des notes d'accompagnement très détaillées. À cette époque, j'enregistrais chez Rudy Van Gelder. Il y eut quatre albums pour commencer : *The Blues and the Abstract Truth* d'Oliver Nelson ; *Genius + Soul = Jazz* (Ray Charles) ; *The Quintessence* de Quincy Jones ; *The Great Kai & J.J.* de Jay Johnson [et Kai Winding] ; et *Out of the Cool* de Gil Evans.

Il y avait des gens comme John Coltrane qui enregistraient pour Impulse !

Je n'ai produit qu'un seul disque de Coltrane chez Impulse !. C'était très bien organisé parce qu'Eric Dolphy était l'arrangeur, et qu'il était aussi un musicien très discipliné. Il est venu au studio avec les arrangements et a fait exactement ce qu'il voulait. Il a parlé avec Coltrane de ce à quoi il pensait que la musique devait ressembler dans le studio, et il a mis son plan en œuvre. Et rapidement en plus.

Vous êtes un ami intime des musiciens. Est-ce que vous connaissiez bien Coltrane ?

Je ne le connaissais pas si bien que ça. Nous étions en bons termes. Je ne sortais pas avec les musiciens le soir.

Vous avez toujours travaillé avec des arrangeurs exceptionnels, comme Claus Ogerman et Don Sebesky. L'arrangeur joue un rôle essentiel dans le déroulement de l'enregistrement, n'est-ce pas?

Oui c'est sûr, c'est lui qui jette les fondations. J'ai travaillé sur une multitude d'albums avec Don Sebesky. Ces séances d'enregistrement étaient sculptées par une espèce de critique invisible et inaudible.

Sur la côte ouest, le son était complètement différent de celui de New York.

Oui, tout à fait. Cela avait beaucoup à voir avec les musiciens. Mais en y réfléchissant bien, je ne trouve pas un son différent à moins de lui mettre une étiquette. New York possède une pulsation que la Californie n'a pas. Nous avons Harlem et les églises noires. New York était plutôt un foyer de joueurs de soul. Ils se donnaient rendez-vous dans les quartiers chics, vers 12th Street. En Californie, ils se donnaient rendez-vous sur la plage Redondo, au soleil. Ce n'est pas qu'il n'y avait pas d'églises en Californie, mais la culture était très différente de celle de New York.

Puis vous êtes passé d'Impulse! à Verve Records, et avez pris une direction complètement différente. Pourquoi?

C'est très simple. Norman Granz avait vendu Verve à MGM, et MGM n'avait personne pour diriger Verve. Les bureaux de MGM étaient en face du bâtiment d'ABC-Paramount, ce qui facilitait beaucoup la communication. Nous avons passé un accord à l'amiable. Cela ne me dérangeait pas, parce que c'était un grand défi.

Ensuite, vous avez créé un phénomène énorme en mélangeant du jazz et de la bossa-nova. C'était complètement révolutionnaire à l'époque. Comment cela s'est-il passé?

Charlie Byrd, le guitariste, était parti en tournée au Brésil. C'est là qu'il a rencontré António Carlos Jobim, qui lui a donné quelques chansons. Il les a ramenées à Washington et m'a appelé pour me dire : « J'ai des chansons très, très intéressantes. Tu penses qu'on pourrait les enregistrer? » Je lui ai répondu : « Bien sûr, pourquoi pas? » Cette musique me plaisait, tout simplement. À Washington, j'ai appelé un ingénieur du son que je connaissais, et il a amené son équipement dans une église noire. Stan Getz était un génie absolu de la musique. Il était capable d'entendre une chanson une seule fois et de l'enregistrer en une prise. Et on se retrouvait tout d'un coup avec un disque.

DON SEBESKY, *The Rape Of El Morro*, 1975, CTI (see page 397)

Quelle relation aviez-vous avec António Carlos Jobim, cet autre génie de la musique?

On se voyait. J'aimais bien Jobim. C'était quelqu'un d'exceptionnel. Je l'appelais António, pas Tom. Je n'ai jamais réussi à l'appeler comme ça. Dès que le disque a commencé à passer à la radio AM à l'époque, aux États-Unis, il s'est retrouvé en tête des classements. Mais le conseil d'administration de MGM était absolument contre. Nous avons appelé cela du jazz samba, parce qu'on ne pouvait pas juste dire «samba». Après cela, on pouvait faire tout ce qu'on voulait sans l'étiqueter en tant que jazz, car le jazz était devenu une marchandise commerciale. Ce qui a vraiment été le début de tout dans le monde entier, c'était «The Girl from Ipanema», trois ans après. Les Brésiliens avaient commencé à débarquer à New York. C'était comme un carnaval permanent. 46th Street était un petit Brésil à l'époque.

En quoi résidait l'attrait de la musique brésilienne?
À ce moment-là, tout le monde pensait que la musique brésilienne c'était Carmen Miranda, avec ses bananes dans les cheveux. Jobim a changé tout ça. Il a fait disparaître l'image comique qui, ironiquement, avait été imposée au public américain par MGM. Il écrivait de la bonne musique et avait vendu beaucoup de disques au Brésil. Cela a eu un impact positif. Le gouvernement brésilien a tellement aimé qu'il a rebaptisé de son nom l'aéroport international de Rio.

Puis, de Verve vous êtes passé à CTI, un projet totalement différent cette fois encore.
Au début, c'était A&M Records. Ce n'était pas vraiment un projet complètement différent. Le spectre était plus large, peut-être.

Vous souvenez-vous du premier titre que vous ayez enregistré pour CTI?
Je crois que c'était *A Day in the Life* de Wes Montgomery, et là aussi la pochette était de Pete Turner, avec les cigarettes dans le cendrier...

Chez CTI la qualité était impressionnante, depuis les arrangements et la production jusqu'aux photos sur les pochettes. Les concerts aussi étaient exceptionnels. Là encore, vous travailliez avec Rudy Van Gelder. Vous avez eu un grand impact sur le marché.
J'aimais beaucoup ce que je faisais. Je n'essayais pas de faire quelque chose qui aurait un succès commercial immédiat. Je m'engageais dans quelque chose que j'aimais, et dans lequel je croyais.

Pourquoi pensez-vous qu'à l'époque les gens croyaient que le jazz était mort, à cause de l'apparition de la fusion?
Non, c'était avant la fusion. *Down Beat* soutenait toujours le jazz, et pendant ce temps-là la pop rapportait beaucoup d'argent. Mais les musiciens de jazz commençaient à gagner des sommes paradisiaques, parce que le public était de plus en plus large.

Pensez-vous que l'arrivée de la fusion ait tué le jazz?
Le terme lui-même est un mélange de plusieurs éléments. Alors, cela dépend de qui fusionne la fusion. Ce sont les maisons de disques et la presse qui ont décidé d'apposer l'étiquette «fusion» à certains disques et concerts, parce que ces musiciens arrivaient à traverser les frontières entre les genres, c'est tout.

Quel conseil pourriez-vous donner à un jeune qui souhaiterait commencer à produire des disques de jazz?
Qu'il ou elle doit prendre ses propres décisions. Je ne sais pas... C'est un instinct et une passion que j'avais, et que j'ai toujours. Ça ne me semble pas très naturel d'essayer de donner un conseil technique à quelqu'un qui veut commencer.

HUBERT LAWS, *Afro-Classic*, 1970, CTI
(see page 277)

RECORD COVERS
A-Z

MUHAL RICHARD ABRAMS

title AFRISONG / *year* 1982 / *label* Indiana Navigation

CANNONBALL ADDERLEY

title PHENIX / *year* 1975 / *label* Fantasy / *ad* Phil Carroll / *photo* Phil Bray, Bruce Talamon

HIGH FIDELITY

CANNONBALL ADDERLEY

title CANNONBALL'S
SHARPSHOOTERS /
year 1959 / *label* EmArcy

STEREO

THE CANNONBALL ADDERLEY QUINTET
74 MILES AWAY
WALK TALL

Capitol RECORDS

THE CANNONBALL ADDERLEY QUINTET

title 74 MILES AWAY / *year* 1982 /
label Indiana Navigation

In the wake of the quintet's biggest commercial hit
with *Live at the Club* (Capitol, 1967), which featured
Joe Zawinul's chart-topping "Mercy Mercy Mercy",
the Cannonball and Nat Adderley fraternity is
joined once again by Zawinul on electric piano, with
production by the amazing David Axelrod. Zawinul
also penned two of the album's hits, including
"Walk Tall" and the title track, "74 Miles Away". **O**
Nach dem größten kommerziellen Hit des Quintetts
– *Live at the Club* (Capitol, 1967), auf dem Joe Zawinuls Chart-Erfolg „Mercy Mercy Mercy" enthalten
ist – bringen die Adderley-Brüder Cannonball und
Nat noch einmal Zawinul am elektrischen Piano an
ihre Seite. Das Album wurde meisterhaft von David
Axelrod produziert. Aus Zawinuls Feder stammen
zwei der Album-Hits: „Walk Tall" und das Titel-
stück „74 Miles Away". **O**
Après le plus grand succès commercial du quintet,
Live at the Club (Capitol, 1967), avec le tube « Mercy
Mercy Mercy » de Joe Zawinul, les frères Cannonball et Nat Adderley sont encore une fois rejoints
par Zawinul au piano électrique, et la production
est à la charge du formidable David Axelrod. Zawinul a aussi écrit deux des tubes de l'album, « Walk
Tall » et le morceau titre, « 74 Miles Away ».

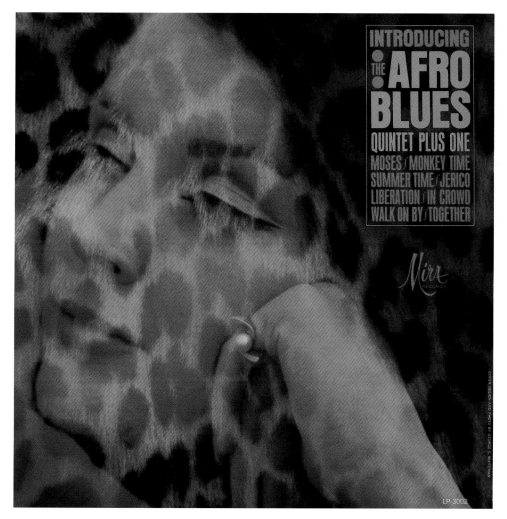

INTRODUCING THE AFRO BLUES QUINTET PLUS ONE
MOSES / MONKEY TIME
SUMMER TIME / JERICO
LIBERATION / IN CROWD
WALK ON BY / TOGETHER

LP-3002

THE AFRO BLUES QUINTET PLUS ONE

title INTRODUCING THE AFRO BLUES
QUINTET PLUS ONE / *year* 1965 / *label* Mira /
design George Whiteman / *photo* George Whiteman

The cover montage by designer George Whiteman
exemplifies a typical 1960s post-exotica style.
Whiteman was active as a photographer-designer
during the 1960s, producing covers for both jazz
and blues artists, such as Jimmy Reed and B.B.
King. ○

Die Fotomontage des Designers George Whiteman
ist im typischen Post-Exotica-Stil der 60er Jahre
gehalten. Whiteman, der Plattencover für Jazz-
und Blueskünstler wie Jimmy Reed und B.B. King
gestaltete, war während der 60er Jahre als Fotograf und Designer aktiv. ○

Ce montage, réalisé par le graphiste George Whiteman, est un exemple typique de style post-exotique
des années 1960. George Whiteman était un photo-
graphe-graphiste actif dans les années 1960. Il a
créé des pochettes pour des artistes de jazz et de
blues, notamment Jimmy Reed et B.B. King.

STORYVILLE RECORDS
Jazz in High Fidelity | STLP 918

Toshiko
her trio her quartet

"Composition" by Joan Miró

courtesy Museum of Fine Arts, Boston

TOSHIKO AKIYOSHI

title TOSHIKO AKIYOSHI HER TRIO HER
QUARTET/ *year* 1956 / *label* Storyville /
art Joan Miró

Jazz and modern art are inextricably linked. Many
artists are inspired by jazz and vice versa, and this
is evident in the history of jazz cover design. In this
instance it is Joan Miró's painting *Composition* that
adorns the cover of this very early recording by the
Japanese American pianist, composer, arranger and
bandleader. **o**

Jazz und moderne Kunst sind untrennbar miteinander verbunden. Zahlreiche Künstler werden vom
Jazz inspiriert und umgekehrt – dies zeigt sich

auch immer wieder in der Geschichte des Jazz-
Coverdesigns. So wird hier das Cover dieser sehr
frühen Aufnahme der japanisch-amerikanischen
Pianistin, Komponistin, Arrangeurin und Band-
leaderin mit Joan Mirós Gemälde „Komposition"
geschmückt. **o**

Le jazz et l'art moderne sont inextricablement liés.
De nombreux artistes sont inspirés par le jazz,
et vice versa. L'histoire des pochettes de disque
de jazz le montre bien. Ici, c'est le tableau « Composition » de Joan Miró qui orne la couverture de cet
enregistrement, l'un des premiers de cette pianiste,
compositrice, arrangeuse et leader de groupe
nippo-américaine.

MANNY ALBAM AND HIS ORCHESTRA

title JAZZ GOES TO THE MOVIES / *year* 1962 / *label* Impulse / *design* Robert Flynn/ Viceroy / *photo* Bob Gomel

"Manny was one of the good guys. His sweet nature endeared him to everyone who met him, and he wrote music that we loved to play."
— Bill Crow, Bassist

MANNY ALBAM

title THE SOUL OF THE CITY / *year* 1966 / *label* Solid State / *design* Frank Gauna

MANNY ALBAM

title THE BLUES IS EVERYBODY'S BUSINESS /
year 1957 / *label* Coral Records

Without doubt one of Manny Albam's best-known
projects, this recording presents the alto sax of Phil
Woods, Al Cohn on tenor, and Bob Brookmeyer on
valve trombone. Albam's endearing presence was
such that he introduced all three of the featured
musicians to the art of arranging. **○**
Diese Platte ist eines der bekanntesten Projekte von
Manny Albam mit Phil Woods am Altsaxofon, Al

Cohn am Tenorsaxofon und Bob Brookmeyer an der
Ventilposaune. Mit seiner gewinnenden Art brachte
Albam alle drei beteiligten Musiker dazu, sich in die
Kunst des Arrangierens einzuarbeiten. **○**
Cet enregistrement est sans aucun doute l'un des
projets les plus connus de Manny Albam. On y
trouve Phil Woods au saxo alto, Al Cohn au saxo
ténor et Bob Brookmeyer au trombone à coulisse.
Manny Albam était un homme charmant, et c'est
lui qui initia ces trois musiciens à l'art de
l'arrangement.

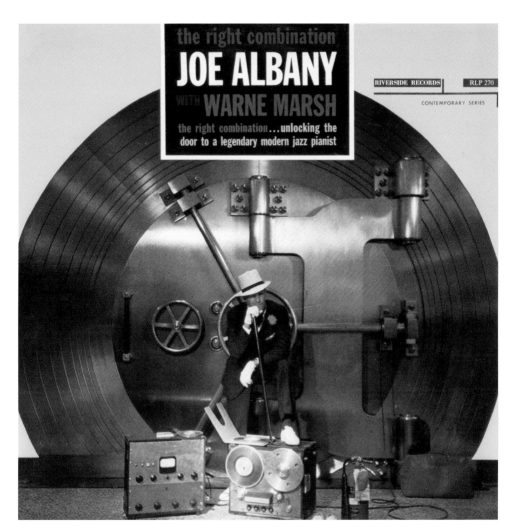

the right combination

JOE ALBANY

WITH WARNE MARSH

the right combination...unlocking the
door to a legendary modern jazz pianist

RIVERSIDE RECORDS   RLP 270

CONTEMPORARY SERIES

JOE ALBANY
title THE RIGHT
COMBINATION / *year* 1957 /
label Riverside / *design* Paul
Bacon / *photo* Paul Weller

LOREZ
ALEXANDRIA
THE GREAT

MCA
impulse!
MCA-29000

LOREZ ALEXANDRIA

title THE GREAT / *year* 1964 / *label* Impulse! /
design Robert Flynn / *photo* Roger Marshutz

Designer Robert Flynn adds a simple typographical
touch to Roger Marshutz's dignified and regal pro-
file shot of one of jazz's vocal gems. Lorez Alexandria grew up singing in gospel choirs before moving
to forge a career in the clubs of Chicago. Although
she never reached the heights of stardom, Lorez
was widely acknowledged by jazz musicians and
fans alike. ○
Der Designer Robert Flynn versah das Cover dieses
Kleinods des Vocal Jazz, auf dem ihr würdevoll-
königliches Profil von Roger Marshutz abgebildet

ist, mit einer eher einfachen typografischen Note.
Lorez Alexandria sang während ihrer gesamten
Kindheit in Gospelchören, bevor sie ihre Karriere in
den Clubs von Chicago begann. Obwohl sie es nie-
mals schaffte, eine Berühmtheit zu werden, war
Lorez in der Szene der Jazzmusiker und -anhänger
weithin bekannt. ○
Le graphiste Robert Flynn ajoute une simple touche
typographique à ce majestueux portrait de profil
que Roger Marshutz avait réalisé de l'une des perles
du jazz vocal. Lorez Alexandria passa son enfance
dans les chœurs de gospel avant de se bâtir une
carrière dans les clubs de Chicago. Bien qu'elle ne
soit jamais devenue une star, elle était très appré-
ciée des musiciens et des amateurs de jazz.

THE AUSTRALIAN
JAZZ QUARTET

title THE AUSTRALIAN
JAZZ QUARTET / *year*
1957 / *label* Bethlehem /
design Burt Goldblatt

ROY AYERS
title VIRGO VIBES / *year* 1967 /
label Atlantic / *art* Dick Luppi /
design Haig Adishian

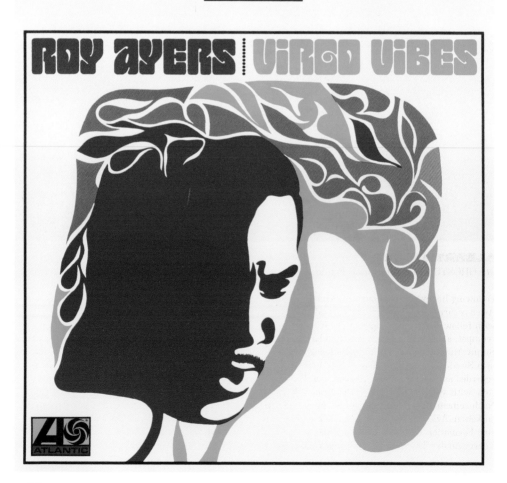

GHOSTS ALBERT AYLER DON CHERRY GARY PEACOCK SONNY MURRAY

GHOSTS
CHILDREN
HOLY SPIRIT
GHOSTS
VIBRATIONS
MOTHERS

fontana
JAZZ

ALBERT AYLER
title GHOSTS / *year* 1964 / *label* Fontana

Following his extended sojourn in Scandinavia, Ayler returned to New York and formed an outfit with fellow free jazz horn player Don Cherry on trumpet, along with Gary Peacock on bass and Sunny Murray on drums. The title track, inspired by a Swedish folk song, "Ghosts" (aka Vibrations), is regarded as a classic of the free jazz stable: a boppy tune with swirling mariachi-style phrases. **O**
Nach seinem ausgiebigen Aufenthalt in Skandinavien kehrte Ayler nach New York zurück und bildete eine Formation mit dem Free-Jazz-Bläser Don Cherry an der Trompete, Gary Peacock am Bass

und Sunny Murray am Schlagzeug. Der Titelsong „Ghosts" (alias „Vibrations"), ein Klassiker des Free Jazz, wurde von einem schwedischen Volkslied inspiriert und kombiniert Bebop-Anklänge mit wirbelnden Mariachi-Stilelementen. **O**
Après un séjour prolongé en Scandinavie, Albert Ayler retourna à New York et forma un groupe avec le trompettiste de free jazz Don Cherry, le contrebassiste Gary Peacock et le batteur Sunny Murray. « Ghosts » (aussi connu sous le titre « Vibrations »), le morceau titre inspiré d'une chanson populaire suédoise, est considéré comme un classique du free jazz. C'est un air de be-bop avec des phrases tourbillonnantes dans un style très mariachi.

ALBERT AYLER

title SPIRITS / *year* 1964 / *label* Debut /
design Nina Aae

Nina Aae's hauntingly beautiful cover illustration
adorns the cover of this recording on the Danish
Debut label. A siren-like winged sorceress is seen
blowing out a maelstrom of spirits, devils and flow-
ers from a saxophone. An intense visualization of
Ayler's emotional over-blowing tenor sax play.
Following his surprising disappearance on Novem-
ber 5, 1970, Ayler's body was found in New York
City's East River almost three weeks later. **o**
Nina Aaes wunderschöne Illustration schmückt das
Cover dieser LP des dänischen Labels Debut. Eine
sirenenähnliche geflügelte Zauberin bläst aus einem

Saxofon einen Wirbel von Geistern, Teufeln und
Blumen – eine eindringliche Visualisierung von
Aylers emotional überblasenem Tenorsaxofonspiel.
Nach seinem mysteriösen Verschwinden am
5. November 1970 wurde Aylers Leiche drei Wochen später im East River in New York gefunden. **o**
Cet album, sorti chez le label Danish Debut, est
orné d'une illustration d'une beauté envoûtante de
Nina Aae. On y voit une sorcière ailée aux allures
de sirène soufflant dans un saxophone pour en faire
sortir un tourbillon d'esprits, de diables et de fleurs.
C'est une vision intense de la puissance et de l'émo-
tion du jeu d'Albert Ayler. Albert Ayler disparut le
5 novembre 1970, et son corps fut retrouvé presque
trois semaines plus tard à New York, dans l'East
River.

TRIBUTE
TO
SOMEONE

GIORGIO
AZZOLINI

with
Franco Ambrosetti, tromba
"Gato" Barbieri, sax tenore
Dino Piana, trombone
"Pocho" Gatti, piano
Renato Sellani, piano
Giorgio Azzolini, basso
Lionello Bionda, batteria

GIORGIO AZZOLINI
title TRIBUTE TO SOMEONE / *year* 1964 /
label Rearward/Schema

The uncredited cinematic cover design on this early
Rearward Schema release shows a composed band
leader with his trademark double bass in the back-
ground. Giorgio Azzolini is a widely recognized
Italian bassist. He studied composition and arrangement in Florence and Milan before establishing the
famous Basso Valdambrini quintet. On this offering,
Azzolini alters the sextet line-up for different
tunes. **O**
Das mit Filmelementen versehene Cover dieser
Rearward-Schema-Platte, dessen Designer unbekannt ist, zeigt den gelassen blickenden Bandleader
und dessen Markenzeichen – den Kontrabass – im
Hintergrund. Giorgio Azzolini war ein namhafter
italienischer Bassist. Er studierte Komposition und
Arrangement in Florenz und Mailand, bevor er das
berühmte Basso Valdambrini-Quintett gründete.
Für die verschiedenen Stücke dieser Scheibe verändert er die Formation des Sextetts. **O**
On ne sait pas qui est l'auteur de la couverture
cinématographique de cet album sorti chez
Rearward Schema. Elle montre le leader du groupe
dans une attitude tranquille, avec sa fameuse
contrebasse à l'arrière-plan. Giorgio Azzolini était
un contrebassiste italien qui bénéficiait d'une large
reconnaissance. Il étudia la composition et l'arrangement à Florence et à Milan avant de créer le
fameux quintet Basso Valdambrini.

CHET BAKER

title CHET BAKER SINGS
AND PLAYS WITH BUD
SHANK, RUSS FREEMAN
AND STRINGS / *year* 1956 /
label Vogue / *art* William Claxton

COLUMBIA

CL 549

LP

A HIGH FIDELITY
RECORDING

YOU DON'T KNOW WHAT LOVE IS
I'M THRU WITH LOVE
LOVE WALKED IN
YOU BETTER GO NOW
I MARRIED AN ANGEL
LOVE
I LOVE YOU
WHAT A DIFF'RENCE A DAY MADE
WHY SHOULDN'T I
A LITTLE DUET
THE WIND
TRICKLEYDIDLIER

PHOTO: WILLIAM JAMES CLAXTON

CHET BAKER

title CHET BAKER &
STRINGS / *year* 1953 / *label*
Columbia / *photo* William
Claxton

PR 7460

groovin' with the chet baker quintet

PRESTIGE

DESIGN/PHOTO: DON SCHLITTEN

THE CHET BAKER QUINTET

title GROOVIN' WITH THE CHET BAKER
QUINTET / *year* 1966 / *label* Prestige

Groovin' was released back to back with *Smokin'
with the Chet Baker Quintet*, and here features Baker
playing a selection of mid-tempo grooves on flugel-
horn. In supporting roles on this Prestige release
are George Coleman on tenor sax, Kirk Lightsey on
piano, Herman Wright on bass and Roy Brooks on
drums. **O**
Groovin' wurde direkt nach *Smokin' with the Chet
Baker Quintet* veröffentlicht. Hier spielte Baker eine

Auswahl von langsamen Grooves am Flügelhorn
ein. Auf dieser Prestige-Veröffentlichung sind George Coleman am Tenorsaxofon, Kirk Lightsey am
Klavier, Herman Wright am Bass und Roy Brooks
am Schlagzeug zu hören. **O**
Groovin' est sorti juste après *Smokin' with the Chet
Baker Quintet*, et l'on y retrouve Chet Baker jouant
au bugle une sélection de morceaux groovy au tem-
po modéré. George Coleman au saxo ténor, Kirk
Lightsey au piano, Herman Wright à la contrebasse
et Roy Brooks à la batterie.

CHET BAKER & ART PEPPER

title PLAYBOYS / *year* 1956 / *label* World Pacific / *design* Chuck Hyman / *photo* Peter Gowland

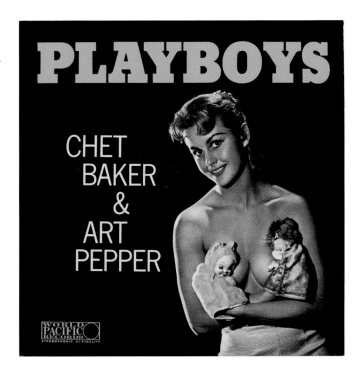

GATO BARBIERI

title FENIX / *year* 1971 / *label* Philips / *design* Haig Adishian / *photo* Charles Stewart

GARY BARTZ

title ANOTHER EARTH /
year 1968 / *label* Milestone /
design John Murello

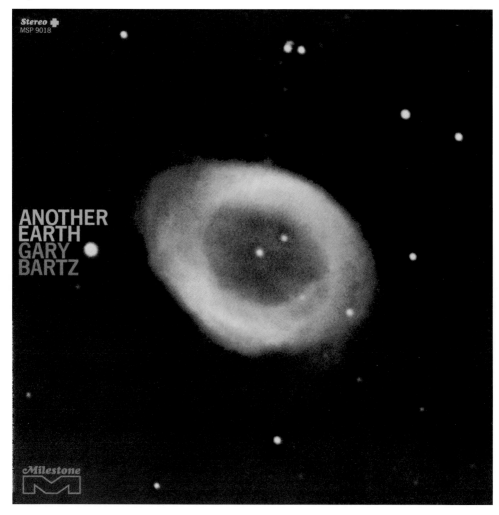

Gary Bartz

Music Is My Sanctuary

GARY BARTZ

title MUSIC IS MY SANCTUARY / *year* 1977 /
label Capitol / *ad* Roy Kohara / *art* Michael Bryan /
photo Vicki Seabrook Bartz

The Capitol Records personnel acknowledged for
bringing this wonderful urban cover image to life
are photographer Vicki Seabrook Bartz, art director
Roy Kohara, and illustrator Michael Bryan. Following a stint with Miles Davis' electric band at the
turn of the 1970s, Bartz eventually switched from
Milestone to Prestige records, though he began to
lose critical opinion as he forayed wider into the
softer pop arena, as is exemplified by this album. **O**
Fotograf Vicki Seabrook Bartz, Art Director Roy
Kohara und Grafiker Michael Bryan von Capital

Records ist dieses wunderbar urbane Coverbild zu
verdanken. Nach einer Arbeitsphase mit Miles
Davis' elektrischer Band Anfang der 1970er wechselte Bartz von Milestone zu Prestige Records. Allerdings verlor er die Gunst der Kritiker, als seine
Musik weiter in Richtung Soft Pop abdriftete. **O**
L'équipe de Capital Records à qui l'on doit cette
superbe couverture urbaine est composée de la
photographe Vicki Seabrook Bartz, du directeur
artistique Roy Kohara et de l'illustrateur Michael
Bryan. Après une incursion dans le groupe électrique de Miles Davis au tournant des années 1970,
Gary Bartz finit par quitter Milestone pour la maison de disques Prestige, mais commença à perdre le
soutien de la critique lorsqu'il s'aventura plus avant
dans la pop, dont cet album est un exemple.

BASIE one more time

music from the pen of
QUINCY JONES

Série Internationale
MODE disques
MDR 9 237

COUNT BASIE

title BASIE ONE MORE
TIME / *year* 1958 / *label*
Mode Disques / *photo* Chuck
Stewart

george wein presents **JAZZ AT STORYVILLE**

SIDNEY **BECHET**

VIC DICKENSON

SIDNEY BECHET
title GEORGE WEIN
PRESENTS JAZZ AT
STORYVILLE /
year 1953 / *label* Storyville /
design Marguerite Ryan

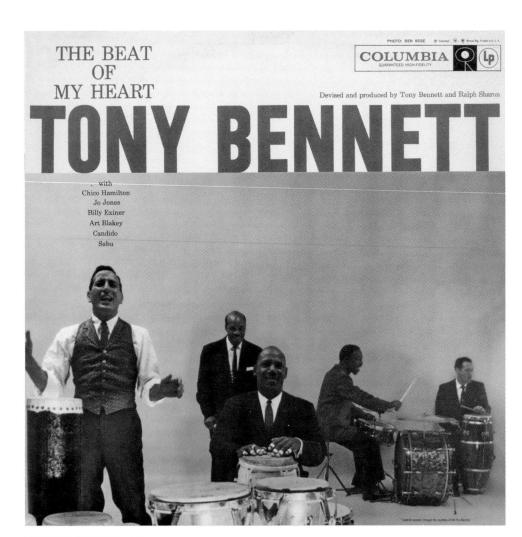

PHOTO: BEN ROSE

COLUMBIA (Lp)
GUARANTEED HIGH-FIDELITY

THE BEAT OF MY HEART

Devised and produced by Tony Bennett and Ralph Sharon

TONY BENNETT

with
Chico Hamilton
Jo Jones
Billy Exiner
Art Blakey
Candido
Sabu

TONY BENNETT

title THE BEAT OF MY HEART / *year* 1957 /
label Columbia / *photo* Ben Rose

Ben Rose's cover photo shows an elated Tony Bennett with a quite unique all-star line formation of guest drummers. Art Blakey, Jo Jones, Chico Hamilton and Candido add a distinctly Latin touch to the crooner's renditions of Broadway and popular hits. A lifelong jazz lover, this is also Bennett's personal all-time favorite recording. **o**
Ben Roses Coverfoto zeigt den beschwingten Tony Bennett mit einer einmaligen All-Star-Gastbesetzung an den Schlagzeugen und Drums. Art Blakey,

Jo Jones, Chico Hamilton und Candido fügen den Broadway- und anderen berühmten Hits eine leichte Latin-Note hinzu. Das Album ist eine Kollektion persönlicher Favoriten des Jazzliebhabers Bennett. **o**
La photographie que Ben Rose a prise pour cette pochette montre un Tony Bennett ravi, accompagné d'une formation rare de percussionnistes de tout premier choix. Art Blakey, Jo Jones, Chico Hamilton et Candido ajoutent une touche très latine aux interprétations que le crooner fait de tubes populaires et de Broadway. Tony Bennett a été un amant du jazz toute sa vie, et cet enregistrement est son préféré.

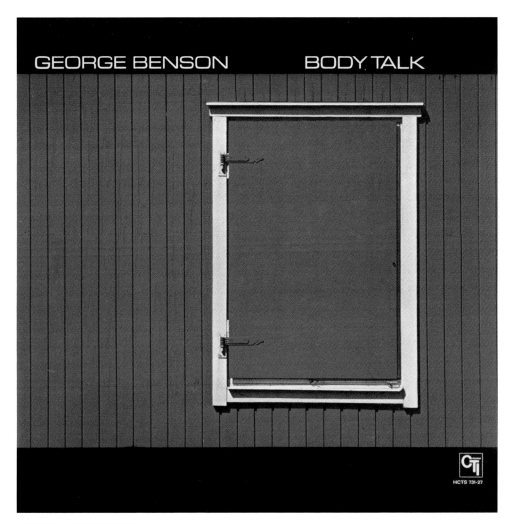

GEORGE BENSON   BODY TALK

HCTS 731-27

GEORGE BENSON

title BODY TALK / *year* 1976 / *label* CTI /
design Bob Ciano / *photo* Pete Turner

For this CTI outing, Benson continued to fuse jazz
with rhythm and blues. Missing from the cover
image is a hook which appears near the barn door
in Pete Turner's original shot. However, designer
Bob Ciano had the image cropped so that it actually
appears on the rear cover, extending the image to
create a sense of continuum. **O**
Für diese CTI-Veröffentlichung vereinte der Gitar-
renvirtuose einmal mehr Jazz mit Rhythm'n'Blues.
Auf dem Coverbild fehlt ein Haken, der auf dem
Originalfoto von Pete Turner neben der Scheunen-
tür zu sehen ist. Designer Bob Ciano hat das Foto
so geschnitten, dass dieser nun auf der Rückseite
der Plattenhülle erscheint – dadurch werden Vor-
der- und Rückseite der Plattenhülle optisch miteinander verbunden. **O**
Sur cet album sorti chez CTI, George Benson conti-
nue à fusionner le jazz et le rhythm and blues. Sur
la couverture manque un crochet qui apparaît près
de la porte de la grange dans le cliché original de
Pete Turner. Le graphiste Bob Ciano a cependant
recadré l'image de façon à ce que le crochet soit
présent à l'arrière de la pochette, ce qui prolonge
l'image et donne une impression de continuité.

THE JOHN BETSCH SOCIETY

title EARTH BLOSSOM /
year 1974 / *label* Strata-East /
art Arlene Turner

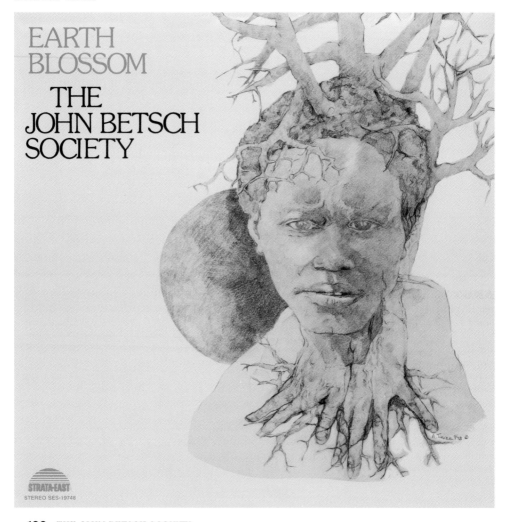

ANDY BEY
title EXPERIENCE AND JUDGMENT /
year 1974 / *label* Atlantic / *design* Bob Defrin

Bob Defrin's cover painting shows the singer encircled with planetary rings, perpetuating the album's musical theme: a sublime blend of cosmic jazz funk is the potion for singer Andy Bey's universal musings on this Atlantic pressing. Unlike his contemporaries such as Leon Thomas, Bey is underrated as a vocalist and musician, despite a prolific career. **O** Auf Bob Defrins Coverillustration ist der Sänger von Planetenringen umgeben, die das musikalische Thema des Albums verewigen. Das bei Atlantic erschienene Kunstwerk des Sängers Andy Bey stellt eine sublime Melange des Cosmic-Jazz-Funk dar. Im Vergleich zu Zeitgenossen wie Leon Thomas wird Bey als Sänger gewaltig unterschätzt, obwohl er eine produktive Karriere hinter sich hat. **O** Cette peinture de Bob Defrin montre le chanteur encerclé par des anneaux planétaires, prolongeant le thème musical de l'album. Sur cet enregistrement sorti chez Atlantic Andy Bey s'est concocté un mélange sublime de jazz funk cosmique pour ses rêveries universelles. À la différence de ses contemporains tels que Leon Thomas, Andy Bey est très sous-estimé en tant que vocaliste et musicien, malgré une carrière prolifique.

BST 84245

BLP 4245

THE FINEST IN JAZZ SINCE 1939
BLUE NOTE
A PRODUCT OF LIBERTY RECORDS

ART BLAKEY AND THE JAZZ MESSENGERS
LEE MORGAN/WAYNE SHORTER/BOBBY TIMMONS/JYMIE MERRITT
LIKESOMEONEINLOVE

PRINTED IN U.S.A.

©LIBERTY RECORDS, INC

ART BLAKEY AND THE JAZZ MESSENGERS

title LIKE SOMEONE IN LOVE /
year 1960 / *label* Blue Note /
design Reid Miles / *photo* Francis
Wolff

PAUL BLEY TRIO:CLOSER

PAUL BLEY TRIO
title CLOSER / *year* 1966 / *label* ESP-Disk' /
ad J. Dillon

The credited art director, J. Dillon, opts for a
moody cover portrait of the young pianist for this
trio recording on the ESP-Disk' label. The New
York label opened for business in 1966, recording
and releasing a staggering 45 albums in its first 18
months. Most of the tracks featured here are penned
by Paul's then wife, jazz pianist Carla Bley. **O**
Art Director J. Dillon entschied sich, ein ernstes
Porträt des jungen Pianisten auf das Cover dieser
Trio-Einspielung zu platzieren, die bei ESP-Disk'

erschienen ist. Das New Yorker Label wurde 1966
gegründet und brachte in den ersten 18 Monaten
die beachtliche Anzahl von 45 Alben heraus. Die
meisten der auf *Closer* enthaltenen Stücke wurden
von Pauls damaliger Frau Carla Bley komponiert. **O**
Le directeur artistique, J. Dillon, a choisi ici un
portrait grave du jeune pianiste pour cet album en
trio sorti sous le label ESP-Disk'. Ce label new-yorkais ouvrit ses portes en 1966, et enregistra et mit
sur le marché 45 albums en 18 mois, une véritable
performance. La plupart des titres de cet album
furent composés par la pianiste de jazz Carla Bley,
qui était alors la femme de Paul Bley.

CHIVO BORRARO

title EL NUEVO SONIDO DEL "CHIVO" BORRARO / *year* 1966 / *label* Microfon 107

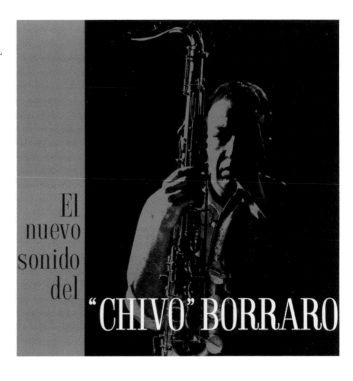

LESTER BOWIE

title THE 5TH POWER / *year* 1978 / *label* Black Saint / *ad* Adriano Benedetti / *photo* Giuseppe G. Pino

"All's fair in love and war – and music is both. So use anything, as long as it works."
—Lester Bowie

RONNIE BOYKINS

title THE WILL COME, IS
NOW / *year* 1975 / *label* ESP-
Disk' / *photo* Gyda Droscher

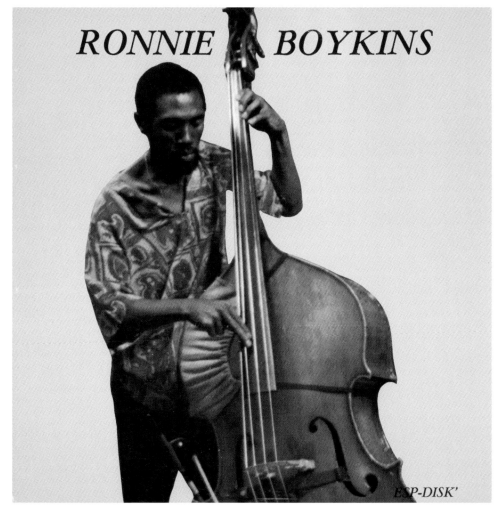

SOWETO/DOLLAR BRAND
abdullah ibrahim

DOLLAR BRAND

title SOWETO / *year* 1965 / *label* Chiaroscuro / *design* Ron Warwell

Ron Warwell's graphic art illustration on this 1965 record seems to convey a sonic reverberation across an African landscape. Chiaroscuro was one of a handful of independent jazz labels to emerge at the dawn of the 1970s. Dollar Brand, who called himself Abdullah Ibrahim later, is a South African pianist and composer whose music reflects many of his childhood influences around the multicultural port areas of Cape Town. **O**
Ron Warwells Grafik auf dieser LP von 1965 legt eine Art akustische Musterung über eine afrikani-

sche Landschaft. Chiaroscuro war eines von wenigen Independent-Jazz-Labels, die Anfang der 1970er entstanden. Die Musik des südafrikanischen Pianisten und Komponisten Dollar Brand, der sich später Abdullah Ibrahim nannte, spiegelt die Einflüsse seiner Kindheit im multikulturellen Hafenviertel von Kapstadt wider. **O**
Sur l'illustration graphique de Ron Warwell pour cet album de 1965 une onde sonore semble se propager sur un paysage africain. Chiaroscuro a fait partie de la poignée de labels de jazz indépendants nés à l'aube des années 1970. Dollar Brand est un pianiste et compositeur sud-africain dont la musique reflète la variété des influences des quartiers portuaires multiculturels de Cape Town.

THE BRASS COMPANY

title COLORS / *year* 1975 / *label* Strata-East /
design Sandra Williams / *photo* Curtis A. Brown

Sandra Williams is responsible for this colorful,
trippy cover design, featuring a photo arrangement
of brass instruments on a very 1970s patterned
backdrop by Curtis A. Brown. This is a very rare
release from Strata-East, featuring an obscure
big-band formation including sax player Clifford
Jordan, who had previously performed with Eric
Dolphy in Charles Mingus' band. ○
Sandra Williams ist für dieses farbenfrohe psychedelische Coverdesign verantwortlich – ein Fotoar-
rangement mit Blechblasinstrumenten ist in den

1970er-Jahre-Hintergrund von Curtis A. Brown
eingebettet. An der eher unbekannten Bigband-
Besetzung dieser sehr seltenen Strata East-Veröf-
fentlichung ist der Saxofonspieler Clifford Jordan
beteiligt, der vorher mit Eric Dolphy in Charles
Mingus' Band spielte. ○
C'est Sandra Williams qui a créé cette pochette
colorée et psychédélique, avec une photo de cuivres
disposés sur un fond aux motifs très années 1970
de Curtis A. Brown. Il s'agit d'un album très rare
sorti chez Strata-East, où l'on entend un big band
peu connu avec au saxophone Clifford Jordan, qui
avait auparavant joué avec Eric Dolphy dans le
groupe de Charles Mingus.

ANTHONY BRAXTON

title ANTHONY BRAXTON /
year 1969 / *label* America
Records

CLIFFORD BROWN & MAX ROACH

title CLIFFORD BROWN
AND MAX ROACH AT BASIN
STREET / *year* 1956 / *label*
EmArcy

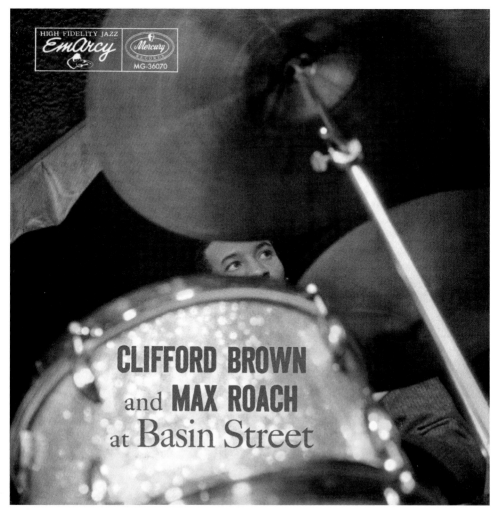

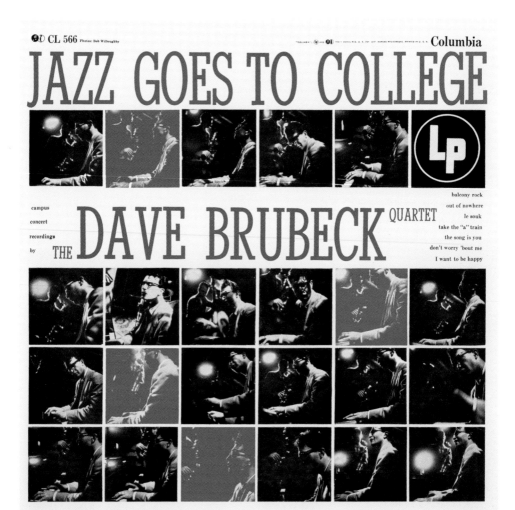

THE DAVE BRUBECK QUARTET
title JAZZ GOES TO COLLEGE /
year 1953 / *label* Columbia

RAY BRYANT

title LONESOME TRAVELER /
year 1966 / *label* Cadet / *design*
Don Bronstein / *photo* Don
Bronstein

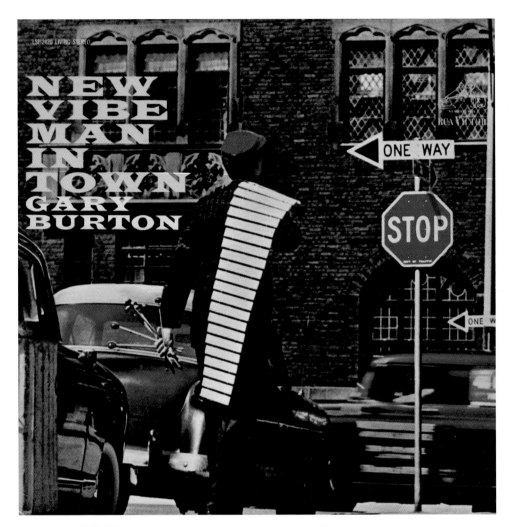

GARY BURTON
title NEW VIBE MAN IN
TOWN / *year* 1962 / *label*
RCA Victor

Nice work if you can get it
Rose de Picardie
...
...

I'm in the mood for love
C'est vous, chérie
Tenderly
...

THIS IS... DON BYAS

DON BYAS

title THIS IS... DON BYAS /
year 1952 / *label* Vogue

DONALD BYRD

DONALD BYRD

title CARICATURES / *year* 1976 / *label* Blue Note /
art Al Hirschfeld / *design* Ria Lewerke

A befittingly illustrated cover by Al Hirschfeld, one of the 20th-century's best known caricaturists. Hirschfeld is best known for his black-and-white line portraits of celebrities and Broadway stars. Joe Pass and Ella Fitzgerald have also been subjects of his affectionately exaggerated treatment on their album covers. In 1996, the caricaturist's work appeared on a series of Jazz reissues by RCA Victor. ⦿ Ein von Al Hirschfeld, einem der bekanntesten Karikaturisten des 20. Jahrhunderts, illustriertes Cover. Seine schwarz-weiß gezeichneten Porträts von Berühmtheiten und Broadway-Stars, die zu seinem Markenzeichen wurden, machten Hirschfeld berühmt. Joe Pass und Ella Fitzgerald wurden ebenfalls als Objekte von Hirschfelds respektvoll-übertriebenen Zeichnungen auf Plattencovern abgebildet. 1996 erschien das Werk des Karikaturisten in einer Serie von Jazz-Neuauflagen bei RCA Victor. ⦿ L'illustration d'Al Hirschfeld, l'un des caricaturistes les plus célèbres du XXe siècle, est parfaite pour cet album. Il est plus connu pour ses fameux portraits en noir et blanc de célébrités et de vedettes de Broadway. Joe Pass et Ella Fitzgerald furent également les cibles du traitement affectueusement exagéré d'Al Hirschfeld sur des couvertures de leurs albums. En 1996, les œuvres du caricaturiste apparurent sur une série de rééditions de jazz sorties chez RCA Victor.

DONALD BYRD
title A NEW PERSPECTIVE /
year 1963 / *label* Blue Note /
design Reid Miles / *photo* Reid
Miles

DONALD BYRD
title BYRDS EYE VIEW /
year 1955 / *label* Esquire /
design Harry Peck

DONALD BYRD
title THE MOTOR CITY
SCENES... / *year* 1960 /
label Esquire

IAN CARR
WITH NUCLEUS+

title SOLAR PLEXUS /
year 1970 / *label* Vertigo /
design B.E. Ltd

*"Long-playing records were just starting to come
out at that time and the covers were very crude.
I remember I was very impressed with Alex
Steinweiss, not about the content of what was on
the cover, that didn't impress me. He did
photograms, where you lay objects on photo paper
and you develop it."*
— Burt Goldblatt

SERGE CHALOFF
AND BOOTS MUSSULLI

title SERGE CHALOFF AND BOOTS
MUSSULLI / *year* 1954 / *label* Storyville /
design Burt Goldblatt

Sax players Chaloff and Mussulli paired regularly
at the height of the bebop era, the period during
which this extremely rare recording was made.
Chaloff, a talented baritone player, had his career
cut short through spinal paralysis in 1957. Mussulli gradually migrated to teaching and died of
cancer at the age of 49. **O**
Die Saxofonspieler Chaloff und Mussulli spielten in
der Glanzzeit des Bebop regelmäßig zusammen. In

dieser Periode entstand diese extrem seltene Platte.
Die Karriere Chaloffs, begnadeter Baritonsaxofo-
nist, wurde 1957 durch seine Querschnittslähmung
abrupt beendet. Mussulli zog sich langsam aus dem
Musikgeschäft zurück und begann, als Lehrer zu
arbeiten, bevor er im Alter von 49 Jahren an Krebs
starb. **O**
Cet enregistrement date de la grande époque du
be-bop, pendant laquelle les saxophonistes Serge
Chaloff et Boots Mussulli firent équipe régulièrement. Serge Chaloff, talentueux joueur de saxo
baryton, vit sa carrière stoppée nette par une
paralysie de la colonne vertébrale en 1957. Boots
Mussulli se tourna peu à peu vers l'enseignement et
décéda des suites d'un cancer à l'âge de 49 ans.

RAY CHARLES

title GENIUS + SOUL = JAZZ /
year 1961 / *label* Impulse! / *design*
Fran Scott

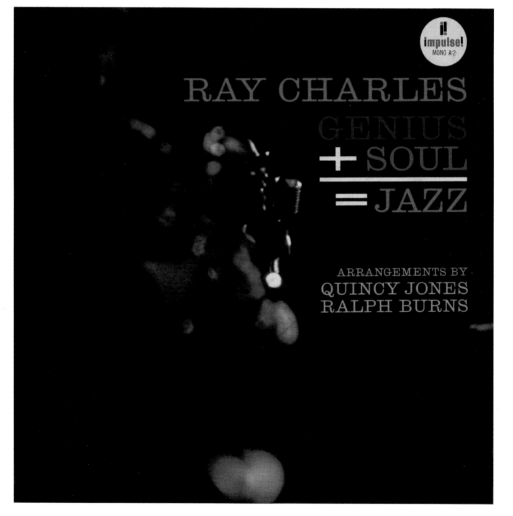

MONO/STEREO **GET 301**

DON CHERRY

title "MU" FIRST PART / *year* 1969 /
label Actuel / *art* Moki

While touring Europe with Albert Ayler in 1964, Cherry met his future wife Monika "Moki" Karlsson. Moki also played percussion and vocals on some of Cherry's recordings. Moki's daughter and Don's stepdaughter is pop star Neneh Cherry. Ranked among his best works, this is the first of two duet recordings Cherry made with drummer Ed Blackwell in 1969 on the French BYG label's Actuel series. **O** Während der Europa-Tournee mit Albert Ayler 1964 lernte Cherry seine zukünftige Frau Monika „Moki" Karlsson kennen. Moki wirkt als Perkussionistin und Sängerin auf einigen von Cherrys Alben

mit. Der Popstar Neneh Cherry ist Mokis Tochter und Dons Stieftochter. Diese erste von zwei Aufnahmen, die Cherry mit dem Schlagzeuger Ed Blackwell 1969 bei der Serie Actuel von BYG veröffentlicht hat, ist eines von seinen besten Werken. **O** C'est lors d'une tournée en Europe avec Albert Ayler en 1964 que Don Cherry rencontra sa femme Monika « Moki » Karlsson. Moki joua également des percussions et chanta sur certains de ses enregistrements. La fille de Moki et belle-fille de Don est la star de la pop Neneh Cherry. Cet album est le premier de deux volumes enregistrés en duo avec le batteur Ed Blackwell en 1969 pour la série Actuel du label français BYG. Il est considéré comme l'une de ses meilleures œuvres.

THE KENNY CLARKE FRANCY BOLAND BIG BAND

title ALL SMILES / *year* 1968 /
label MPS / *design* Heinz Bähr /
photo Sam Haskins

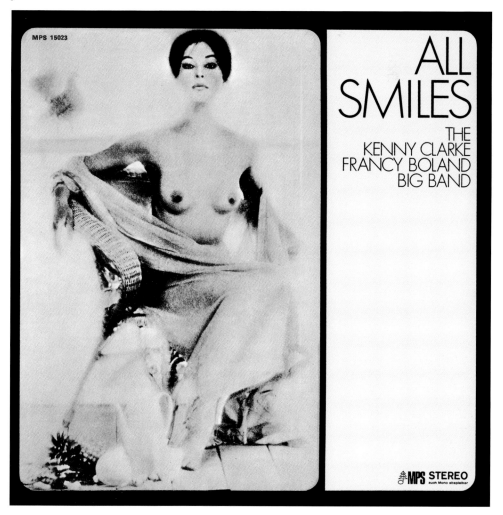

SAX NO END

THE KENNY CLARKE FRANCY BOLAND BIG BAND

title SAX NO END / *year* 1967 / *label* MPS /
design Heinz Bähr / *photo* Chargesheimer

German designer Heinz Bähr has been a notable
influence on the development of typography and
graphic design in Europe over the past four decades.
The cover photo for *Sax No End* was taken by Karl-
Heinz Hargesheimer, aka Chargesheimer. He is
famous for his post-war portraits of ordinary people
and bourgeoisie in the Ruhr Valley. ○
Der deutsche Designer Heinz Bähr beeinflusste die
Entwicklung des typografischen und grafischen

Designs in Europa in den letzten 40 Jahren maßgeblich. Das Coverfoto von *Sax No End* ist eine
Aufnahme von Karl Heinz Hargesheimer, alias
Chargesheimer. Chargesheimer erlangte Berühmtheit unter anderem durch seine schonungslosen
Porträts im Ruhrgebiet der Nachkriegszeit. ○
Le graphiste allemand Heinz Bähr a eu une influence notable sur l'évolution de la typographie et
du graphisme en Europe ces quarante dernières
années. La photo de la pochette de *Sax No End* a été
prise par Karl Heinz Hargesheimer, également
connu sous le nom de Chargesheimer. Il est célèbre
pour ses portraits de gens ordinaires et de bourgeois
réalisés après la guerre dans la vallée de la Ruhr.

MR. MUSIC

AL
COHN
AND HIS ORCHESTRA

AL COHN AND HIS ORCHESTRA

title MR. MUSIC / *year* 1954 / *label* His Master's Voice / *design* Gersten / *photo* David B. Hecht

Al Cohn also recorded under the pseudonym of Ike Horowitz. One of the Four Brothers sax section of Woody Herman's late-1940s orchestra, Cohn was closely associated with fellow swinging tenorist, Zoot Sims. After trying his hand at the family textile business during the 1950s he realigned his musical career and became a popular arranger. ○
Al Cohn nahm für einige Projekte das Pseudonym Ike Horowitz an. Cohn arbeitete als Mitglied von Woody Hermans Saxofonformation Four Brothers in den späten 1940ern eng mit dem Tenorsaxofonisten Zoot Sims zusammen. Nachdem er in den 1950ern sein Glück im familieneigenen Textilgeschäft versucht hatte, kehrte er in den Musikbetrieb zurück, um als Arrangeur berühmt zu werden. ○
Al Cohn a également enregistré sous le pseudonyme Ike Horowitz. Il était l'un des Four Brothers, les saxophonistes de l'orchestre de Woody Herman à la fin des années 1940, et était très proche de son compagnon du swing, le saxophoniste ténor Zoot Sims. Après s'être essayé au commerce textile familial pendant les années 1950, il réorienta sa carrière musicale et devint un arrangeur très prisé.

BOBBY COLE TRIO
title NEW! NEW! NEW! /
year 1960 / *label* Columbia /
photo Leon Kuzmanoff

ORNETTE COLEMAN

title SKIES OF AMERICA /
year 1972 / *label* Columbia /
ad Michael Gross / *design* Ed Lee

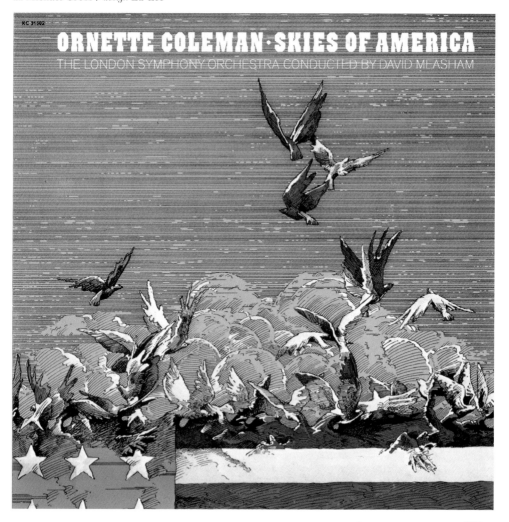

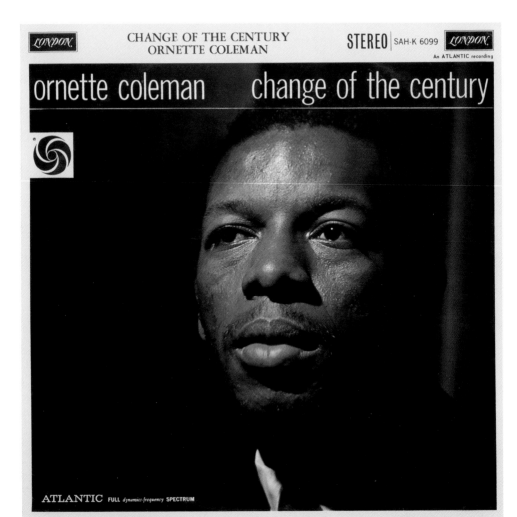

ATLANTIC FULL dynamics-frequency SPECTRUM

ORNETTE COLEMAN

title CHANGE OF THE CENTURY /
year 1959 / *label* Atlantic / *photo* Lee Friedlander

Lee Friedlander is acknowledged as one of America's leading photographers. He has published several photographic collections and written essays on a variety of subjects. **O**

Lee Friedlander ist einer der wichtigsten Fotografen Amerikas. Er veröffentlichte zahlreiche Fotobände und verfasste Essays zu verschiedenen Themen. **O**

Lee Friedlander est reconnu comme l'un des plus grands photographes américains. Il a publié plusieurs collections de photographies et a écrit des essais sur différents sujets.

"It seems to me that in the western world, culture has something to do with appearance. A person that's out creating good stuff has got to appreciate someone when they take the time to have an appearance that goes with what they're doing."
— Ornette Coleman

ORNETTE COLEMAN
title BODY META / *year* 1976 /
label Verve

THIS IS OUR MUSIC

THE ORNETTE COLEMAN QUARTET

WITH DONALD CHERRY / ED BLACKWELL / CHARLIE HADEN

ATLANTIC 1353 FULL dynamics-frequency SPECTRUM

THE ORNETTE COLEMAN QUARTET

title THIS IS OUR MUSIC / *year* 1960 / *label* Atlantic / *design* Loring Eutemey / *photo* Lee Friedlander

On the occasions that Loring Eutemey and Lee Friedlander were assigned on a cover project together, the results were unique and quite special. The designer's ability to frame the photo subject is quite astounding. Friedlander's group portrait of Coleman and his suave band of free jazz pioneers is elegantly bordered with subtlety and visual finesse. **o**

Wenn Loring Eutemey und Lee Friedlander die Gelegenheit hatten, Coverbilder zusammen zu ge-

stalten, kamen dabei stets sagenhaft gute und sehr besondere Ergebnisse heraus. Ihre Fähigkeit, Fotos durch Umrahmungen in Szene zu setzen, ist einzigartig. Friedlanders Gruppenporträt von Coleman und seiner Band aus ausgesuchten Free-Jazz-Pionieren wird von einem eleganten Rahmen umgeben, der dem Ganzen eine dezente Noblesse verleiht. **o**

Lorsque Loring Eutemey et Lee Friedlander travaillaient ensemble sur un projet de pochette, le résultat était toujours original et très spécial. Le graphiste a recadré la photo avec un talent assez stupéfiant. Le portrait de groupe que Lee Friedlander avait réalisé d'Ornette Coleman et de son groupe de dandys pionniers du free jazz est élégamment bordé avec subtilité et finesse visuelle.

ALICE COLTRANE

title UNIVERSAL CONSCIOUSNESS / *year* 1971 / *label* Impulse! / *design* Philip Melnick / *photo* Philip Melnick

Philip Melnick has been involved in music and photography since he was a teenager. He started publishing his photos in the 1950s and since the mid-1960s has had exhibitions throughout the United States. By the time she recorded *Universal Consciousness*, Alice Coltrane had finally shaken off her perceived image, as being the wife of John Coltrane, and had come into her own as a highly talented musician and composer of spiritual music. **O** Philip Melnick begann schon zu Jugendzeiten, zu fotografieren und zu musizieren. In den 1950ern

stellte er seine ersten Fotos aus und tourte seit Mitte der 1960er mit verschiedenen Ausstellungen durch die USA. Mit der Aufnahme von *Universal Consciousness* schaffte es Alice Coltrane endlich, aus dem Schatten von Ehemann John Coltrane herauszutreten und als eigenständige Spiritual-Musikerin und Komponistin anerkannt zu werden. **O** Philip Melnick a pratiqué la musique et la photographie dès son adolescence. Il commença à publier ses photos dans les années 1950 et les a exposées dans tous les États-Unis depuis le milieu des années 1960. Au moment où elle enregistra *Universal Consciousness*, Alice Coltrane avait enfin réussi à se débarrasser de son image de femme du défunt John Coltrane et elle était reconnue pour elle-même, en tant que musicienne et compositrice de grand talent.

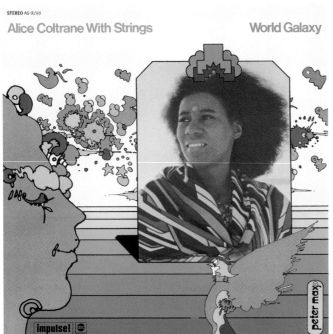

STEREO AS-9218

Alice Coltrane With Strings   World Galaxy

ALICE COLTRANE
title WORLD GALAXY / *year*
1971 / *label* Impulse! / *design*
Peter Max / *photo* Philip
Melnick

JOHN COLTRANE
title LUSH LIFE / *year* 1957 /
label Prestige / *design* Esmond
Edwards / *photo* Esmond
Edwards

JOHN COLTRANE
title ASCENSION / *year* 1965 /
label Impulse! / *design* Robert
Flynn/Viceroy / *photo* Charles
Stewart

stereo

Ascension
John Coltrane

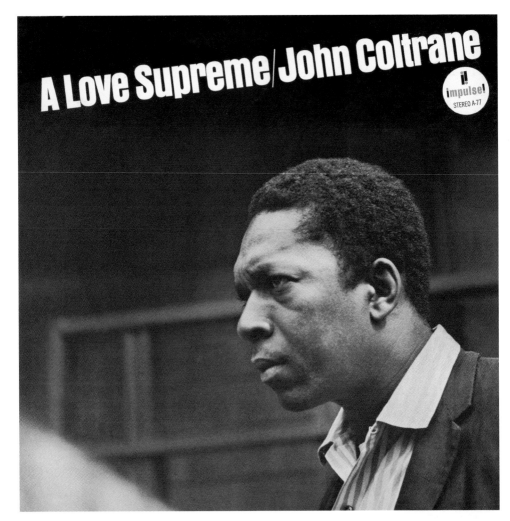

A Love Supreme/John Coltrane

impulse!
STEREO A-77

JOHN COLTRANE

title A LOVE SUPREME / *year* 1964 /
label Impulse! / *design* George Gray/Viceroy /
photo Bob Thiele

It was Bob Thiele, head producer at ABC/Impulse!
from 1961-69, who gave John Coltrane total artistic freedom. Thiele's now instantly recognizable
cover photo was taken during the historic recording
session on December 9, 1964 at Rudy Van Gelder's
studio in Englewood Cliffs, New Jersey. The image
captures the intensity and focus of a creative genius
in a devotional state. **O**
Bob Thiele, 1961 bis 1969 Chefproduzent von
ABC/Impulse!, gab John Coltrane komplette künstlerische Freiheit. Dieses von Thiele geschossene

Coverfoto, das einen hohen Wiedererkennungswert
besitzt, wurde am 9. Dezember 1964 während der
historischen Aufnahmesession in Rudy Van Gelders
Studio in Englewood Cliffs, New Jersey, aufgenommen. Das Bild fängt die Angespanntheit und den
Blick des kreativen Genies in einem Moment höchs-
ter Konzentration ein. **O**
C'est Bob Thiele, le producteur en chef d'ABC/
Impulse! de 1961 à 1969, qui donna à John Coltrane une liberté artistique totale. Il prit cette
photographie aujourd'hui archiconnue pendant la
session d'enregistrement historique du 9 décembre
1964, au studio de Rudy Van Gelder à Englewood
Cliffs, dans le New Jersey. Elle capture l'intensité
et la concentration d'un génie créatif en plein état
de grâce.

JOHN COLTRANE

title KULU SÉ MAMA /
year 1966 / *label* Impulse! /
design Robert Flynn/Viceroy /
photo Charles Stewart

JOHN COLTRANE GIANT STEPS

FULL *dynamics·frequency* SPECTRUM   ATLANTIC 1311

STEREO

JOHN COLTRANE
title GIANT STEPS / *year* 1959 / *label* Atlantic /
design Marvin Israel / *photo* Lee Friedlander

Lee Friedlander's upward close-up of Coltrane
seems larger than Marvin Israel's minimally designed frame can seem to hold with its red border
and typeface. Coltrane's sonic language has inspired
many visual artists. Children's book illustrator
Chris Raschka explored the tune "Giant Steps" as a
dynamic visual journey for children. **O**
Lee Friedlanders von unten aufgenommene Nahaufnahme von Coltrane wirkt, als wäre sie zu groß,
um von Marvin Israels minimalistischem roten
Rahmen mit roter Schrift gehalten zu werden.

Durch Coltranes musikalische Sprache wurden
zahlreiche Künstler inspiriert. Kinderbuchillustra-
tor Chris Raschka verarbeitete den Track „Giant
Steps" zu einem dynamischen visuellen Erlebnis für
Kinder. **O**
Ce gros plan en contre-plongée de Coltrane, réalisé
par Lee Friedlander, semble plus grand que ce que
peut accueillir le cadre minimaliste de Marvin
Israel, avec sa bordure et ses lettres rouges. Le
langage sonique de Coltrane a inspiré de nombreux
artistes graphiques. Chris Raschka, illustrateur de
livres pour enfants, a exploré le morceau «Giant
Steps» sous l'angle d'un voyage visuel dynamique
pour les enfants.

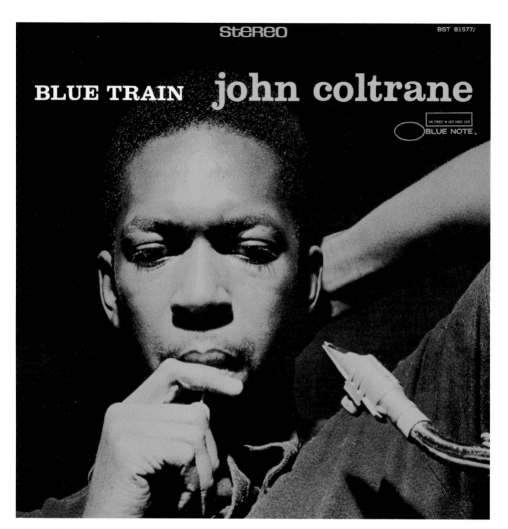

STEREO BST 81577*

BLUE TRAIN **john coltrane**

THE FINEST IN JAZZ SINCE 1939
BLUE NOTE.

JOHN COLTRANE
title BLUE TRAIN / *year* 1957 / *label* Blue Note / *design* Reid Miles / *photo* Francis Wolff

Reid Miles' greatest achievement was the harmonious blending of modernism with a distinct personality. Not for all his compositional flair, Miles also knew when to play hands-off, letting Wolff's expressive photography drive sleeves such as John Coltrane's legendary *Blue Train*. That's why Miles' sleeves fit so well; they visually represent jazz, at once personal and progressive, vernacular and global. **O**

Reid Miles' bewundernswerte Fähigkeit war es, einen modernistischen Stil mit seiner unverkennbaren persönlichen Note zu versehen. Bei all seiner Fähigkeit wusste Miles trotzdem ganz genau, wann er die Zügel aus der Hand geben und Wolffs ausdrucksstarke Fotografie für sich sprechen lassen musste, wie es bei dem Cover von Coltranes legendärem *Blue Train* der Fall ist. Daher passen seine Plattenhüllen so hervorragend zu ihrem Inhalt: Sie stellen eine visuelle Umsetzung des Jazz dar. **O**

La plus grande qualité du travail de Reid Miles était le mélange harmonieux de la modernité et d'une personnalité originale. Grâce à son sens de la composition, il a également su laisser le champ libre à la photographie expressive de Francis Wolff pour des couvertures telles que le légendaire *Blue Train* de John Coltrane. C'est pour cela que ses pochettes sont si parfaites : ce sont des représentations visuelles du jazz.

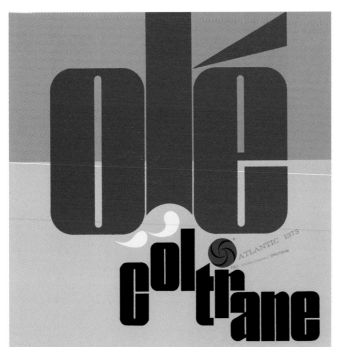

JOHN COLTRANE

title OLÉ / *year* 1961 / *label* Atlantic / *design* Jagel & Slutzky Graphics

JOHN COLTRANE AND JOHNNY HARTMAN

title JOHN COLTRANE AND JOHNNY HARTMAN / *year* 1963 / *label* Impulse! / *design* Robert Flynn/Viceroy / *photo* Joe Alper

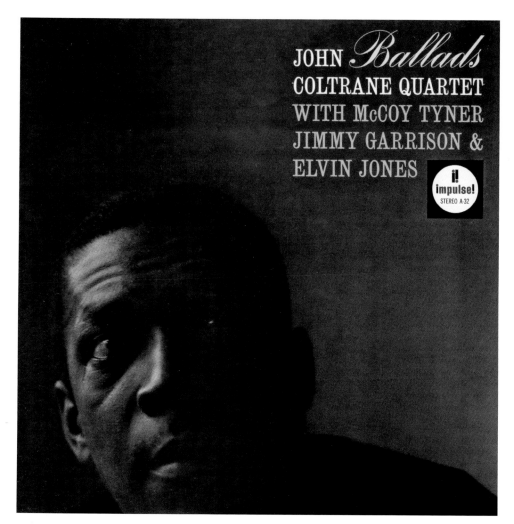

JOHN COLTRANE QUARTET

title BALLADS / *year* 1962 / *label* Impulse! /
ad Hollis King / *design* Jim Marshall, Charles
Stewart

Veteran art director, Hollis King, brings together
the mighty talents of Monterey Festival photographer, Jim Marshall, and Charles Stewart for the
design of this dark and unusual portrait of Trane.
As a response to a ferocious critical attack on his
music, where some traditionalist reviewers labeled
his music as being "anti-jazz", Coltrane recorded
this hauntingly beautiful set of standard ballads. **○**
Der altgediente Art Director Hollis King vereinte
die großartigen Talente Jim Marshalls, Fotograf
beim Monterey-Festival, und Charles Stewarts

miteinander, um dieses dunkle, ungewöhnliche
Porträt von Trane zu verwirklichen. Als Antwort
auf die grausame Kritikerattacke, bei der seine
Musik von einigen als „Anti-Jazz" bezeichnet
wurde, nahm Coltrane diese eindringlichen, wun-
dervollen Standards auf. **○**
Le directeur artistique vétéran Hollis King rassemble ici les grands talents du photographe du
festival de Monterey, Jim Marshall, et du graphiste
Charles Stewart pour ce portrait sombre et inhabi-
tuel de Coltrane. En réponse à des critiques féroces
de sa musique, que certains commentateurs tradi-
tionalistes avaient taxée d'«anti-jazz», Coltrane
enregistra ces ballades classiques à la beauté
envoûtante.

EDDIE CONDON'S ALL-STARS

title JAM SESSION COAST-
TO-COAST / *year* 1953 /
label Columbia

CHICK COREA

title TONES FOR JOAN'S
BONES / *year* 1968 / *label*
Vortex / *art* Dick Luppi /
design Haig Adishian

CORTEX
title TROUPEAU BLEU / *year*
1975 / *label* Disques Esperance

CORTEX

troupeau bleu

JACK COSTANZO

title LEARN-PLAY BONGOS
WITH "MR. BONGO" JACK
COSTANZO / *year* 1961 /
label Liberty / *design* Pate/
Francis & Associates / *photo*
Garrett-Howard

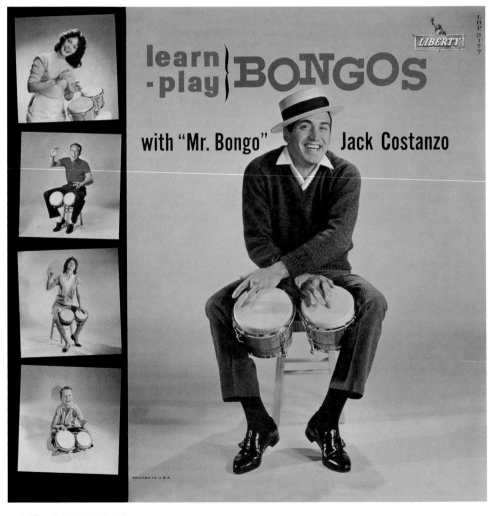

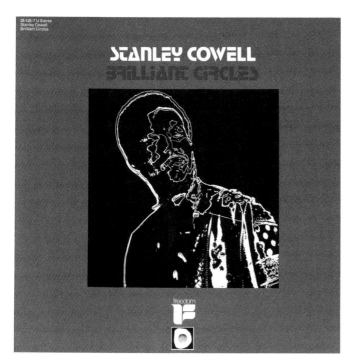

STANLEY COWELL

title BRILLIANT CIRCLES /
year 1969 / *label* Freedom

NEAL CREQUE

title CONTRAST! / *year*
1972 / *label* Cobblestone /
design Don Schlitten / *photo*
Don Schlitten

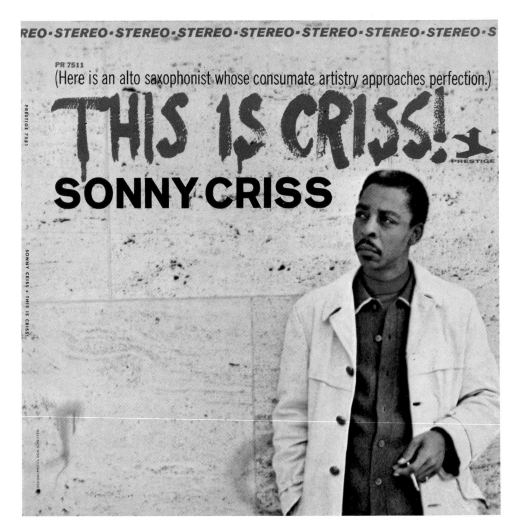

REO·STEREO·STEREO·STEREO·STEREO·STEREO·STEREO·STEREO·S

PR 7511

(Here is an alto saxophonist whose consumate artistry approaches perfection.)

THIS IS CRISS!

SONNY CRISS

PRESTIGE

PRESTIGE 7531

SONNY CRISS • THIS IS CRISS!

DESIGN/PHOTO: DON SCHLITTEN

SONNY CRISS

title THIS IS CRISS! / *year*
1966 / *label* Prestige / *design* Don
Schlitten / *photo* Don Schlitten

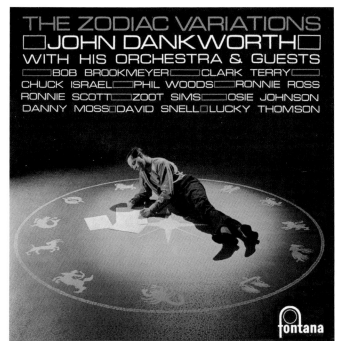

JOHN DANKWORTH
title THE ZODIAC
VARIATIONS / *year* 1964 /
label Fontana

**JOHNNY
DANKWORTH AND
HIS ORCHESTRA**
title JAZZ ROUTES / *year*
1959 / *label* Columbia

Johnny Dankworth and his Orchestra

Johnny
Dankworth:
ENGLAND'S
AMBASSADOR
of JAZZ

ROULETTE
BIRDLAND SERIES

**JOHNNY
DANKWORTH AND
HIS ORCHESTRA**
title JOHNNY DANKWORTH:
ENGLAND'S AMBASSADOR
OF JAZZ / *year* 1958 / *label*
Roulette / *photo* Alex Greco

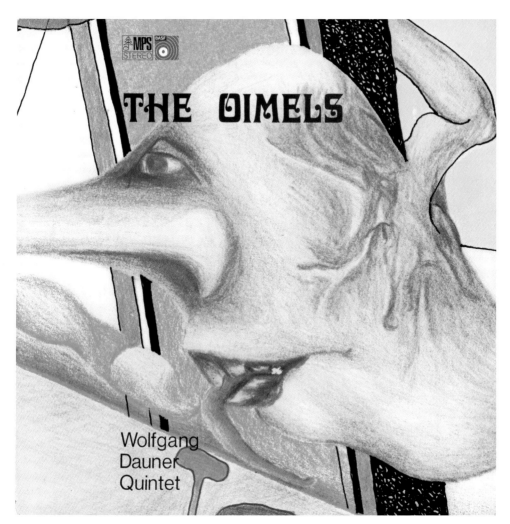

MPS STEREO BASF

THE OIMELS

Wolfgang
Dauner
Quintet

**WOLFGANG
DAUNER QUINTET**

title THE OIMELS /
year 1970 / *label* MPS /

FREE ACTION

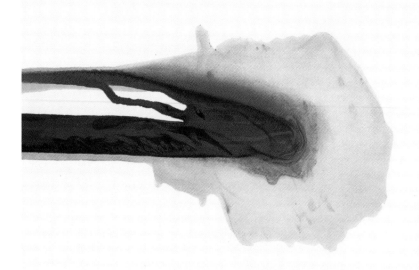

WOLFGANG DAUNER

WOLFGANG DAUNER
title FREE ACTION / *year* 1967 /
label MPS / *design* Gigi Berendt /
photo Paul Deker

MILES DAVIS

title BIRTH OF THE COOL / *year* 1949 /
label Capitol / *photo* Aram Avakian

Aram Avakian's photo evokes the movement and
energy of a young Miles about to change the whole
direction of jazz. As with the music itself, the now
classic cover was a design revelation in 1950. *Birth
of the Cool* is a landmark recording which collects
the 12 sides recorded by the Miles Davis nonet for
Capitol Records in 1949 and 1950. **o**
In Aram Avakians Foto sind die Aktivität und die
Energie eines noch jungen Miles zu spüren, der den
gesamten Jazz umkrempeln wird. Im Jahr 1950
stellte der mittlerweile zum Klassiker gewordene

Stil des Plattencovers genau wie die darauf enthaltene Musik eine stilistische Neuheit dar. Der
Meilenstein *Birth of the Cool* enthält zwölf Stücke,
die 1949 und 1950 vom Miles-Davis-Nonett für
Capitol Records aufgenommen wurden. **o**
La photographie d'Aram Avakian évoque le mouvement et l'énergie d'un jeune Miles Davis sur le point
de bouleverser le cours du jazz. Tout comme la
musique de l'album, cette couverture aujourd'hui
devenue classique fut une véritable révélation dans
le secteur du graphisme des années 1950. *Birth of
the Cool* est un enregistrement majeur qui rassemble les douze morceaux que le nonet de Miles
Davis avait enregistrés pour Capitol Records en
1949 et 1950.

MILES DAVIS
title ODYSSEY! / *year* 1955 /
label Prestige / *design* Don
Schlitten / *photo* Don Schlitten

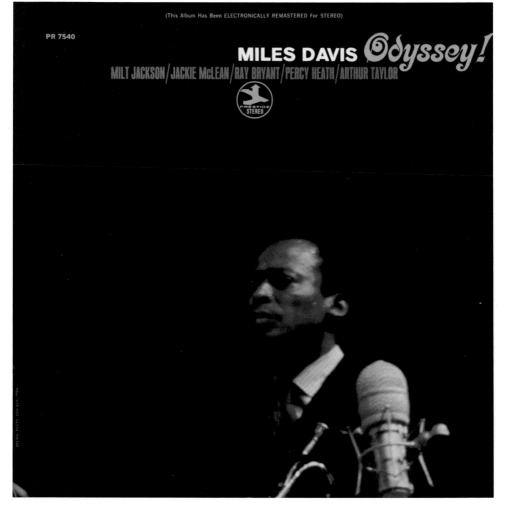

MILES DAVIS

title LIFT TO THE SCAFFOLD /
year 1958 / *label* Fontana

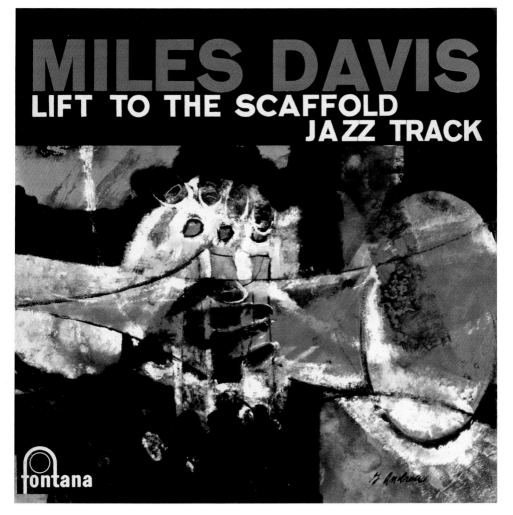

Miles Davis/E.S.P.

MILES DAVIS

title E.S.P. / *year* 1965 /
label CBS / *photo* Bob Cato

E.S.P. was the first recording of the Miles Davis quintet, consisting of Wayne Shorter, Herbie Hancock, Ron Carter and Tony Williams. Bob Cato's composed double portrait shows Miles relaxing with his then first wife, the dancer Frances Taylor. ○

E.S.P. war die erste Aufnahme von Miles' Quintett, das aus Wayne Shorter, Herbie Hancock, Ron Carter und Tony Williams bestand. Bob Catos Doppelporträt zeigt Miles ganz entspannt mit seiner ersten Frau, der Tänzerin Frances Taylor. ○

E.S.P. était le premier enregistrement du quintette de Miles Davis, composé de Wayne Shorter, Herbie Hancock, Ron Carter et Tony Williams. Le double portrait montre Miles détendu, aux côtés de sa première femme, la danseuse Frances Taylor.

MILES DAVIS
ALL
STARS

PRESTIGE HI-FI LP 7076

JAY JAY JOHNSON LUCKY THOMPSON HORACE SILVER PERCY HEATH KENNY CLARKE

WALKIN'

Hannan

MILES DAVIS
title WALKIN' / *year* 1954 /
label Prestige

After a long fluctuating battle with heroin, *Walkin'* announced Miles Davis' return to recording with a new verve. The recent introduction of the 33 1/3 rpm long-player also meant that musicians were able to perform extended tracks, such as can be heard on the 13-minute title track. ○
Nach einem langen, von Rückschlägen geprägten Kampf gegen die Heroinsucht kündigte *Walkin'*

Miles Davis' Rückkehr zur Musik sowie einen zu neuem Schwung gelangten Davis an. Durch die Einführung der 33 1/3 rpm-Langspielplatte war es den Musikern möglich auch sehr lange Stücke zu spielen – der 13-minütige Titelsong zeugt davon. ○
Après une longue bataille contre l'héroïne, *Walkin'* annonçait le retour de Miles Davis avec une nouvelle énergie. L'apparition du 33 tours signifiait également que les plages pouvaient durer plus longtemps, comme le montre le morceau titre de treize minutes, aujourd'hui devenu un classique.

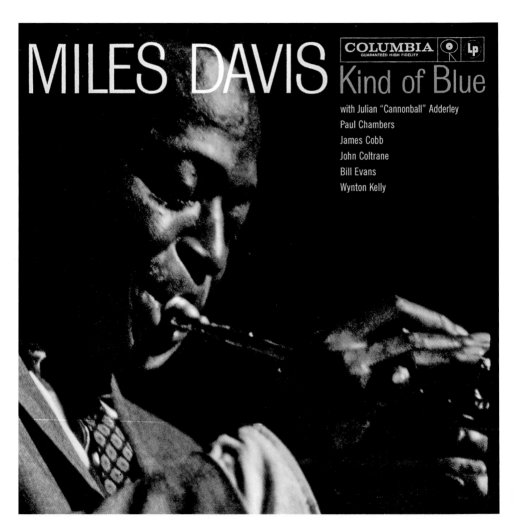

MILES DAVIS Kind of Blue

COLUMBIA GUARANTEED HIGH FIDELITY lp

with Julian "Cannonball" Adderley
Paul Chambers
James Cobb
John Coltrane
Bill Evans
Wynton Kelly

MILES DAVIS
title KIND OF BLUE' / *year*
1959 / *label* Columbia

"Take a walk down a city street with Miles Davis and listen to the language of the people on the sidewalk. Listen to music that captures the joy, the pain, the beauty of people who live on 'The Block'. Listen to one of the most beautiful places in the world..."
— CBS records promotional poster for *On the Corner* (1972)

MILES DAVIS
title ON THE CORNER /
year 1972 / *label* CBS / *art*
Corky McCoy

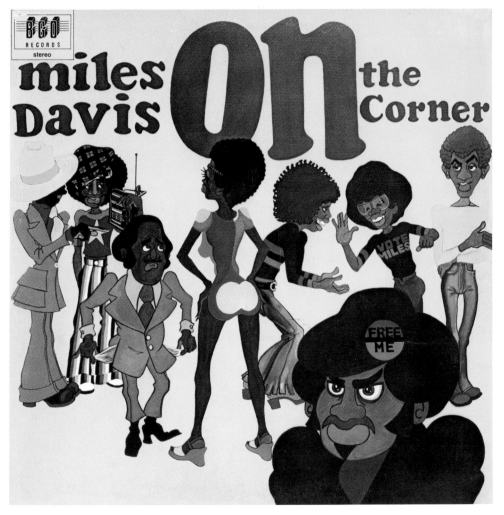

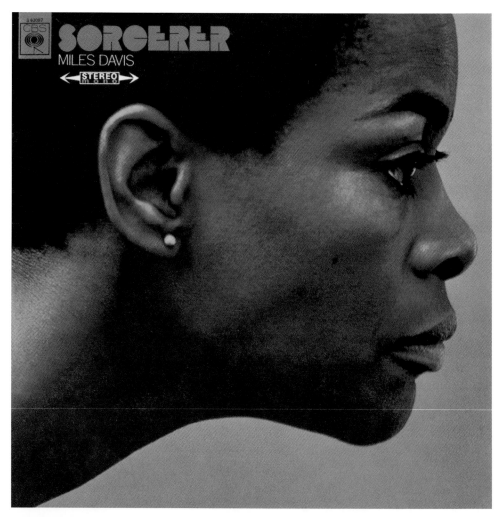

MILES DAVIS

title SORCERER / *year* 1967 /
label CBS

MILES DAVIS
title WE WANT MILES /
year 1982 / *label* CBS / *photo*
Yoshihisa Yoneda

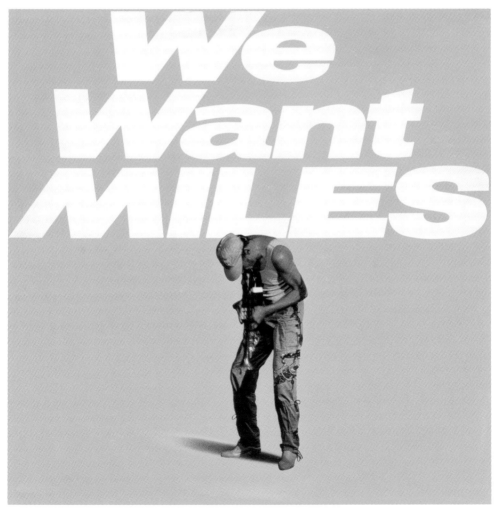

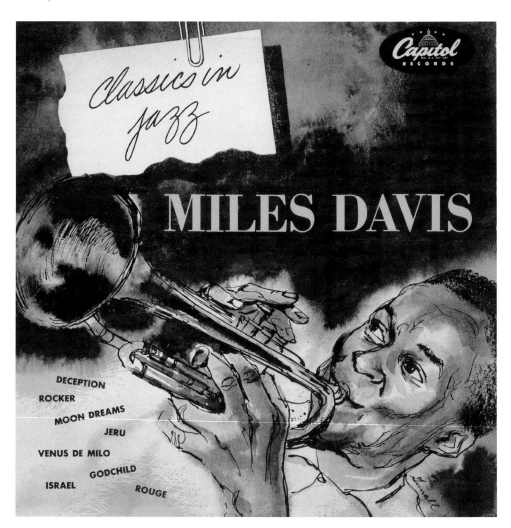

MILES DAVIS
title CLASSICS IN JAZZ /
year 1949 / *label* Capitol

**MILES DAVIS
QUINTET /
ART BLAKEY
AND THE JAZZ
MESSENGERS**
title ASCENSEUR POUR
L'ÉCHAFAUD / *year* 1955 /
label Fontana / *photo* Stan
Wiezniak

**MILES DAVIS
QUINTET**
title STEAMIN' WITH THE
MILES DAVIS QUINTET /
year 1956 / *label* Prestige /
design Don Schlitten / *photo*
Don Schlitten

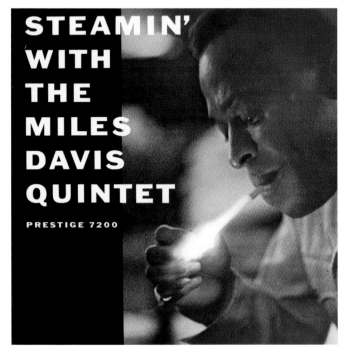

PRESTIGE
LP 161

MILES DAVIS QUARTET

WITH
JOHN LEWIS
HORACE SILVER
PERCY HEATH
MAX ROACH
ART BLAKEY

MILES DAVIS QUARTET

title MILES DAVIS QUARTET /
year 1954 / *label* Prestige /
photo Bob Weinstock

RICHARD DAVIS
title MUSES FOR RICHARD
DAVIS / *year* 1969 / *label* MPS /
design Tilman Michalski

DEODATO
title DEODATO / *year* 1972 /
label CTI / *design* Bob Ciano /
photo Pete Turner

DEODATO

CTI
AC 30-018
STEREO

WALT DICKERSON
title THIS IS WALT DICKERSON! / *year* 1961 / *label* New Jazz

DOLDINGER QUARTET
title DIG DOLDINGER / *year* 1963 / *label* Philips

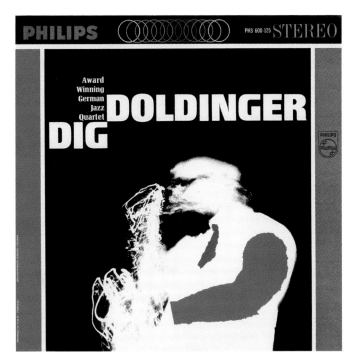

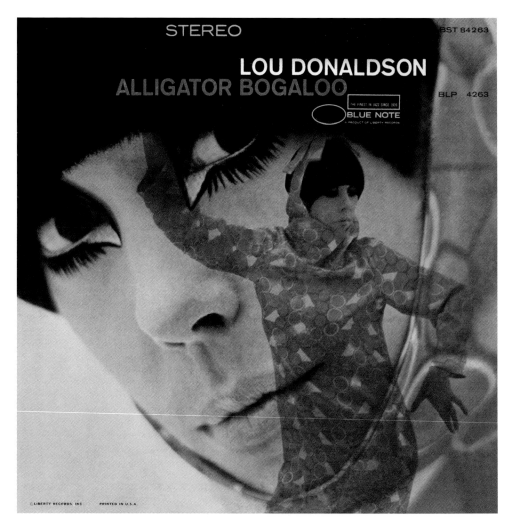

LOU DONALDSON

title ALLIGATOR BOGALOO /
year 1967 / *label* Blue Note /
design Reid Miles / *photo*
Francis Wolff

LOU DONALDSON

title COSMOS / *year* 1971 / *label* Blue Note

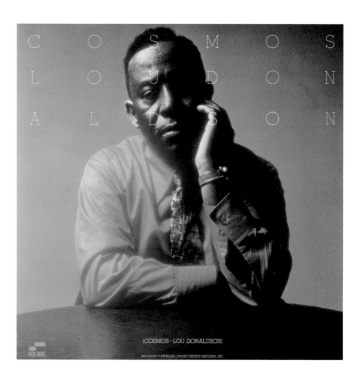

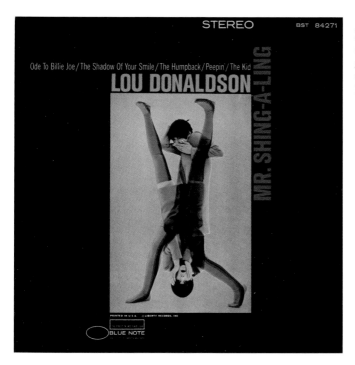

LOU DONALDSON

title MR. SHING-A-LING / *year* 1967 / *label* Blue Note / *design* Reid Miles / *photo* Reid Miles

BLUE NOTE 5055

lou donaldson

SEXTET

vol. 2

with
kenny dorham
matthew gee
elmo hope
percy heath
art blakey

LOU DONALDSON
SEXTET

title LOU DONALDSON
SEXTET VOL. 2 / *year* 1954 /
label Blue Note

*"Blues is the backbone,
and if you don't have it
in jazz it's like taking sugar
out of a cake."*

— Lou Donaldson

KENNY DORHAM

title JAZZ CONTRASTS / *year* 1957 /
label Riverside / *design* Paul Bacon / *photo*
Paul Weller

A jazz fan in his teens, Paul Bacon took up playing the ukulele. He moved from New York to Newark, New Jersey, where he befriended fellow jazz aficionado, John Hermansader, with whom he would join the Blue Note design team after WWII. Bacon cleverly arranges Paul Weller's double portrait of trumpeter Kenny Dorham, emphasizing the album's title. The "contrast" on this occasion refers to the addition of harp playing on the album. ○

Paul Bacon erlernte früh das Ukulele-Spiel. Er zog von New York nach Newark, New Jersey, wo er sich mit Jazzliebhaber John Hermansader zusammentat, um mit ihm nach dem Zweiten Weltkrieg in das Designteam von Blue Note einzusteigen. Bacon arrangiert zwei Porträts von Kenny Dorham auf pfiffige Weise, um den Titel des Albums, *Jazz Contrasts*, inhaltlich hervorzuheben. Der „Kontrast" bezieht sich hier auf das Harfenspiel des Albums. ○

Adolescent, Paul Bacon écoutait du jazz et commença à apprendre à jouer du ukulélé. De New York, il partit à Newark dans le New Jersey, où il rencontra John Hernamsader, un autre amateur de jazz, avec lequel il allait rejoindre l'équipe graphique de Blue Note après la Deuxième Guerre mondiale. Pour faire écho au titre de l'album, il fait un arrangement astucieux de deux portraits de Kenny Dorham. Ici, le «contraste» se réfère à l'ajout de la harpe.

KENNY DORHAM

title AFRO-CUBAN / *year* 1955 /
label Blue Note / *design* Gil
Mellé / *photo* Francis Wolff

**KENNY DORHAM
& JACKIE MCLEAN**

title INTA SOMETHIN' /
year 1962 / *label* Pacific Jazz /
design Woody Woodward /
photo Woody Woodward

BOB DOROUGH
title DEVIL MAY CARE /
year 1956 / *label* Bethlehem

"*After eating a wonderful meal in a Chinese restaurant in Glasgow, I beckoned the waitress to my table and asked her if she accepted American Express. She replied 'No, but we have Canada Dry.'*"
— Bob Downes

BOB DOWNES OPEN MUSIC

title ELECTRIC CITY / *year* 1971 / *label* Vertigo / *design* Nigel Rollings, Rob Lett

**THE KENNY
DREW TRIO**
title NEW FACES, NEW
SOUNDS / *year* 1953 / *label*
Blue Note

URSZULA DUDZIAK
title NEWBORN LIGHT /
year 1974 / *label* Columbia /
design Eloise Vega Smith / *photo*
Don Hunstein

URSZULA DUDZIAK NEWBORN LIGHT

GEORGE DUKE

title THE AURA WILL
PREVAIL / *year* 1975 / *label*
MPS / *design* Wilfried Satty

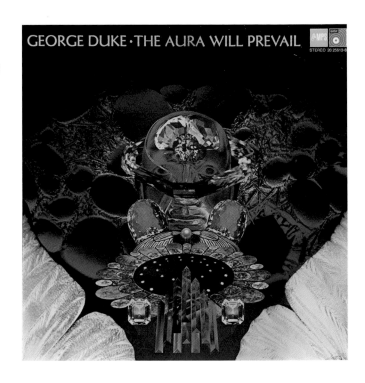

GEORGE DUKE · THE AURA WILL PREVAIL

STEREO 20 25613-6

Keno Duke/Contemporaries

with George Coleman, Frank Strozier, Harold Mabern, and Lisle Atkinson

Sense of Values

STRATA-EAST
STEREO SES-7416

From an original painting by Roland Bloch

KENO DUKE

title SENSE OF VALUES /
year 1974 / *label* Strata-East /
art Roland Bloch / *design*
Theodore Plair

*"The concept
of identity is
not a mystery.
Neither is
the direction
in which we
are headed."*
— Keno Duke

CHARLES EARLAND

title ODYSSEY / *year* 1976 / *label* Mercury / *design* Roberto / *photo* Benno Friedman

TEDDY EDWARDS & HOWARD MCGHEE

title TOGETHER AGAIN!!!! / *year* 1961 / *label* Contemporary / *design* George Kershaw, Guidi/Tri-Arts / *photo* Roger Marshutz

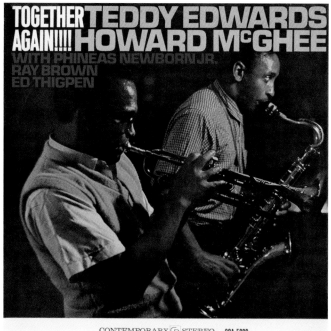

DUKE ELLINGTON
title ANATOMY OF A
MURDER / *year* 1959 / *label*
Columbia / *design* Saul Bass /
photo Sam Leavitt

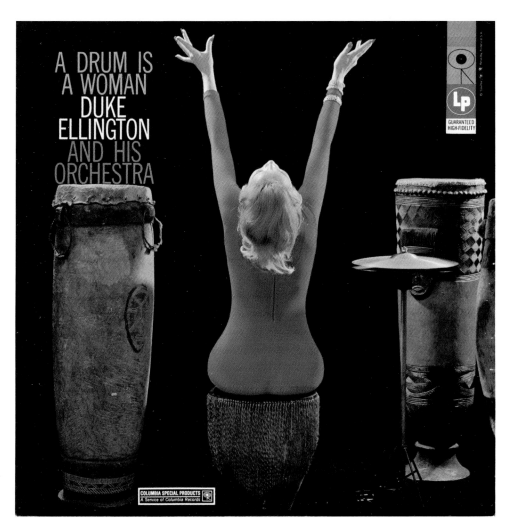

DUKE ELLINGTON
AND HIS ORCHESTRA

title A DRUM IS A WOMAN /
year 1956 / *label* Columbia

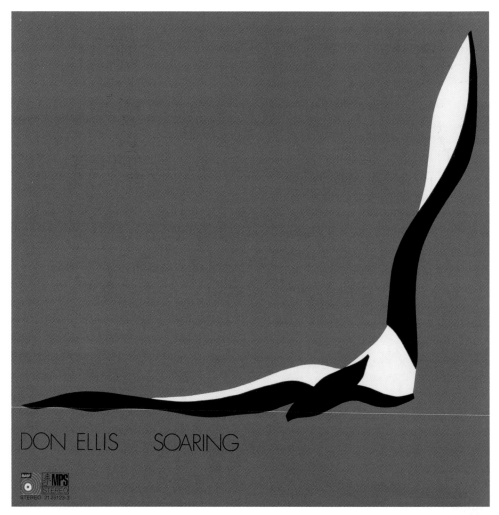

DON ELLIS
title SOARING / *year* 1973 /
label MPS / *design* Maria Eckstein

DON ELLIS ORCHESTRA

title ELECTRIC BATH /
year 1967 / *label* CBS

THE ENSEMBLE AL-SALAAM

title THE SOJOURNER /
year 1974 / *label* Strata-East /
design Freedom Sunday, Jawara
Kenyatta, William Ennett

The Ensemble Al-Salaam
The Sojourner

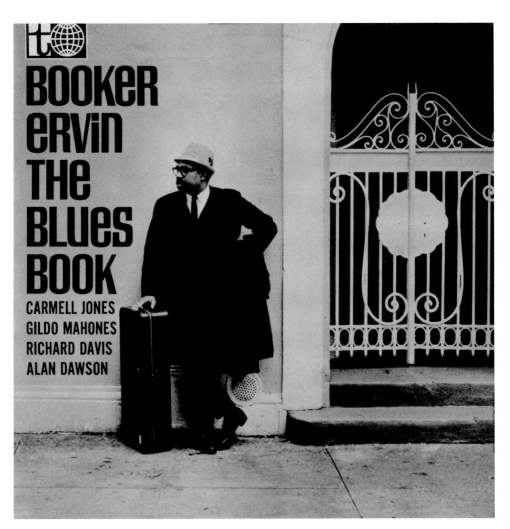

BOOKER ERVIN
THE BLUES BOOK
CARMELL JONES
GILDO MAHONES
RICHARD DAVIS
ALAN DAWSON

BOOKER ERVIN
title THE BLUES BOOK /
year 1964 / *label* Prestige

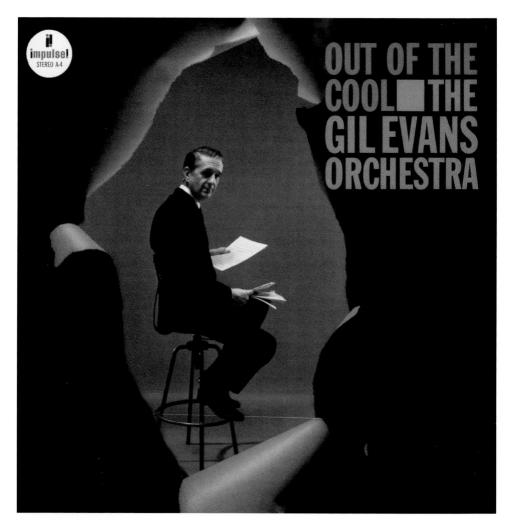

OUT OF THE
COOL■THE
GIL EVANS
ORCHESTRA

impulse!
STEREO A-4

THE GIL EVANS ORCHESTRA

title OUT OF THE COOL /
year 1960 / *label* Impulse! /
design Robert Flynn/Viceroy /
photo Arnold Newman

THE GIL EVANS ORCHESTRA

title INTO THE HOT / *year* 1961 / *label* Impulse! /
design Robert Flynn/Viceroy / *photo* Arnold
Newman

The work of celebrated photographer Arnold
Newman has often been called environmental
portraiture, a term used to describe his approach of
photographing his subjects within their physical
environments, whether professional, domestic or
constructed. Once again, Newman provides the
image for this sequel to *Out of the Cool* (1960) under
the art direction of Impulse!'s design guru, Robert
Flynn. ●
Das Werk des gefeierten Fotografen Arnold Newman wurde häufig als „environmental portraiture"
(Umgebungs-Porträtfotografie) bezeichnet. Er fotografierte seine Objekte entweder in ihrer beruf-
lichen oder privaten Umgebung oder konstruierte
eine entsprechende Kulisse. Auch für dieses Album
lieferte Newman unter der Leitung des Impulse!-
Designgurus Robert Flynn das Coverfoto. ●
On a souvent dit que le grand photographe Arnold
Newman faisait des portraits environnementaux,
un terme utilisé pour décrire son approche consis-
tant à photographier ses sujets dans leur environne-
ment physique, qu'il soit professionnel, domestique
ou mis en scène. Pour cette suite de *Out of the Cool*
(1960), c'est encore lui qui était derrière l'objectif,
sous la direction artistique de Robert Flynn.

TAL FARLOW
title THE SWINGING GUITAR
OF TAL FARLOW / *year* 1957 /
label Verve / *ad* Sheldon Marks /
photo Herman Leonard

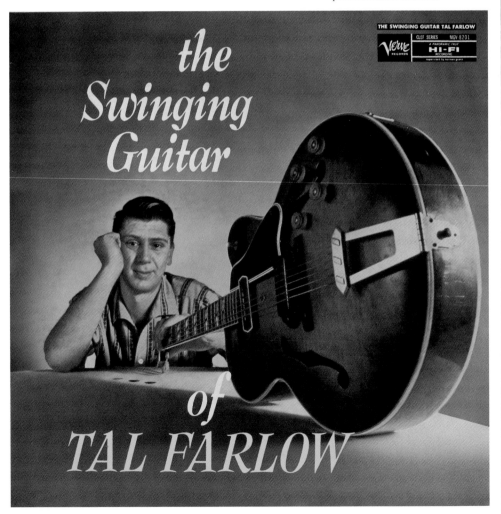

THE TAL FARLOW QUARTET

title COOKIN' ON ALL
BURNERS / *year* 1983 /
label Concord Jazz / *ad* Dick
Hendler / *photo* Bruce Burr

THE ART FARMER QUARTET

title SING ME SOFTLY OF
THE BLUES / *year* 1966 /
label Atlantic / *design* Haig
Adishian / *photo* Pete Sahula

SHAMEK FARRAH
title FIRST IMPRESSIONS /
year 1974 / *label* Strata-East /
design Jerry Harris

F 9035

MAYNARD
FERGUSON
title MAYNARD FERGUSON
PLAYS JAZZ FOR DANCING /
year 1959 / *label* Forum

CLARE FISCHER
title SALSA PICANTE / *year* 1978 / *label* Discovery / *design* Holger Matthies, Müller, Von Frankenberg

CLARE FISCHER
title FIRST TIME OUT / *year*
1962 / *label* Pacific Jazz / *design*
Woody Woodward / *photo* Woody
Woodward

ELLA FITZGERALD

title ELLA SWINGS LIGHTLY /
year 1958 / *label* Verve /
ad Sheldon Marks / *photo* Phil
Stern

BLUE NOTE 5043
33⅓ MICROGROOVE
modern jazz series

here comes
FRANK FOSTER

FRANK FOSTER QUINTET
title HERE COMES FRANK FOSTER /
year 1954 / *label* Blue Note / *design* John
Hermansader / *photo* Francis Wolff

John Hermansader was one of Blue Note's first
great cover designers. Reid Miles, a former assistant
of Hermansader, succeeded him at the label in
1956. While Hermansader was a jazz fan to the
core, it was classical loving Reid Miles, who together with the photography of Francis Wolff,
defined the Blue Note style. Nonetheless, Hermansader set the standard with his dynamic graphic
ability. ○
John Hermansader war einer der großartigsten
Coverdesigner bei Blue Note. Reid Miles, früherer

Assistent von Hermansader, folgte ihm und begann
1956, ebenfalls bei dem Label zu arbeiten. Obwohl
Hermansader der eingefleischte Jazzfan war, prägte
Reid Miles, der klassische Musik bevorzugte, zusammen mit dem Fotografen Francis Wolff den Stil
von Blue Note. Hermansader aber setzte mit seinem Geschick den grafischen Standard. ○
John Hermansader fut l'un des premiers grands
créateurs de pochettes de Blue Note. Reid Miles,
son ancien assistant, lui succéda en 1956. Alors
que John Hermansader était un passionné de jazz,
c'est Reid Miles, qui n'aimait que la musique classique, qui allait définir le style Blue Note avec l'aide
du photographe Francis Wolff. John Hermansader a
cependant posé les bases de ce style grâce à ses
graphismes dynamiques.

BETHLEHEM BCP 29
DELUXE SERIES
HI FIDELITY

BUD FREEMAN

BUD FREEMAN

title BUD FREEMAN / *year* 1955 /
label Bethlehem / *design* Burt Goldblatt

Designer Burt Goldblatt won a Gold Medal from the
New York Art Directors Club for this innovative
graphic assemblage. Bud Freeman was a big-band
sax player known for his long improvised solos.
Goldblatt used the same technique for the cover
of *Mel Tormé with the Marty Paich Dektette*
(Bethlehem, 1956), which is composed of con-
vertible cars. **O**
Der New York Art Directors Club verlieh dem
Designer Burt Goldblatt für dessen innovatives
grafisches Werk eine Goldmedaille. Big-Band-

Saxofonist Bud Freeman wurde bekannt durch
seine langen, improvisierten Soli. Goldblatt nutzte
dieselbe Technik bei dem Cover für *Mel Tormé with
the Marty Paich Dek-tette* (Bethlehem, 1956), auf
dem ein aus Cabriolets zusammengesetztes Gesicht
zu sehen ist. **O**
Le graphiste Burt Goldblatt gagna une médaille d'or
de l'Art Directors Club pour cette composition
graphique innovante. Bud Freeman était un saxophoniste de big band connu pour ses longs solos
improvisés. Burt Goldblatt utilisa la même technique pour la pochette de *Mel Tormé with the Marty
Paich Dek-tette* (Bethlehem, 1956), mais cette fois
avec des voitures décapotables.

FOUR FRESHMEN
title FOUR FRESHMEN AND
5 TROMBONES / *year* 1956 /
label Capitol

*"Mingus once said to me, something I feel very
good about: 'You know, Burt. I like you. You
come into a session, you take pictures. I never
even know that you're there.' And that was
the most flattering thing that he ever said."*
— Burt Goldblatt

CARLOS GARNETT
title JOURNEY TO
ENLIGHTENMENT / *year*
1974 / *label* Muse / *design* Ron
Warwell

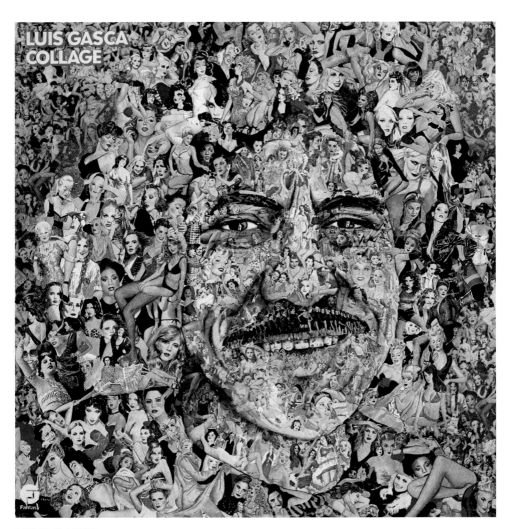

LUIS GASCA
title COLLAGE /
year 1976 / *label* Fantasy

THE HERB GELLER SEXTETTE

title THE HERB GELLER SEXTETTE / *year* 1962 / *label* EmArcy / *photo* Herman Leonard

CUSTOM EmArcy HIGH FIDELITY

MG-36040

THE Herb Geller SEXTETTE

OUTPOST INCIDENT
CRAZY HE CALLS ME
GIN FOR FUGUELHORNS
TARDI AT ZARDI'S
VONE MAE
ROCKIN' CHAIR
OWL EYES
YOU'D BE SO NICE
    TO COME HOME TO

Herb Geller, alto sax; Lorraine Geller, piano;
Ziggy Vines, tenor sax; Conte Candoli,
trumpet; Eldridge Freeman, drums; Leroy
Vinnegar, Keith Mitchell, bass.

EmArcy . . A PRODUCT OF MERCURY RECORD CORPORATION, CHICAGO, ILLINOIS

PHOTO—HERMAN LEONARD

STAN GETZ
title STAN GETZ PLAYS /
year 1954 / *label* Verve /
design Tom Hughes / *photo* Phil
Stern

STAN GETZ

title FOCUS / *year* 1961 /
label Barclay–Verve / *design*
Walter Coleman

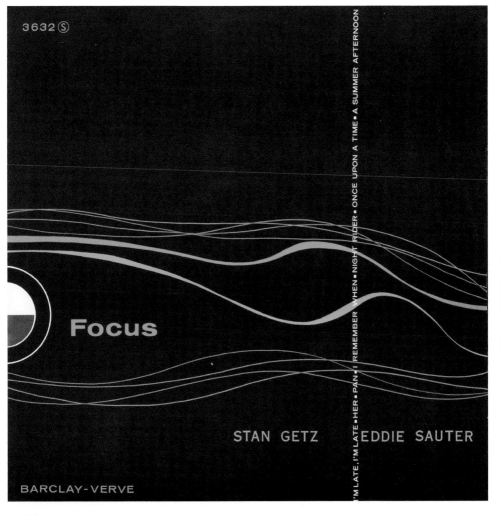

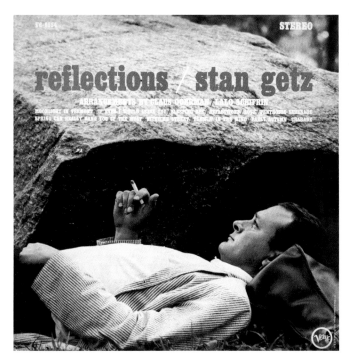

**TERRY GIBBS
QUARTET**
title TAKE IT FROM ME /
year 1964 / *label* Impuls! /
design Robert Flynn/Viceroy /
photo Frank Gauna

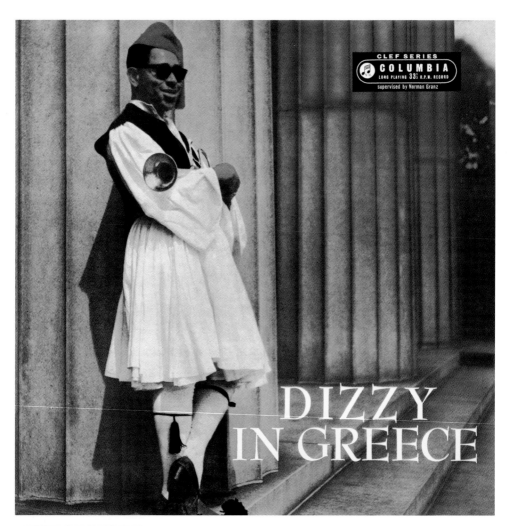

DIZZY
IN GREECE

DIZZY GILLESPIE
title DIZZY IN GREECE /
year 1957 / *label* Columbia

ENFIN!

JEF GILSON

JEAN-LOUIS CHAUTEMPS - FRANÇOIS JEANNEAU - JEAN-LUC PONTY - BERNARD VITET

30 J 1002

mono

JEF GILSON

title ENFIN! / *year* 1962 / *label* CED /
design Pierre Caron / *photo* Jean-Pierre Leloir

Music lover Jean-Pierre Leloir began taking photos in the early 1950s. He has photographed many of the world's musical icons, from Billie Holiday to Jimi Hendri. French pianist Jef Gilson was an active bandleader in the 1960s. He was one of the first bandleaders to showcase the creative talents of electric fusion violinist Jean-Luc Ponty. This early recording on the CED label is now an extreme rarity. ○

Musikliebhaber Jean-Pierre Leloir begann in den frühen 1950ern mit der Fotografie. Er fotografierte zahlreiche Giganten der Musikwelt, von Billie Holiday bis hin zu Jimi Hendrix. Der französische Pianist Jef Gilson war in den 1960ern rege als Bandleader tätig. Er brachte als erster das kreative Talent des Electric-Fusion-Violinisten Jean-Luc Ponty voll zur Geltung. Diese frühe Aufnahme ist mittlerweile zur Rarität geworden. ○

Le mélomane Jean-Pierre Leloir commença à prendre des photos au début des années 1950. Il a photographié beaucoup des icônes de la musique dans le monde entier, de Billie Holiday à Jimi Hendrix. Le pianiste français Jef Gilson dirigeait son groupe dans les années 1960. Il fut l'un des premiers à utiliser les talents créatifs du violoniste de jazz fusion électrique Jean-Luc Ponty. Cet enregistrement sorti sous le label CED est aujourd'hui extrêmement rare.

JIMMY GIUFFRE
title MUSIC FOR PEOPLE,
BIRDS, BUTTERFLIES &
MOSQUITOES / *year* 1972 /
label Choice / *design* Ray Ross

JIMMY GIUFFRE
title THE FOUR BROTHERS
SOUND / *year* 1958 / *label*
Atlantic / *design* Marvin
Israel / *photo* Lee Friedlander

ARGO **take a number from 1 to 10**

BENNY GOLSON
title TAKE A NUMBER FROM
1 TO 10 / *year* 1961 / *label*
Argo / *design* Emmett McBain

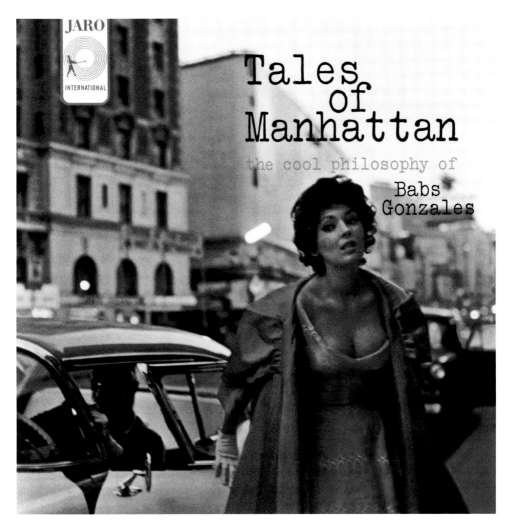

Tales
of
Manhattan

the cool philosophy of
Babs
Gonzales

BABS GONZALES
title TALES OF MANHATTAN /
year 1959 / *label* Jaro / *design*
Maurer Studios

DEXTER GORDON

title ONE FLIGHT UP / *year*
1964 / *label* Blue Note / *design*
Reid Miles / *photo* Francis
Wolff

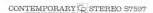

JOE GORDON

title LOOKIN' GOOD! / *year*
1961 / *label* Contemporary /
design Kershaw, Guidi/Tri-
Arts / *photo* Roger Marshutz

MILFORD GRAVES
PERCUSSION ENSEMBLE
WITH
SUNNY MORGAN

MILFORD GRAVES

title PERCUSSION ENSEMBLE / *year* 1965 /
label ESP-Disk' / *photo* Bob Greene

Founded in 1964 by Bernard Stollman, the New
York-based ESP-Disk' label was set up with the
directive of releasing music based upon the constructed language of Esperanto. Bob Greene's gran-
ular cover portrait appropriately frames Milford
Graves behind the blurred arc of a drum. Graves
was a leading figure in the American free jazz
movement during the 1960s. ○
Das 1964 von Bernard Stollman gegründete Plattenlabel ESP-Disk' mit Sitz in New York verfolgte
von Beginn an das Ziel, Musik herauszubringen,

deren Songtexte in der künstlichen Sprache Esperanto geschrieben waren. Bob Greenes körniges
Coverporträt bildet Milford Graves in passendem
Rahmen, nämlich hinter dem verschwommenen
Rund einer Trommel ab. Graves war eine Leitfigur
der amerikanischen Free-Jazz-Bewegung der
1960er Jahre. ○
Fondé en 1964 par Bernard Stollman, le label
new-yorkais ESP-Disk' fut créé pour produire une
musique basée sur l'Esperanto, une langue artifi-
cielle. Ce portrait réalisé par Bob Greene cadre
Milford Graves derrière l'arc flou d'une grosse
caisse. Milford Graves était un personnage important dans le mouvement du free jazz américain des
années 1960.

GLIDIN' ALONG
BENNY GREEN QUINTET

WITH JOHNNY GRIFFIN
AND JUNIOR MANCE

JAZZLAND SERIES 43

**BENNY GREEN
QUINTET**

title GLIDIN' ALONG /
year 1961 / *label* Jazzland

GRANT GREEN

title IRON CITY! / *year* 1967 /
label Cobblestone / *design*
Don Schlitten / *photo* Don
Schlitten

CST 9002
IRON CITY! GRANT GREEN
BIG JOHN PATTON/BEN DIXON
COBBLESTONE

GRANT GREEN **209**

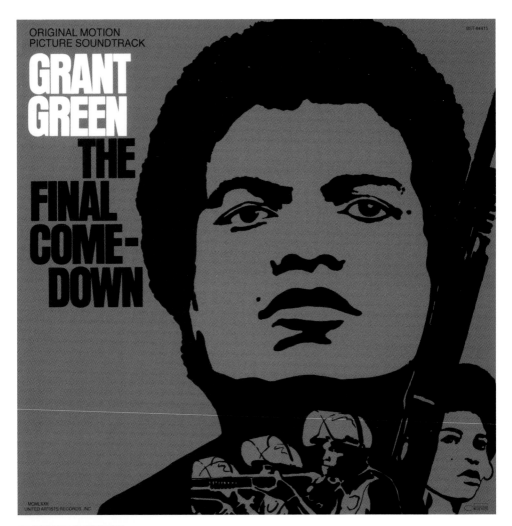

GRANT GREEN
title THE FINAL COMEDOWN /
year 1971 / *label* United Artists

JOHNNY GRIFFIN

title JOHNNY GRIFFIN VOL. 2 /
year 1955 / *label* Blue Note /
photo Harold Feinstein, Francis
Wolff

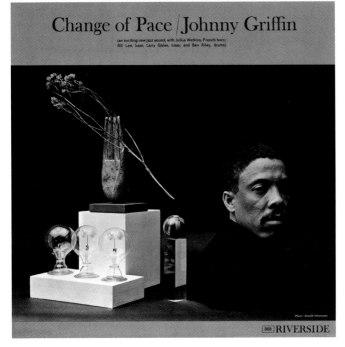

JOHNNY GRIFFIN
title CHANGE OF PACE /
year 1962 / *label* Riverside /
photo Donald Silverstein

JOHNNY GRIFFIN
title INTRODUCING JOHNNY
GRIFFIN / *year* 1956 / *label*
Blue Note / *design* Reid Miles /
photo Francis Wolff

GEORGE GRUNTZ
title FROM STICKSLAND
WITH LOVE – DRUMS AND
FOLKLORE / *year* 1967 /
label SABA / *design* Gus Ramp
Agency / *photo* P. Armbruster

from sticksland
with love
drums and folklore

george gruntz
daniel humair
charly antolini
pierre favre
mani neumeier
alfred sacher

SABA

STEREO

Featuring Thad Jones, trumpet / Frank Foster, tenor sax / Larry Rosen, drums / Bob Cranshaw, bass

DAVE GRUSIN

title KALEIDOSCOPE / *year* 1964 /
label CBS / *photo* Henry Parker

Obscure photographer Henry Parker creates an
interesting title-related composition for this 1964
CBS sleeve. With nearly 100 films to his name,
including *Three Days of the Condor* (1975), *The
Fabulous Baker Boys* (1989), and an Oscar for his
score of *The Milagro Beanfield War* (1988), Dave
Grusin is one of Hollywood's most celebrated film
composer-arrangers. ○
Der unbekannte Fotograf Henry Parker kreierte für
diese 1964 entstandene Plattenhülle eine interes-
sante Bildkomposition, die mit dem Namen des

Albums eine Verbindung herstellt. Mit nahezu 100
Filmmusiken, darunter *Die drei Tage des Condor*
(1975), *Die fabelhaften Baker Boys* (1989) und einem
Oscar für seinen Soundtrack zu *Milagro – Der Krieg
im Bohnenfeld* (1988) ist Grusin einer der gefeiert-
sten Filmkomponisten und Arrangeure. ○
Henry Parker, un photographe obscur, a créé une
composition intéressante qui illustre bien le titre de
cet album sorti chez CBS en 1964. Avec près de
100 films à son actif, notamment *Les Trois Jours du
Condor* (1975), *Susie et les Baker Boys* (1989) et
Milagro (1988), pour lequel il reçut un Oscar, Dave
Grusin est l'un des plus célèbres compositeurs-
arrangeurs d'Hollywood.

FRIEDRICH GULDA
title PIANO AND BIG
BAND!! / *year* 1963 / *label*
Scepter Records / *design* Burt
Goldblatt

FRIEDRICH GULDA
title FROM VIENNA WITH
JAZZ! / *year* 1964 / *label*
Columbia / *photo* Henry Parker

THE CHICO HAMILTON QUINTET

title THE CHICO HAMILTON QUINTET WITH STRINGS ATTACHED / *year* 1959 / *label* Warner Bros. / *photo* Gene Kornman

THE FURTHER ADVENTURES
OF EL CHICO CHICO HAMILTON
featuring Gabor Szabo and CLARK TERRY, RON CARTER,
CHARLIE MARIANO, JEROME RICHARDSON

MONDAY MONDAY ■ DAYDREAM ■ GOT MY MOJO WORKIN'
THAT BOY WITH THAT LONG HAIR ■ WHO CAN I TURN TO (WHEN NOBODY NEEDS ME)
EVIL EYE ■ MANILA ■ THE SHADOW OF YOUR SMILE ■ STELLA BY STARLIGHT ■ MY ROMANCE

impulse!
A-9114

Monaural

CHICO HAMILTON

title THE FURTHER
ADVENTURES OF EL
CHICO / *year* 1966 / *label*
Impulse! / *design* Robert
Flynn/Viceroy / *photo* Michael
Wollman

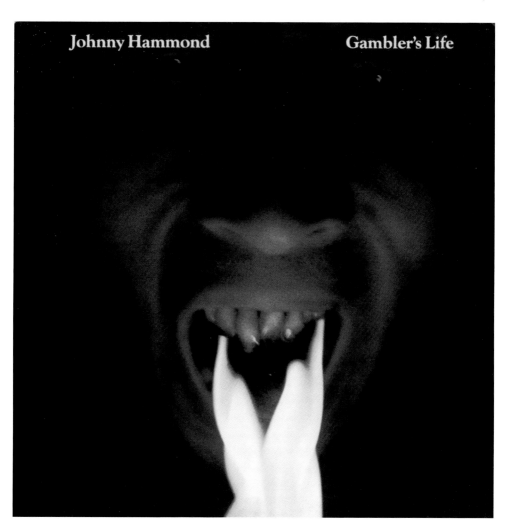

JOHNNY HAMMOND
title GAMBLER'S LIFE /
year 1974 / *label* Salvation /
design Sibbie McDonough / *photo*
Pete Turner

HERBIE HANCOCK

title MAN-CHILD / *year* 1975 /
label CBS / *design* Dario Campanile

"*The spirit
of jazz is the
spirit of
openness.*"
— Herbie Hancock

THE NEW JOHN HANDY QUINTET

title NEW VIEW! / *year*
1967 / *label* Columbia / *design*
Thomas Molesky

NOBUO HARA /
HOZAN YAMAMOTO

title NEW JAZZ IN JAPAN /
year 1968 / *label* Columbia

PARTITA
MULTANI
GANA
ACKA RAGA
SUBJECT

JOE HARRIOTT
– JOHN MAYER
DOUBLE QUINTET

title INDO-JAZZ FUSIONS /
year 1967 / *label* Atlantic / *design*
Haig Adishian / *photo* Michael
Joseph

GENE HARRIS
title ASTRAL SIGNAL /
year 1974 / *label* Blue Note /
design Bob Cato

COLEMAN HAWKINS
title THE HAWK IN PARIS /
year 1956 / *label* Vik / *photo*
Lester Bookbinder

**TUBBY HAYES
AND THE ALL STARS**
title RETURN VISIT! /
year 1962 / *label* Fontana

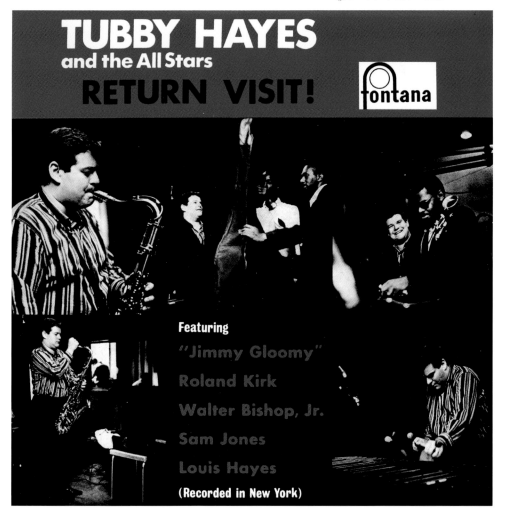

THE LOUIS HAYES GROUP

title VARIETY IS THE SPICE /
year 1979 / *label* Gryphon /
art Michael Mendel

PETER HERBOLZHEIMER RHYTHM COMBINATION & BRASS

title I HEAR VOICES / *year* 1978 / *label* Polydor / *photo* Dieter Lutthen & Jürgen Tegge

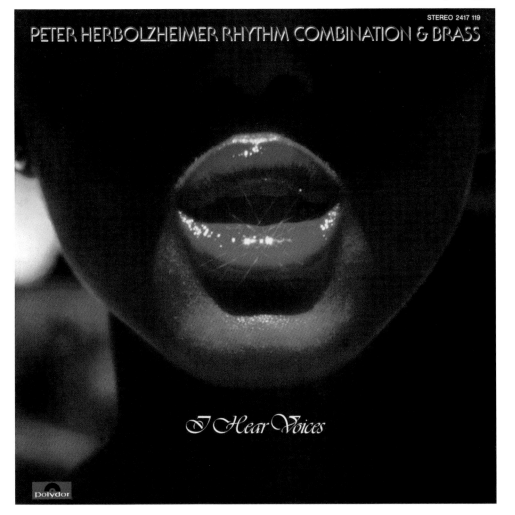

STEREO 2417 119

PETER HERBOLZHEIMER RHYTHM COMBINATION & BRASS

ℐ Hear Voices

polydor

JOE HENDERSON
title BLACK MIRACLE /
year 1976 / *label* Milestone /
ad Phil Carroll / *design* Tony
Lane / *photo* Tony Lane

ANDREW HILL
title COMPULSION!!!!! /
year 1965 / *label* Blue Note /
design Reid Miles / *photo* Reid
Miles

EARL HINES
title ONCE UPON A TIME /
year 1966 / *label* Impulse! /
design Robert Flynn/Viceroy /
photo Charles Stewart

STEREO

Earl
Hines

Once **Upon a Time** in the days of the Great Society, the citizens of Fun City were subjected to many and various hardships. After sources of light and power had wholly failed them, and they had been cast into Stygian Darkness, they were next deprived of their normal means of transport. Some strode long miles to their places of Labor through streets choked with the chariots and carts of farmers, shepherds and peasants from all the countryside around. Others meditated in lonely chambers on ways to improve the lot of their harassed fellow-men.

One such, with much faith in the healing power of Music, had a vision of bringing together so noble a company of musicians that the minds of the citizens could not but be lifted up out of the Slough of Despond.

It happened that there was within the city a Consort of Players whose leader and certain others were many leagues away, beyond communication. The Visionary decided to summon the most famous of those who remained to make plans for a Musical Celebration, and he sent messengers running through the streets to the houses of John Cornelius Hodges and Lawrence Brown. These twain came in due course to the appointed meeting place.

Now at that time the Fatha, Earl Hines, a great player of the piano, had come to the East, and him they had known for many years, and him they forthwith chose to head their company. There was also, within the northern boundaries of the city, an associate of yesterday, a formidable beater of hides, one Sonny Greer, and they sent word that he should come to them with all dispatch, bringing his tambours large and small.

(continued on back cover)

impulse!
A-9108

GL 1137

COLUMBIA lp

Lady in Satin
Billie
Holiday

Ray Ellis
and his orchestra

BILLIE HOLIDAY

title LADY IN SATIN / *year* 1958 /
label Columbia / *photo* Arnold Newman

Arnold Newman photographed some of the world's
most famous people during the latter half of the
20th century. This image of Billie Holiday encapsu-
lates the pain within the woman and the beauty of
her expression. *Lady in Satin* would be her last
studio album. Within a year she was dead. **O**
Arnold Newman fotografierte in der zweiten Hälfte
des 20. Jahrhunderts einige der berühmtesten
Menschen der Welt. In diesem Porträt wird eine

schwermütige Billie Holiday gezeigt, die trotz
ihres tragischen Schicksals nichts von ihrer
Schönheit verloren hat. *Lady in Satin* war Holidays
letztes Studioalbum – ein Jahr später war sie
bereits tot. **O**
Arnold Newman a photographié quelques-unes des
plus grandes personnalités du monde entier pendant
la seconde moitié du XXe siècle. Cette photographie
de Billie Holiday traduit la douleur qu'elle portait
en elle et la beauté de son expression. *Lady in Satin*
est son dernier album enregistré en studio. Elle
décéda l'année suivante.

The Madison Time
Oklahoma Toad
98.6-Lazy Day
Sunday Mornin'
Groovin' Time
The Odd Couple
I'm In The Mood For Love
Upward Bound

GROOVE WITH GROOVE

HOLMES SWEET HOLMES

**RICHARD 'GROOVE'
HOLMES**
title HOLMES SWEET
HOLMES / *year* 1974 / *label*
World Pacific / *ad* Woody
Woodward / *art* Jon Dahlstrom /
design Gabor Halmos

RICHARD 'GROOVE' HOLMES

title A BOWL OF SOUL /
year 1966 / *label* Valiant /
design Paul May

TERUMASA HINO QUARTET

title ALONE, ALONE
AND ALONE / *year* 1967 /
label Tact Jazz Series

FREDDIE HUBBARD

title BACKLASH / *year* 1967 / *label* Atlantic /
design Loring Eutemey / *photo* Lee Friedlander

Atlantic's art director, Loring Eutemey, joins forces
with celebrated photographer Lee Friedlander for
this jazz R&B excursion by the former member of
Art Blakey's Jazz Messengers. Eutemey's flair for
creating often bold and colorful typographical layouts would draw the viewer into the image itself. ⊙
Loring Eutemey, Art Director bei Atlantic, tat sich
mit dem gefeierten Fotografen Lee Friedlander
zusammen und gestaltete das Cover dieser Platte.

Backlash stellt einen R'n'B-Abstecher Hubbards dar,
der ursprünglich bei Art Blakeys Jazz Messengers
spielte. Eutemey, der einen Hang zu einer gewag-
ten, farbenfrohen Typografie hatte, zieht den Be-
trachter mit diesem Schriftzug förmlich in das Bild
hinein. ⊙
Loring Eutemey, le directeur artistique d'Atlantic,
fait équipe avec le célèbre photographe Lee
Friedlander pour cette excursion dans le jazz R&B,
conduite par l'ancien membre des Jazz Messengers
d'Art Blakey. Il avait le don de créer des maquettes
typographiques audacieuses et colorées qui faisaient
plonger le spectateur dans l'image.

FREDDIE HUBBARD
title THE HUB OF HUBBARD / *year* 1969 / *label* MPS / *design* Heinz Bähr

FREDDIE HUBBARD
title HUB-TONES / *year* 1962 / *label* Blue Note / *design* Reid Miles / *photo* Francis Wolff

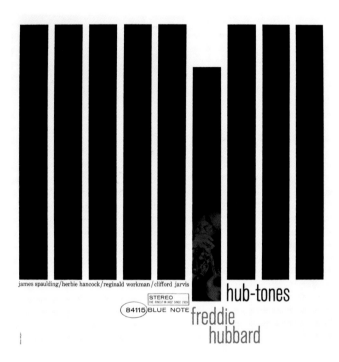

Freddie
Hubbard

Sky Dive

With
Ron Carter
Billy Cobham*
George Benson
Keith Jarrett*
Ray Barretto**
Airto
Hubert Laws

CTI
HCTS 731-21

FREDDIE HUBBARD

title SKY DIVE / *year* 1976 / *label* CTI /
design Bob Ciano / *photo* Pete Turner

The eye-catching cover image illustrates the range
of Pete Turner's creative flair and technical bril-
liance. For Turner, experimenting with images he'd
taken of racing cars on the Salt Lake Flats in Utah
resulted in something both embryonic and rocket-
like. Joining Hubbard on this jam are fellow CTI
frontmen, George Benson and Hubert Laws, and
featuring Keith Jarrett on keyboards. **O**

Pete Turners kreatives Gespür und sein technisches
Geschick kommen auf diesem auffälligen Coverbild
besonders gut zur Geltung. Der für seine visuellen
Experimente bekannte Turner fotografierte an den
Sandbänken des Salt Lake in Utah Rennautos – das
Ergebnis ist ein verblüffendes Gebilde, das in seiner
Form gleichermaßen an einen Embryo wie an eine
Rakete erinnert. Bei diesem Jam wird Hubbard von
seinen CTI-Kollegen, den Bandleadern George Ben-
son und Hubert Laws, sowie von Keith Jarrett an
den Keyboards begleitet. **O**

Cette image accrocheuse illustre le talent créatif et
le génie technique de Pete Turner. Le résultat
obtenu à partir de son expérience visuelle des voitures de courses qu'il avait lui-même photogra-
phiées sur la plaine de Salt Lake Flats dans l' Utah
donne à penser à la fois à un embryon et à une
fusée. Pour cette session, Freddie Hubbard est
rejoint par ses acolytes de CTI George Benson et
Hubert Laws, ainsi que Keith Jarrett aux claviers.

FREDDIE HUBBARD

title KEEP YOUR SOUL
TOGETHER / *year* 1973 /
label CTI / *design* Bob Ciano /
photo Pete Turner

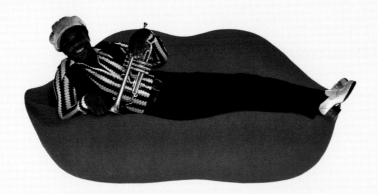

Freddie Hubbard
Keep Your Soul Together

CTI 6036

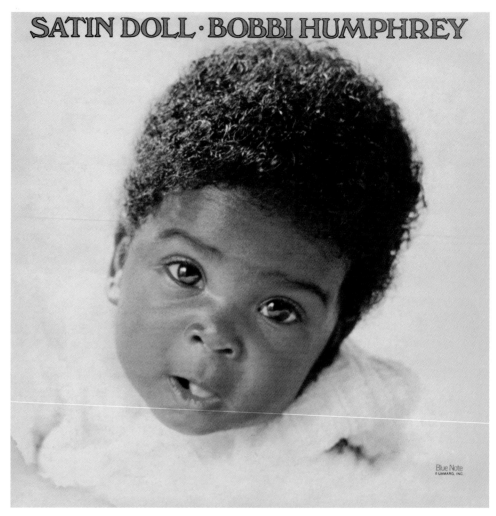

BOBBI HUMPHREY
title SATIN DOLL / *year* 1974 /
label Blue Note / *ad* Bob Cato /
photo Josef Schneider

BST 84244

STICK-UP!

BOBBY HUTCHERSON
JOE HENDERSON
McCOY TYNER
HERBIE LEWIS
BILLY HIGGINS

THE FINEST IN JAZZ SINCE 1939
BLUE NOTE

PRINTED IN U.S.A.

LIBERTY RECORDS, INC.

BOBBY HUTCHERSON

title STICK-UP! / *year* 1966 / *label* Blue Note / *design* Reid Miles / *photo* Francis Wolff

The covers for vibes and marimba player Bobby Hutcherson show the depth of Reid Miles' visual awareness, both in branding: the cinema-poster-style type on *Dialogue*, and in his play on musicality – the positioning of type on *Stick-Up!* looks like Bobby Hutcherson is playing his own name in the titles. **O**
Die Cover für den Vibraphon- und Marimbaspieler Bobby Hutcherson veranschaulichen das visuelle Verständnis von Reid Miles sowohl bei der Bildung

eines Markenbewusstseins, etwa bei dem Kinopla-kat-Stil auf *Dialogue*, als auch sein Spiel mit Musi-kalität: Die Positionierung des Bildes auf *Stick-Up!* erweckt den Eindruck, als spiele Bobby Hutcherson seinen eigenen Albumtitel. **O**
Ces deux pochettes pour le joueur de vibraphone et de marimba Bobby Hutchinson montrent la profon-deur de la sensibilité visuelle de Reid Miles, à la fois pour ce qui est de la stratégie de marque, avec la police de caractères typique d'une affiche de cinéma sur *Dialogue*, et dans son jeu sur l'aspect musical: la position des lettres sur *Stick-Up!* donne l'impres-sion que Bobby Hutcherson joue sur son propre nom.

**BOBBY
HUTCHERSON**
title DIALOGUE / *year* 1965 /
label Blue Note / *design* Reid
Miles / *photo* Francis Wolff

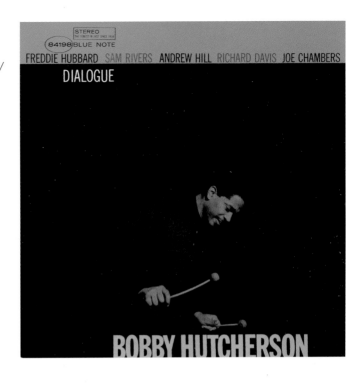

**BOBBY
HUTCHERSON**
title HEAD ON / *year* 1971 /
label Blue Note

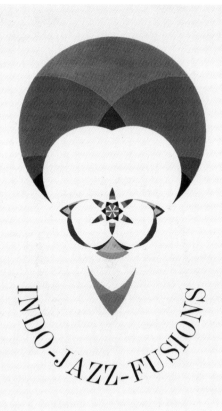

INDO-JAZZ-FUSIONS

INDO-JAZZ-FUSIONS

title INDO-JAZZ-FUSIONS /
label Bam Bam Records /
design Rv Beaugendre

*"My art is motivated
by curiosity and
provokes the mystery
that is the life of the
mind."*
— Dennis Pohl

WELDON IRVINE
title COSMIC VORTEX /
year 1974 / *label* RCA Victor /
ad Acy Lehman / *design* Dennis
Pohl

MILT JACKSON

title BAGS & FLUTES / *year* 1957 / *label* Atlantic /
design Marvin Israel / *photo* Elbert Budin

According to some of his associates, Marvin Israel
often appeared as a grumpy, shabby character,
accompanied by his ugly little dog, also named
Marvin. The art director would tease people by
warning them his dog would bite. This wonderful
prop arrangement creates a light-hearted visual
reference for vibes player Milt Jackson's outing,
featuring an alternating Bobby Jaspar and Frank
Wess on flute. ○
Laut Aussage einiger seiner Mitarbeiter machte
Marvin Israel häufig einen kauzigen, herunterge-
kommenen Eindruck, meist in Begleitung seines
hässlichen kleinen Hundes. Der künstlerische Leiter zog die Leute mit der Warnung auf, dass sein
Hund sie beißen würde. Dieses Arrangement von
Flöten nimmt einen visuellen Bezug auf Vibrafon-
Spieler Milt Jacksons musikalischen Ausflug, wobei
er abwechselnd von Bobby Jaspar und Frank Wess
an der Flöte begleitet wird. ○
Selon certains de ses collègues, Marvin Israel appa-
raissait souvent comme un personnage bougon et
mesquin, flanqué de son horrible petit chien également appelé Marvin. Ce directeur artistique taqui-
nait les gens en leur disant que son chien mordait.
Cette superbe composition donne une référence
visuelle ludique à cet opus du vibraphoniste Milt
Jackson, où Bobby Jaspar et Frank Wess se relaient
à la flûte.

MILT JACKSON
title WIZARD OF THE
VIBES / *year* 1952 / *label*
Blue Note / *design* Paul
Bacon / *photo* Francis Wolff

AHMAD JAMAL

title OUTERTIME
INNERSPACE / *year* 1971 /
label Impulse! / *design* Terry
Lamb

*"I would like to be a scholar in whatever
I do, a scholar is never finished, he is always
seeking and I am always seeking."*
— Ahmad Jamal

AHMAD JAMAL
title AHMAD JAMAL '73 /
year 1973 / *label* 20th Century /
design Philip Ching, Rod Dyer
Inc. / *photo* Norman Seeff

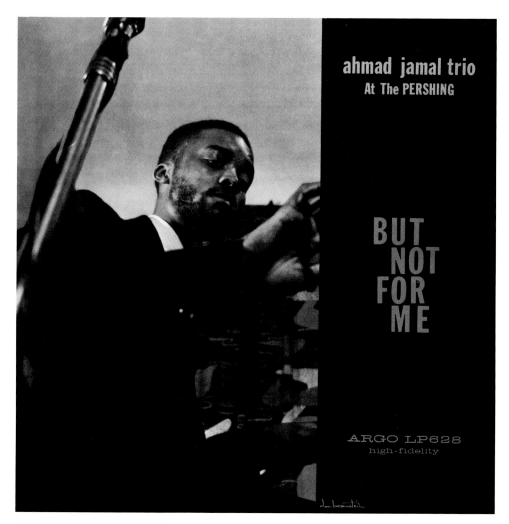

ahmad jamal trio
At The PERSHING

BUT
NOT
FOR
ME

ARGO LP628
high-fidelity

AHMAD JAMAL TRIO

title BUT NOT FOR ME / *year* 1958 / *label* Argo /
design Don Bronstein / *photo* Don Bronstein

This 1958 live recording in Chicago by Ahmad
Jamal and his trio was an instant hit for both the
pianist and the Chess label. Miles Davis was particularly influenced by the record and later inter-
preted most of its material. **O**
Diese 1958er Liveaufnahme aus Chicago von
Ahmad Jamal und seinem Trio war sowohl für den

Pianisten als auch für das Chess-Label ein um-
gehender Erfolg. Miles Davis wurde besonders von
dieser Aufnahme beeinflusst und interpretierte
später einen Großteil des Materials. **O**
Cet album qu'Ahmad Jamal et son trio enregis-
trèrent en public en 1958 fut un succès immédiat
pour le pianiste et le label Chess. Miles Davis a été
très influencé par cet album et a interprété la
plupart de ses morceaux.

AHMAD JAMAL

title HEAT WAVE / *year* 1966 /
label Cadet / *design* Reid Design

FACING
YOU

KEITH
JARRETT
PIANO

ECM 1017 ST

KEITH JARRETT
title FACING YOU / *year* 1972 / *label* ECM /
design Barbara Wojirsch / *photo* Danny Michael

Keith Jarrett is without doubt one of the most
important jazz, classical and contemporary cross-
over musicians of the modern age. *Facing You*, his
first album for ECM, marked the start of a relationship that has lasted for three decades. The
monochrome cover is an instantly recognizable
image from ECM's designer, Barbara Wojirsch.
Jarrett is renowned for his animated presence at
the piano. **o**
Keith Jarrett ist zweifellos einer der wichtigsten
Jazz-, Klassik- und Crossover-Musiker der heutigen

Zeit. *Facing You*, seine erste Platte für ECM, war
der Grundstein für eine Zusammenarbeit, die drei
Jahrzehnte andauern sollte. Das monochrome Cover
ist unverkennbar ein Bild der ECM-Designerin
Barbara Wojirsch. Jarrett ist für seine lebhafte
Präsenz am Klavier berühmt. **o**
Keith Jarrett est sans aucun doute l'un des musiciens de jazz, de classique et d'hybridations contem-
poraines les plus importants de l'ère moderne.
Facing You, son premier album chez ECM, marqua
le début d'une relation qui allait durer trente ans.
Cette couverture monochrome est très caractéris-
tique du style de la graphiste d'ECM, Barbara
Wojirsch. Keith Jarrett est renommé pour sa pré-
sence exaltée au piano.

BOBBY JASPAR
title NEW JAZZ VOL. 2 /
year 1954 / *label* Swing

BST 81507

THE JAZZ MESSE NGERS

BLP 1507

THE JAZZ MESSENGERS AT THE CAFE BOHEMIA VOLUME 1

BLUE NOTE

HORACE SILVER   HANK MOBLEY   ART BLAKEY   KENNY DORHAM   DOUG WATKINS

THE JAZZ MESSENGERS

title AT THE CAFE BOHEMIA VOL. 1 /
year 1955 / *label* Blue Note / *design* John
Hermansader / *photo* Francis Wolff

John Hermansader began designing for Blue Note
in the late 1940s, along with his friend Paul Bacon.
The latter would later become art director for the
Riverside label. Hermansader's early works, notably
his pictorial collaborations with Francis Wolff,
created a new brand awareness in jazz. Volume 2 of
this classic release is identical in design except for
the typography, which is printed in green. **O**
John Hermansader begann in den späten 1940ern,
zusammen mit seinem Freund Paul Bacon für Blue
Note LP-Cover zu gestalten. Letzterer wurde später
künstlerischer Leiter beim Riverside-Label. Die
frühen Arbeiten Hermansaders, besonders seine
bildhaften Arbeiten zusammen mit Francis Wolff,
schufen ein neues Markenbewusstsein im Jazz.
Volume 2 dieser klassischen Veröffentlichung ist
vom Design identisch, abgesehen von der in grün
gehaltenen Typografie. **O**
John Hermansader commença à travailler comme
graphiste pour Blue Note, vers la fin des années
1940, avec son ami Paul Bacon. Ce dernier devien-
drait par la suite directeur artistique chez le label
Riverside. Les premières œuvres de John Hermansader, et notamment ses collaborations avec Francis
Wolff, créèrent un concept de marque nouveau dans
le jazz. Le volume 2 de ce classique est identique,
excepté les lettres qui sont imprimées en vert.

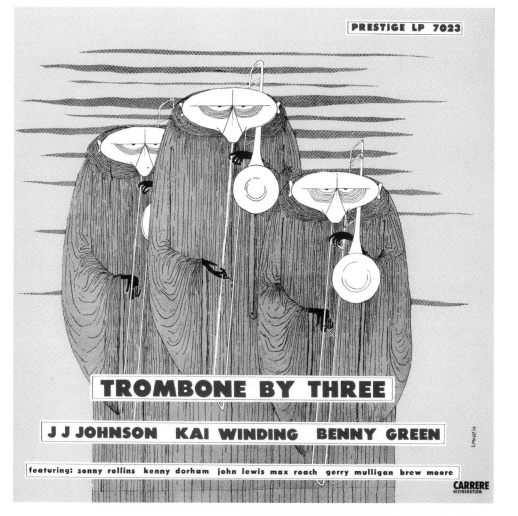

PRESTIGE LP 7023

TROMBONE BY THREE

J J JOHNSON   KAI WINDING   BENNY GREEN

featuring: sonny rollins kenny dorham john lewis max roach gerry mulligan brew moore

CARRERE
DISTRIBUTION

CL 935

COLUMNIA
GUARANTEED
HIGH FIDELITY

THE J.J.
JOHNSON
QUINTET

PHOTOGRAPH: DAN WYNN

THE J.J. JOHNSON QUINTET

title J IS FOR JAZZ /
year 1956 / *label* Columbia /
photo Dan Wynn

JONAH JONES

title JONAH JONES / *year* 1954 /
label Bethlehem / *design* Burt Goldblatt /
photo Burt Goldblatt

Trumpeter and occasional singer, Jones enjoyed
success with the Cab Calloway band in the 1940s.
Early Jones album covers command a greater interest with collectors than his music. **O**
Der Trompeter und gelegentliche Sänger Jones
durchlebte in den 1940ern eine erfolgreiche Zeit
mit der Cab Calloway Band. Die ersten Album-
Cover von Jones lösten jedoch bei den Sammlern
größeres Interesse aus als seine Musik. **O**
Jonah Jones, trompettiste et chanteur occasionnel,
connut le succès avec l'orchestre de Cab Calloway
dans les années 1940. Les collectionneurs s'intéressent davantage aux pochettes de ses premiers
albums qu'à sa musique.

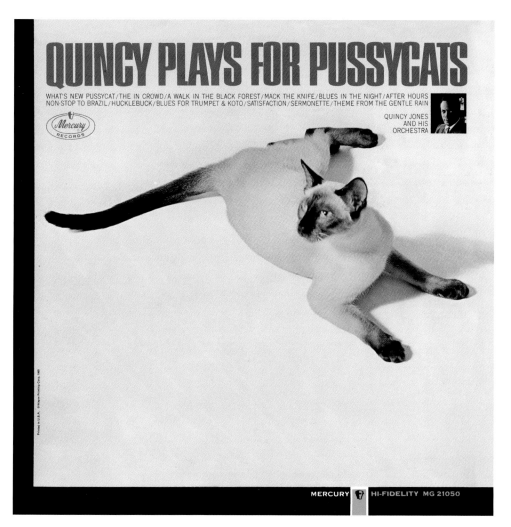

QUINCY PLAYS FOR PUSSYCATS

WHAT'S NEW PUSSYCAT/THE IN CROWD/A WALK IN THE BLACK FOREST/MACK THE KNIFE/BLUES IN THE NIGHT/AFTER HOURS
NON-STOP TO BRAZIL/HUCKLEBUCK/BLUES FOR TRUMPET & KOTO/SATISFACTION/SERMONETTE/THEME FROM THE GENTLE RAIN

Mercury
RECORDS

QUINCY JONES
AND HIS
ORCHESTRA

Printed in U.S.A. ©Wayne Printing Corp. 1965

MERCURY 🍸 HI-FIDELITY MG 21050

QUINCY JONES

title QUINCY PLAYS FOR PUSSYCATS /
year 1962 / *label* Mercury / *photo* Stan Malinowski

Stan Malinowski soon progressed from photographing cats to sex kittens for the covers of *Playboy* and
Penthouse. During the 1970s, he joined the ranks of
the world's leading fashion photographers, his work
has adorned covers from worldwide editions of
Vogue to *Bazaar*. He has worked with models like
Christie Brinkley, Cindy Crawford and Isabella
Rossellini. **o**
Nachdem Stan Malinowski zunächst Katzen fotografiert hatte, ging er bald dazu über, Sex-Kittens
für *Playboy*- und *Penthouse*-Cover abzulichten. In

den 1970ern gehörte er zu den führenden Modefo-
tografen der Welt, dessen Fotos die Cover der weltweit erscheinenden Ausgaben von *Vogue* bis *Bazaar*
verschönerten. Dabei arbeitete er mit Models wie
Christie Brinkley, Cindy Crawford und Isabella
Rossellini. **o**
Stan Malinowski est passé bien vite des chats à des
félins plus langoureux pour les couvertures de
Playboy et *Penthouse*. Dans les années 1970, il
rejoignit les rangs des plus grands photographes de
mode du monde, dont le travail a orné les couvertures de magazines de premier plan, de *Vogue* à
Bazaar. Il a travaillé avec des mannequins de l'envergure de Christie Brinkley, Cindy Crawford et
Isabella Rossellini.

CLIFFORD JORDAN

title SOUL FOUNTAIN /
year 1970 / *label* Vortex /
design Stanislaw Zagorski

MR 5O76

CLIFFORD JORDAN
CEDAR WALTON
SAM JONES
BILLY HIGGINS

DICK KATZ

title KOOL FOR KATZ /
year 1958 / *label* Nixa

WYNTON KELLY

title KELLY GREAT /
year 1959 / *label* VeeJay /
photo Chuck Stewart

STAN KENTON

title ENCORES / *label* Capitol

STAN KENTON
title NEW CONCEPTS OF
ARTISTRY IN RHYTHM /
year 1952 / *label* Capitol

**GUSTAVO
KERESTEZACHI**
title GUSTAVO
KERESTEZACHI Y SU
TRIO / *label* Tonodisc

KING PLEASURE /
ANNIE ROSS

title KING PLEASURE SINGS,
ANNIE ROSS SINGS /
year 1952 / *label* Prestige /
design Marc Rice / *photo* Esmond
Edwards

ROLAND KIRK

title LEFT & RIGHT /
year 1969 / *label* Atlantic /
design Stanislaw Zagorski /
photo Lee Tanner

HANS KOLLER

title PHOENIX / *year* 1972 /
label MPS / *art* Hans Koller /
design MPS / *photo* Hans
Harzheim, G. Hasenfratz

KRZYSZTOF KOMEDA

title KOMEDA JAZZ VOL. 1 /
year 1960 / *label* Muza /
photo Marek Karewicz

DADISI KOMOLAFE

title HASSAN'S WALK /
year 1983 / *label* Nimbus /
art Michael D. Wilcuts

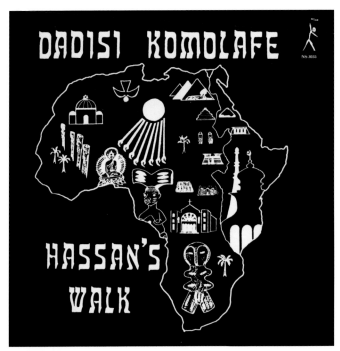

LEE KONITZ

title THE LEE KONITZ DUETS / *year* 1967 / *label* Milestone / *design* Asterisk Associates, Inc. / *photo* Charles Stewart

While many of the larger record companies relied upon the design talents of their in-house art departments, some labels during the 1960s and 1970s outsourced projects to graphic studios, such as this design, in the style of Mondrian, by the unrecognized Asterisk Associates, Inc. This intriguing jazz concept album features sax player Lee Konitz in a series of duets with various musicians. **O**
Während sich zahlreiche der größeren Plattenfirmen auf ihre eigenen Design-Talente verließen,

gaben einige Labels in den 1960ern und 1970ern ihre Projekte an Grafikstudios ab. So auch bei diesem im Stil von Mondrian gehaltenen Design der verkannten Asterisk Associates, Inc. Auf diesem faszinierenden Jazz-Konzeptalbum ist Sax-Spieler Lee Konitz in mehreren Duetten zu hören. **O**
La plupart des grandes maisons de disques utilisaient les talents de leurs services internes de graphisme, mais dans les années 1960-70 certains labels commandaient leurs projets à des studios externes. C'est le cas ici, avec cette couverture au style proche de Mondrian, des inconnus Asterisk Associates, Inc. On retrouve sur cet album de jazz conceptuel fascinant le saxophoniste Lee Konitz dans une série de duos avec différents musiciens.

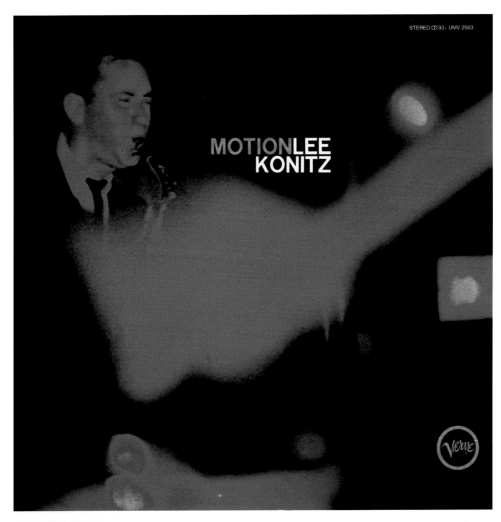

MOTION**LEE KONITZ**

LEE KONITZ

title MOTION / *year* 1961 / *label* Verve /
photo Pete Turner

With soft-focus foreground, similar to Dizzy Gillespie's album *Perceptions* (Verve, 1961), this cover typifies the early portraiture of photographer Pete Turner. *Motion* is regarded as alto sax player Lee Konitz's finest album. A serendipitous encounter with no rehearsal, the key ingredients for this successful album lie within the highly improvized trio interplay with Elvin Jones on drums and Sonny Dallas on bass. ○

Der weichgezeichnete Vordergrund kennzeichnet ähnlich wie auf dem Dizzy-Gillespie-Album *Perceptions* (Verve, 1961) die frühen Porträts des Fotografen Pete Turner. *Motion* wird als schönstes Album des Altsaxofonisten Lee Konitz angesehen. Da diese glückliche musikalische Begegnung ohne jegliche Probe stattfand, liegen die Hauptzutaten für dieses erfolgreiche Album beim stark improvisierten Zusammenspiel mit Elvin Jones am Schlagzeug und Sonny Dallas am Bass. ○

Avec son premier plan flou, comme sur l'album de Dizzy Gillespie *Perceptions* (Verve, 1961), cette pochette est un bel exemple des premiers portraits du photographe Pete Turner. *Motion* est considéré comme le meilleur album du joueur de saxo alto Lee Konitz. Cet album enregistré sans répétition préalable est le fruit d'un hasard heureux, dont le succès est dû au jeu très improvisé du trio, avec Elvin Jones à la batterie et Sonny Dallas à la contrebasse.

JANCSI KÖRÖSSY

title JANCSI KÖRÖSSY NR. 1 /
year 1965 / *label* Electrecord

This cover photo showing Jancsi Körössy at the
piano remains unattributed. Körössy is regarded as
an old master of Romanian jazz. As well as his
orchestra recordings with Electrecord, he has also
released material on the Czech Supraphon label.
Like his compatriot, Johnny "Cretu" Raducanu, his
music has drawn upon Romania's rich folklore.
Körössy has toured extensively throughout the
United States and Mexico. **O**
Dieses Cover mit Jancsi Körössy am Klavier lässt
sich keinem Designer zuordnen. Körössy gilt als
alter Meister des rumänischen Jazz. Zusätzlich zu
seinen Orchesteraufnahmen mit Electrecord hat er
auch Material auf dem tschechischen Label Supraphon veröffentlicht. Wie auch bei seinem Lands-
mann Johnny „Cretu" Raducanu hat sich seine
Musik der vielfältigen Folklore Rumäniens bedient.
Körössy hat ausgedehnte Tourneen durch die Verei-
nigten Staaten und Mexiko unternommen. **O**
Cette photo montrant Jancsi Körössy au piano reste
sans auteur connu. Ce pianiste est considéré comme
un grand maître du jazz roumain. Outre ses enregistrements en orchestre chez Electrecord, il a
également travaillé avec le label tchèque Supraphon.
Tout comme son compatriote Johnny «Cretu»
Raducanu, sa musique s'inspirait du riche folklore
de la Roumanie. Il a donné de nombreux concerts
dans tous les États-Unis et au Mexique.

KARIN KROG
title WE COULD BE FLYING /
year 1974 / *label* Polydor

2382 051 STEREO

"We Could Be Flying"
KARIN KROG – STEVE KUHN
STEVE SWALLOW – JON CHRISTENSEN

Three Waves
Steve Kuhn Trio
featuring Steve Swallow
and Pete La Roca

CONTACT

Mono CM-5

STEVE KUHN TRIO
title THREE WAVES /
year 1966 / *label* Contact /
design Robert Flynn/Viceroy /
photo Charles Stewart

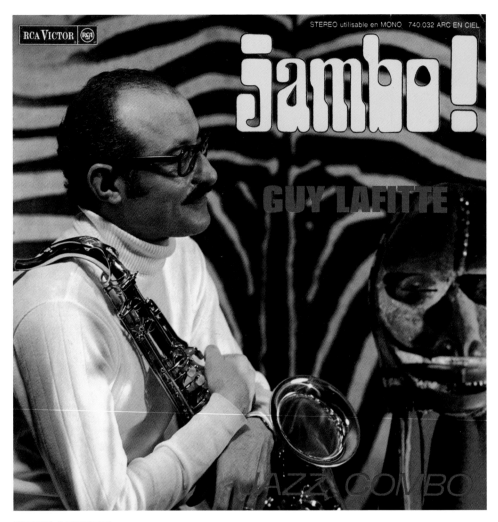

STEREO utilisable en MONO 740.032 ARC EN CIEL

RCA VICTOR [RCA]

jambo!

GUY LAFITTE

JAZZ COMBO

GUY LAFITTE

title JAMBO! / *year* 1968 / *label* RCA Victor /
photo Jean-Pierre Leloir

While the designer of the cover's pronounced yellow typography remains anonymous, the photo showing the suave French tenorist Guy Lafitte is the work of master photographer Jean-Pierre Leloir. Lafitte was a popular sideman for many jazz formations on the European jazz circuit. He collaborated with the likes of American clarinet and sax player Mezz Mezzrow and blues guitarist and singer Big Bill Broonzy. ○

Der Designer der auf dem Cover gelb hervortretenden Typografie ist unbekannt, das Foto des freundlich dreinschauenden französischen Tenorsaxofonis-

ten Guy Laffite ist die Arbeit des Meisterfotografen Jean-Pierre Leloir. Lafitte war ein beliebter Gastmusiker in vielen Jazz-Formationen der europäischen Jazz-Szene. Dabei arbeitete er unter anderem mit dem amerikanischen Klarinettisten und Saxofonisten Mezz Mezzrow und dem Blues-Gitarristen und Sänger Big Bill Broonzy. ○

L'auteur des lettres jaunes de cette couverture reste inconnu, mais la photo montrant le charmant joueur de saxo ténor français Guy Lafitte est l'œuvre du grand photographe Jean-Pierre Leloir. Guy Lafitte a accompagné de nombreuses formations de jazz sur le circuit européen, et il était très apprécié. Il a notamment travaillé avec le clarinettiste et saxophoniste américain Mezz Mezzrow et le guitariste et chanteur de blues Big Bill Broonzy.

**LAMBERT,
HENDRICKS, & ROSS**

title LAMBERT, HENDRICKS, &
ROSS! / *year* 1960 / *label* CBS /
photo Vernon Smith

HAROLD LAND

title HAROLD IN THE LAND
OF JAZZ / *year* 1958 /
label Contemporary / *design*
Guidi/Tri-Arts / *photo* Walter
Zerlinden

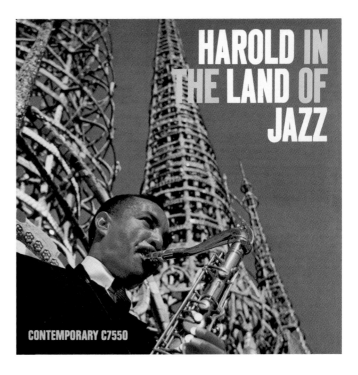

HAROLD LAND

title WEST COAST BLUES! /
year 1960 / *label* Jazzland /
design Ken Deardoff / *photo*
Jerry Stoll

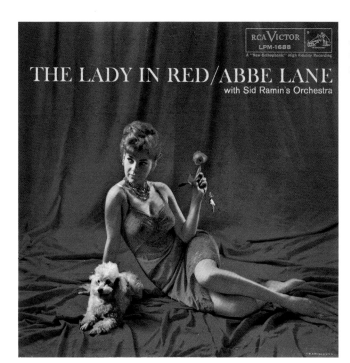

ABBE LANE
title THE LADY IN RED / *year* 1958 / *label* RCA Victor

PRINCE LASHA QUINTET
title THE CRY! / *year* 1963 / *label* Contemporary / *design* George Kershaw / *photo* Roger Marshutz

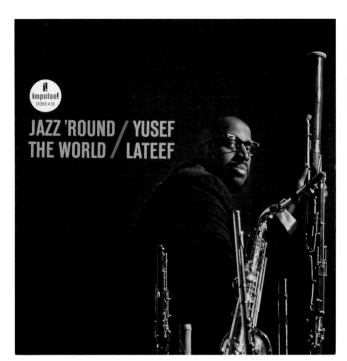

YUSEF LATEEF
title JAZZ 'ROUND THE
WORLD / *year* 1963 /
label Impulse! / *design* Robert
Flynn/Viceroy / *photo* Charles
Stewart

YUSEF LATEEF
title PSYCHICEMOTUS /
year 1965 / *label* Impulse! /
design Robert Flynn/Viceroy /
photo Charles Stewart

HUBERT LAWS
title AFRO-CLASSIC / *year*
1970 / *label* CTI / *design* Bob
Ciano / *photo* Pete Turner

Hubert Laws
Morning Star

Arranged and Conducted
by Don Sebesky
Where Is The Love
Amazing Grace
No More
Morning Star
What Do You Think
Of This World Now?
Let Her Go

CTI 6022

HUBERT LAWS

title MORNING STAR / *year* 1972 / *label* CTI /
design Bob Ciano / *photo* Pete Turner

The stunning lunar backdrop was actually taken while Pete Turner was on a photo assignment at an oil refinery in Libya. Another image from the same series was used as the cover for pianist Walter Wanderley's 1969 CTI recording, *Moondreams.* Hubert Laws' soulful flute is complemented by Bob James' electric piano flourishes over a warm string orchestra on this set, conducted by Don Sebesky. **O**
Diese atemberaubende Mondkulisse wurde von Pete Turner aufgenommen, als er für einen Auftrag eine Ölraffinerie in Libyen besuchte. Ein weiteres Bild dieser Reihe fand als Cover für das 1969 veröffent-

lichte CTI-Album *Moondreams* des brasilianischen Pianisten Walter Wanderley Verwendung. Hubert Laws souliges Flötenspiel, begleitet von Bob James' elektrischem Klavier, entfaltet sich in dieser Aufnahme vor den warmen Klängen eines Streichorchesters, geleitet von Don Sebesky. **O**
Pete Turner a photographié ce magnifique paysage sous la lune alors qu'il travaillait sur un projet dans une raffinerie de pétrole en Libye. Une autre image de la même série fut utilisée pour la couverture de l'album du pianiste brésilien Walter Wanderley sorti chez CTI en 1969, *Moondreams.* La flûte expressive d'Hubert Laws est ici accompagnée par le piano électrique de Bob James, sur le fond chaleureux d'un orchestre de cordes dirigé par Don Sebesky.

MICHEL LEGRAND
title LEGRAND JAZZ /
year 1958 / *label* Columbia /
photo Sabine Weiss

**ERWIN LEHN
ORCHESTER**

title COLOR IN JAZZ /
year 1974 / *label* MPS /
photo Hubertus Mall

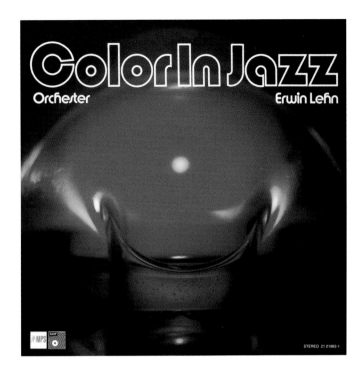

JOHN LEWIS

title A MILANESE STORY /
year 1962 / *label* Atlantic /
design Loring Eutemey /
photo Roberto Barbieri

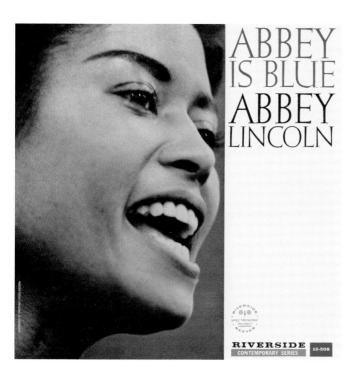

ABBEY LINCOLN
title ABBEY IS BLUE /
year 1959 / *label* Riverside /
design Paul Bacon, Ken
Braren, Harris Lewine /
photo Lawrence Shustack

CHARLES LLOYD
title FOREST FLOWER /
year 1967 / *label* Atlantic /
design Marvin Israel /
photo Jim Marshall

CHARLES LLOYD **281**

JULIE LONDON
title CALENDAR GIRL /
year 1956 / *label* Liberty /
photo Gene Lester

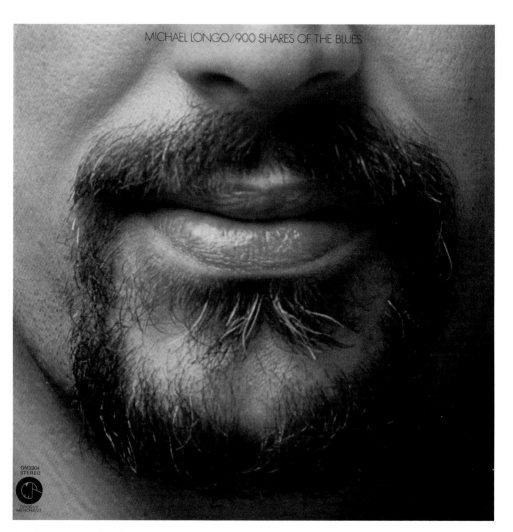

MICHAEL LONGO/900 SHARES OF THE BLUES.

GM3304
STEREO

GROOVE
MERCHANT

MICHAEL LONGO

title 900 SHARES OF THE BLUES / *year* 1974 /
label Groove Merchant / *ad* Frank Daniel /
photo Charles Stewart

Charles Stewart has often been described as a
humanist observer, which shines through in his
natural portraits. As well as his association with
jazz music, Stewart also branched out into travel
and fashion photography. Mike Longo is a jazz
pianist and composer who got his break with
Cannonball Adderley. He later studied under Oscar
Peterson and had a long association with the great
Dizzy Gillespie, for whom he was musical director. ○
Charles Stewart wurde aufgrund seiner natürlich
wirkenden Porträts oft als humanistischer Beob-

achter beschrieben. Neben seiner Verbindung zur
Jazzmusik betätigte er sich auch in den Bereichen
Reise- und Modefotografie. Der Jazz-Pianist und
Komponist Mike Longo schaffte seinen Durchbruch
mit Cannonball Adderley. Später lernte er bei Oscar
Peterson und arbeitete lange als musikalischer
Leiter mit dem großartigen Dizzy Gillespie. ○
Charles Stewart a souvent été décrit comme un
observateur humaniste, qualité qui transparaît
dans ses portraits très naturels. Il a travaillé dans
le domaine du jazz, mais aussi des voyages ou de la
mode. Mike Longo est un compositeur et pianiste de
jazz qui a percé avec Cannonball Adderley. Il a par
la suite été élève d'Oscar Peterson et a longtemps
travaillé avec le grand Dizzy Gillespie, pour qui il a
été directeur musical.

HOWARD LUCRAFT
title SHOWCASE FOR
MODERN JAZZ / *year* 1951 /
label Decca Records / *photo*
Jerry Tiffany

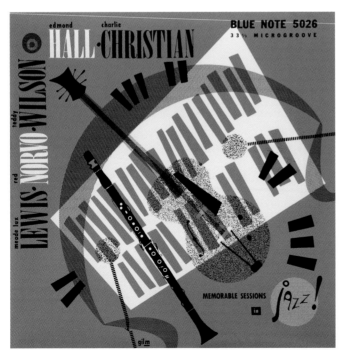

**MEADE LUX LEWIS,
RED NORVO, TEDDY
WILSON, EDMOND
HALL, CHARLIE
CHRISTIAN**
title MEMORABLE
SESSIONS / *year* 1941 /
label Blue Note / *design* Gil
Mellé

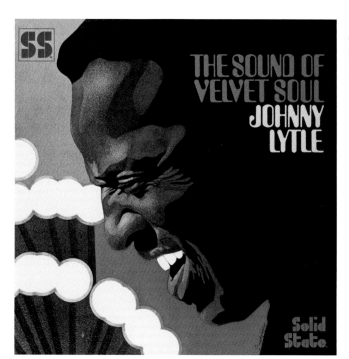

JOHNNY LYTLE
title THE SOUND OF VELVET
SOUL / *year* 1968 / *label* Solid
State

JOHNNY LYTLE
title CLOSE ENOUGH FOR
JAZZ / *year* 1967 / *label* Solid
State / *ad* Frank Gauna

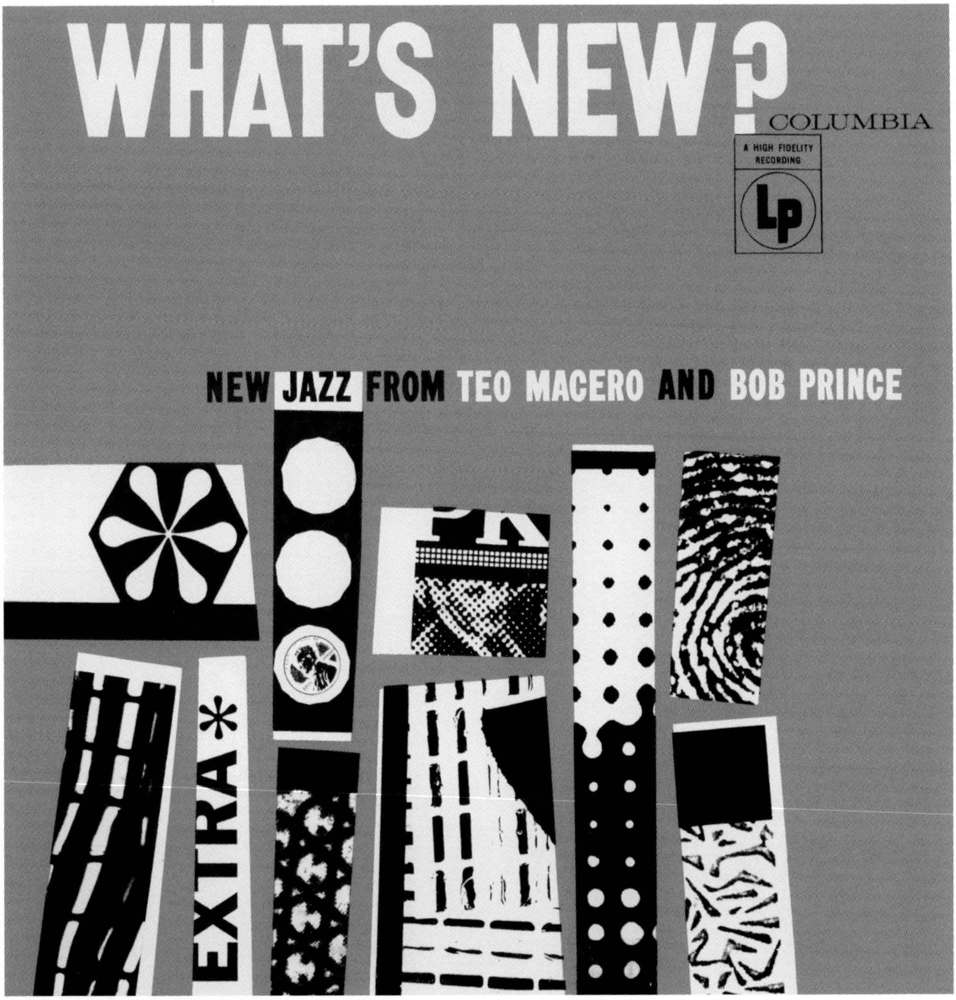

WHAT'S NEW? COLUMBIA

A HIGH FIDELITY RECORDING

Lp

NEW JAZZ FROM TEO MACERO AND BOB PRINCE

**TEO MACERO
AND BOB PRINCE**
title WHAT'S NEW? /
year 1956 / *label* Columbia

NOW, JAZZ RAMWONG
’ALBERT MANGELSDORFF
TROMBONE WINNER OF DOWNBEAT'S 1965 INTERNATIONAL JAZZ CRITICS POLL!

PACIFIC JAZZ
A PRODUCT OF LIBERTY RECORDS

**ALBERT
MANGELSDORFF**

title NOW, JAZZ RAMWONG /
year 1970 / *label* Pacific Jazz /
design Peter Gross

HERBIE MANN
title IMPRESSIONS OF THE
MIDDLE EAST / *year* 1966 /
label Atlantic / *design* Marvin
Israel

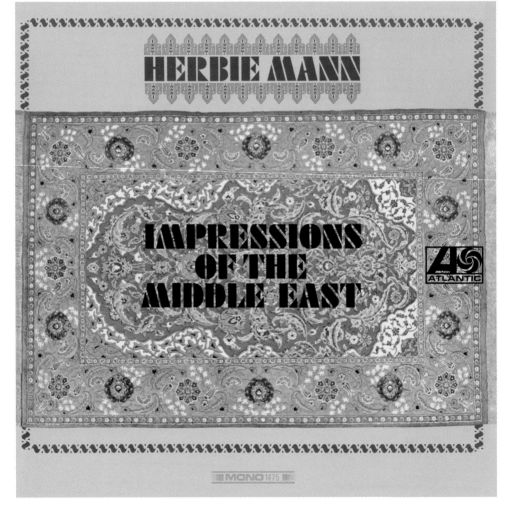

bethlehem bcp 1018

herbie mann

east coast jazz/4

BURT GOLDBLATT

HERBIE MANN
title EAST COAST JAZZ
NO. 4 / *year* 1955 /
label Bethlehem /
design Burt Goldblatt /
photo Burt Goldblatt

SHELLY MANNE
title 234 / *year* 1962 / *label*
Impulse! / *design* Robert
Flynn/Viceroy / *photo* Bob
Gomel

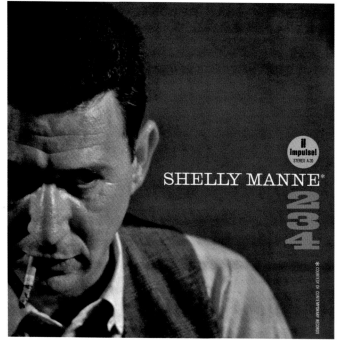

Impulse!
STEREO A-20

SHELLY MANNE*

234

* COURTESY OF CONTEMPORARY RECORDS

SHELLY MANNE
AND HIS MEN

title JAZZ GUNN / *year* 1967 /
label Atlantic / *design* Stanislaw
Zagorski

SHELLY MANNE
& RUSS FREEMAN
title SHELLY MANNE &
RUSS FREEMAN / *year*
1953 / *label* Contemporary

GUIDO MANUSARDI
title FREE JAZZ / *year* 1967 /
label Electrecord / *design* Iuliu
Sinpetru / *photo* Sorin Radu

MAT MATHEWS
title THE MODERN ART OF JAZZ BY MAT MATHEWS / *year* 1956 / *label* Dawn Records / *design* Fran Scott / *photo* Hank Parker

LES MCCANN
title LES MCCANN LTD. IN SAN FRANCISCO / *year* 1961 / *label* Pacific Jazz / *design* Woody Woodward / *photo* Chester Maydole

BROTHER JACK MCDUFF

title A CHANGE IS GONNA
COME / *year* 1966 /
label Atlantic / *design* Loring
Eutemey / *photo* Charles Varon

BROTHER JACK MCDUFF

title TO SEEK A NEW
HOME / *year* 1970 / *label*
Blue Note / *ad* Frank Gauna /
design Reginald Wickman

BROTHER JACK MCDUFF

title DOWN HOME STYLE /
year 1969 / *label* Blue Note /
ad Frank Gauna

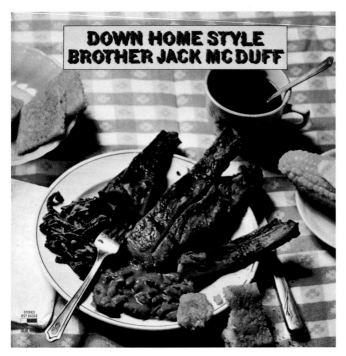

**GARY MCFARLAND /
STEVE KUHN**
title THE OCTOBER SUITE /
year 1966 / *label* Impulse! /
design Robert Flynn/Viceroy /
photo Charles Stewart

THE GARY MCFARLAND SEXTET

title POINT OF DEPARTURE / *year* 1963 / *label* Impulse! / *design* Robert Flynn/Viceroy / *photo* Pete Turner

GARY MCFARLAND / GABOR SZABO

title SIMPÁTICO / *year* 1966 / *label* Impulse! / *design* Robert Flynn/Viceroy / *photo* Bob Ghiraldini

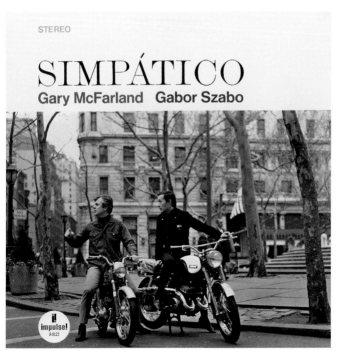

Maggie's back in town!!

HOWARD McGHEE WITH SHELLY MANNE PHINEAS NEWBORN JR. & LEROY VINNEGAR

HOWARD MCGHEE

title MAGGIE'S BACK IN
TOWN!! / *year* 1961 / *label*
Contemporary / *design* Kershaw,
Guidi/Tri-Arts / *photo* William
Claxton

**HOWARD MCGHEE /
FREDDIE REDD**
title MUSIC FROM THE
CONNECTION / *year* 1960 /
label Iris Records

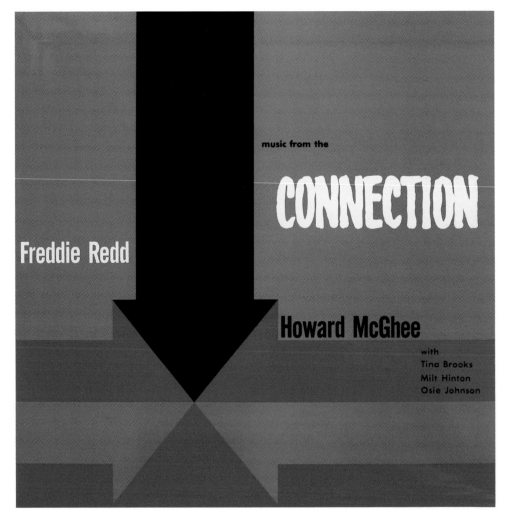

music from the

CONNECTION

Freddie Redd

Howard McGhee

with
Tina Brooks
Milt Hinton
Osie Johnson

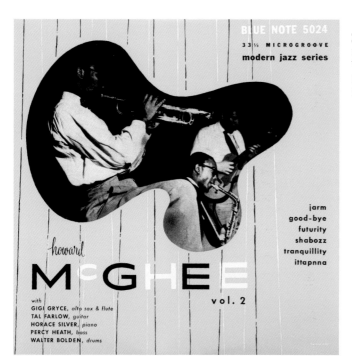

HOWARD MCGHEE

title HOWARD MCGHEE
VOL. 2 / *year* 1953 / *label*
Blue Note / *design* John
Hermansader

JIMMY MCGRIFF

title ELECTRIC FUNK /
year 1969 / *label* Blue Note /
ad Frank Gauna / *photo* Steve
Wasserman

JIMMY MCGRIFF
title TOPKAPI / *year* 1964 /
label Sue Records / *design*
Frank Lerner / *photo* Frank
Lerner

**MAURICE
MCINTYRE**
title HUMILITY IN THE
LIGHT OF CREATOR /
year 1969 / *label* Delmark /
design Zbigniew Jastrzebski /
photo Zbigniew Jastrzebski

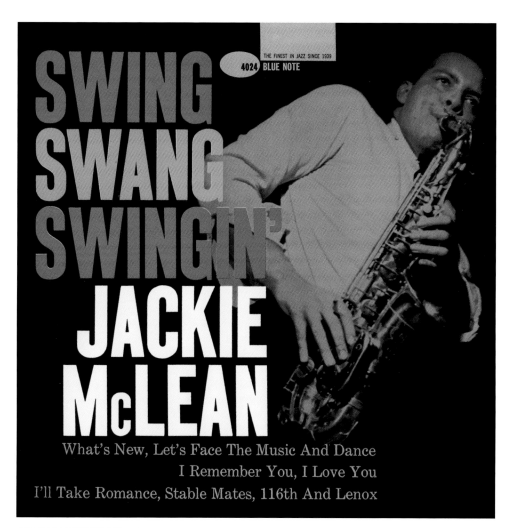

JACKIE MCLEAN
title SWING SWANG
SWINGIN' / *year* 1959 /
label Blue Note / *design* Reid
Miles / *photo* Francis Wolff

**GIL MELLÉ
QUINTET / SEXTET**
title NEW FACES, NEW
SOUNDS / *year* 1953 / *label*
Blue Note / *design* Gil Mellé

GIL MELLÉ
title TOME VI /
year 1967 / *label* Verve

HELEN MERRILL
title HELEN MERRILL /
year 1954 / *label* EmArcy

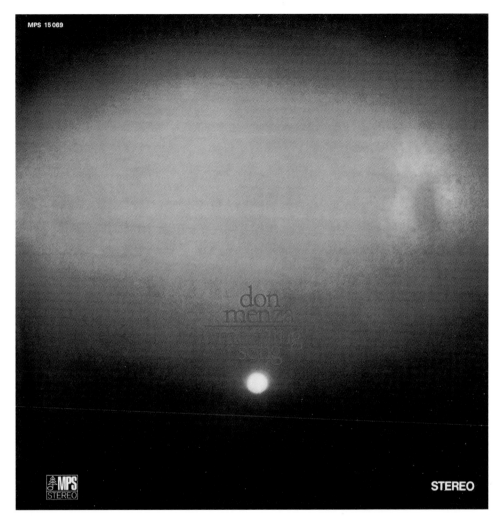

MPS 15069

STEREO

DON MENZA
title MORNING SONG /
year 1966 / *label* MPS /
design William Hopkins /
photo Josef Werkmeister

CHARLES MINGUS
title MINGUS AH UM / *year*
1959 / *label* CBS / *art* S. Neil
Fujita / *design* Randall Martin /
photo Bob Parent

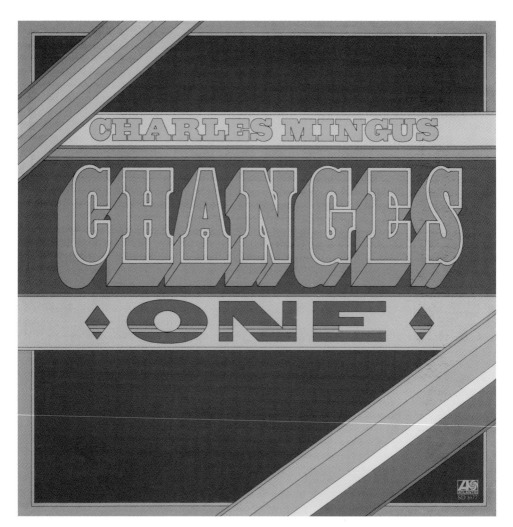

CHARLES MINGUS

title CHANGES ONE /
year 1974 / *label* Atlantic /
design Paula Scher

SAVOY MG 12059

JAZZ COMPOSERS WORKSHOP

CHARLIE MINGUS

WALLY CIRILLO

TEO MACERO

JOHN LA PORTA

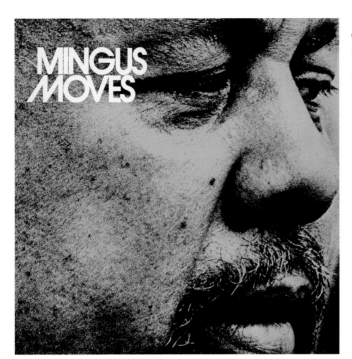

CHARLES MINGUS

title MINGUS MOVES / *year*
1974 / *label* Atlantic / *ad* Bob
Defrin / *photo* Giuseppe Pino

CHARLES MINGUS

title MINGUS DYNASTY /
year 1959 / *label* CBS

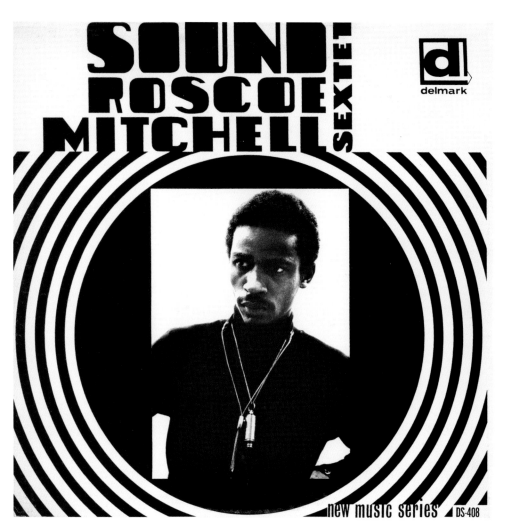

**ROSCOE MITCHELL
SEXTET**

title SOUND / *year* 1966 /
label Delmark / *design* Sylvia
Abernathy / *photo* Bill Abernathy

BLUE MITCHELL
title OUT OF THE BLUE /
year 1958 / *label* Riverside /
design Paul Bacon, Ken
Braren, Harris Lewine

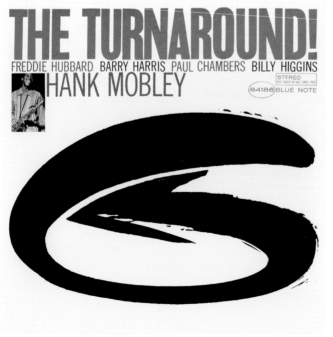

HANK MOBLEY
title THE TURNAROUND! /
year 1965 / *label* Blue Note /
design Reid Miles / *photo*
Francis Wolff

HANK MOBLEY

title NO ROOM FOR
SQUARES / *year* 1963 / *label*
Blue Note / *design* Reid Miles /
photo Francis Wolff

**HANK MOBLEY
QUARTET**

title HANK MOBLEY
QUARTET / *year* 1955 /
label Blue Note / *design* John
Hermansader/Reid Miles /
photo Francis Wolff

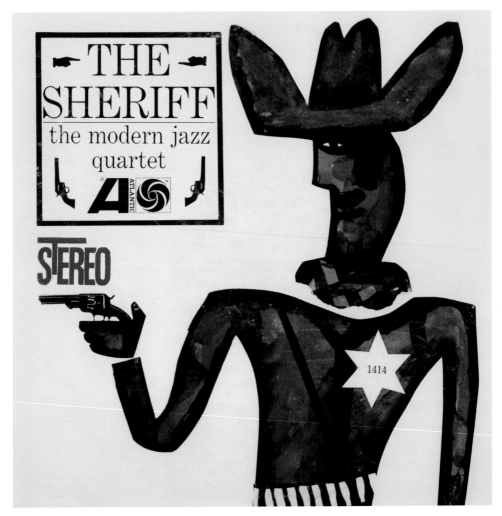

THE MODERN
JAZZ QUARTET

title THE SHERIFF / *year* 1964 /
label Atlantic / *design* Stanislaw
Zagorski

THE MODERN JAZZ SEXTET

title THE MODERN JAZZ
SEXTET / *year* 1956 /
label Verve / *design* David
Stone Martin

THELONIOUS MONK

title MONK / *year* 1953 /
label Prestige

THELONIOUS MONK
title GENIUS OF MODERN
MUSIC VOL. 2 / *year* 1951 /
label Blue Note / *design* Paul
Bacon / *photo* Francis Wolff

"On Thelonious Monk's Underground, *a project with photographers Steve Horn and Norman Griner, the title of the album came from a current jazz movement, which I twisted into a version of the French anti-Nazi underground of World War II. An entire set was built and the scene was full of costumed extras. There was no problem with budgets in those days."*
— John Berg

THELONIOUS MONK
title UNDERGROUND / *year* 1968 / *label* Columbia / *design* John Berg, Dick Mantel / *photo* Horn/Griner

MONK MONTGOMERY

title BASS ODYSSEY / *year*
1971 / *label* Chisa Records /
design Tom Wilkes & Barry
Feinstein / *photo* Tom Wilkes &
Barry Feinstein

MONK MONTGOMERY:
BASS ODYSSEY
CHISA STEREO CS 806

WES MONTGOMERY

title CALIFORNIA DREAMING / *year* 1966 / *label* Verve / *design* Acy Lehman / *photo* Ken Whitmore

A generic cover photo from Ken Whitmore reflects Wes Montgomery's branding in the more mainstream pop arena in the latter stages of his career. The renowned art director never lost sight of the commercial purpose of packaging design and would often commission photographers and graphic artists to fulfill the label's brief. ○

Ein eher konventionelles Coverfoto von Ken Whitmore spiegelt Wes Montgomerys Bewegung Rich-

tung Mainstream-Pop gegen Ende seiner Karriere wider. Der bekannte Art Director verlor nie das kommerzielle Ziel für die Plattenhüllen aus den Augen und beauftragte oft Fotografen und Grafik-künstler, die Ziele des Labels umzusetzen. ○

Cette photo de couverture générique de Ken Whitmore reflète le positionnement de Wes Montgomery dans le secteur plus grand public de la pop vers la fin de sa carrière. Ce directeur artistique de renom ne perdit jamais de vue la fonction commerciale de la pochette et demandait souvent aux photographes et aux graphistes de respecter les lignes directrices du label.

JAMES MOODY
title LAST TRAIN FROM
OVERBROOK / *year* 1958 / *label*
Cadet / *design* Vytas A. Valaitis

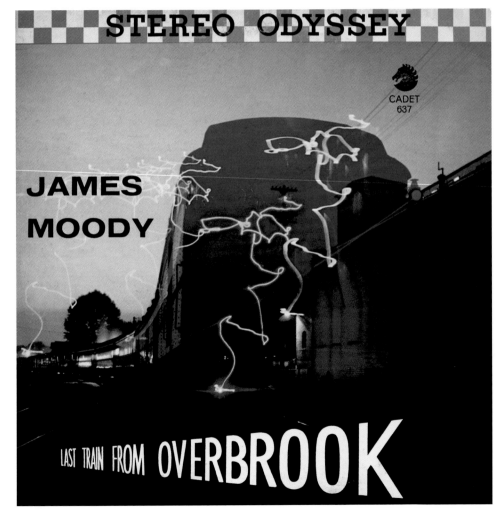

STEREO ODYSSEY

CADET
637

JAMES
MOODY

LAST TRAIN FROM OVERBROOK

JOE MOONEY
title LUSH LIFE / *year* 1956 /
label Atlantic / *design* Bill Hughes

LEE MORGAN
title THE RUMPROLLER /
year 1965 / *label* Blue Note /
design Reid Miles / *photo* Francis
Wolff

LEE MORGAN
title THE GIGOLO / *year*
1965 / *label* Blue Note / *design*
Forlenza Venosa Associates /
photo Francis Wolff

NATE MORGAN
title RETRIBUTION,
REPARATION / *year* 1984 /
label Nimbus

PAUL MOTIAN

title CONCEPTION VESSEL /
year 1973 / *label* ECM /
design B&B Wojirsch / *photo*
A. Raggenbass

**THE MPS RHYTHM
COMBINATION
& BRASS**

title MY KIND OF
SUNSHINE / *year* 1971 /
label MPS / *design* Heinz
Bähr / *photo* Heinz Bähr

IDRIS MUHAMMAD
title PEACE AND RHYTHM /
year 1971 / *label* Prestige / *ad*
Tony Lane / *photo* Burt Goldblatt

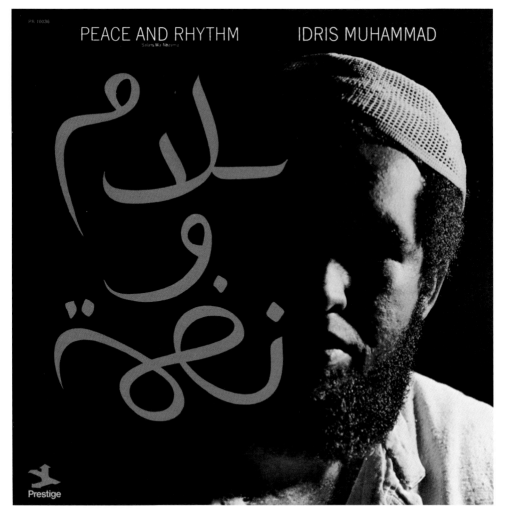

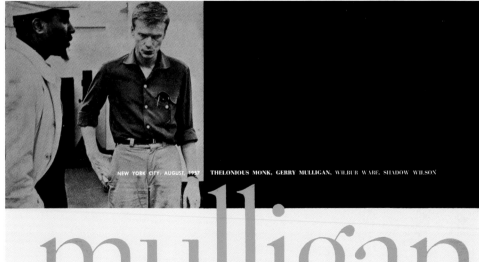

NEW YORK CITY: AUGUST, 1957 — THELONIOUS MONK, GERRY MULLIGAN, WILBUR WARE, SHADOW WILSON

mulligan meets monk

247 RIVERSIDE

GERRY MULLIGAN /
THELONIOUS MONK

title MULLIGAN MEETS
MONK / *year* 1957 / *label*
Riverside / *design* Paul Bacon

GERRY MULLIGAN QUARTET

title REUNION WITH CHET BAKER / *year*
1958 / *label* World Pacific Records / *art* Harlan
R. Crippen / *design* Harlan R. Crippen

This beautifully ornate and colorful mosaic of two
peacocks was the creation of unknown artist Harlan R. Crippen. The World Pacific logo on the top
right hand side of the cover adds a particularly
intricate touch. In the early 1950s, composer and
sax player Gerry Mulligan teamed up with trumpeter and singer Chet Baker to create one of the
most memorable sounds of West Coast cool jazz. ○
Dieses schön verzierte und farbenfrohe, zwei Pfauen
abbildende Mosaik stammt von dem unbekannten
Künstler Harlan R. Crippen. Das raffiniert gestalte-

te Logo von World Pacific oben rechts auf dem
Cover verleiht dem Ganzen eine komplex-
verschlungene Wirkung. Anfang der 1950er Jahre
tat sich der Komponist und Saxofonist Gerry Mulligan mit dem Trompeter und Sänger Chet Baker
zusammen – die beiden erschufen einen der unver-
gesslichsten Sounds des West-Coast-Cool-Jazz. ○
Cette magnifique mosaïque aux couleurs intenses
de deux paons est la création de l'artiste inconnu
Harlan R. Crippen. Le logo World Pacific, en haut à
droite, ajoute un détail très subtil. Au début des
années 1950, le compositeur et saxophoniste Gerry
Mulligan fit équipe avec le trompettiste et chanteur
Chet Baker pour créer l'un des sons les plus mémorables du cool jazz de la côte ouest.

THE GERRY MULLIGAN SEXTET

title PRESENTING THE GERRY
MULLIGAN SEXTET /
year 1955 / *label* EmArcy

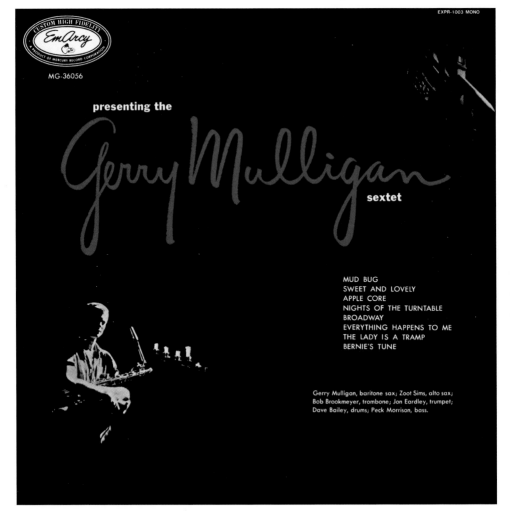

EXPR-1003 MONO

MG-36056

presenting the

Gerry Mulligan

sextet

MUD BUG
SWEET AND LOVELY
APPLE CORE
NIGHTS OF THE TURNTABLE
BROADWAY
EVERYTHING HAPPENS TO ME
THE LADY IS A TRAMP
BERNIE'S TUNE

Gerry Mulligan, baritone sax; Zoot Sims, alto sax;
Bob Brookmeyer, trombone; Jon Eardley, trumpet;
Dave Bailey, drums; Peck Morrison, bass.

MARK MURPHY

title MARK MURPHY'S HIP
PARADE / *year* 1960 /
label Capitol

TERUO
NAKAMURA

title UNICORN /
year 1973 / *label* TBM

MICHAEL NAURA QUARTETT

title CALL / *year* 1970 / *label*
MPS / *design* Wolfgang Baumann

FATS NAVARRO
title MEMORIAL ALBUM /
year 1947 / *label* Blue Note

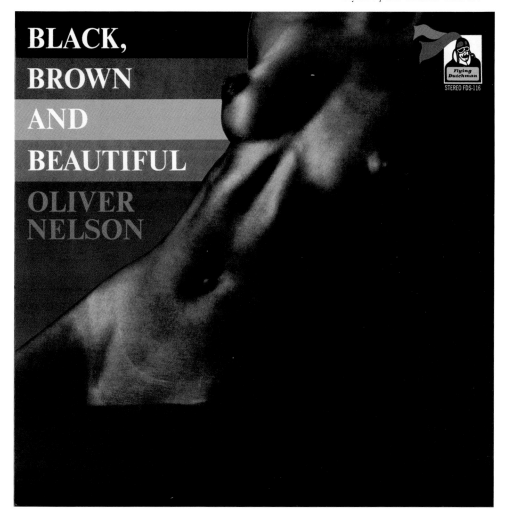

OLIVER NELSON
title BLACK, BROWN AND
BEAUTIFUL / *year* 1969 / *label*
Flying Dutchman / *design* Robert
Flynn / *photo* Charles Stewart

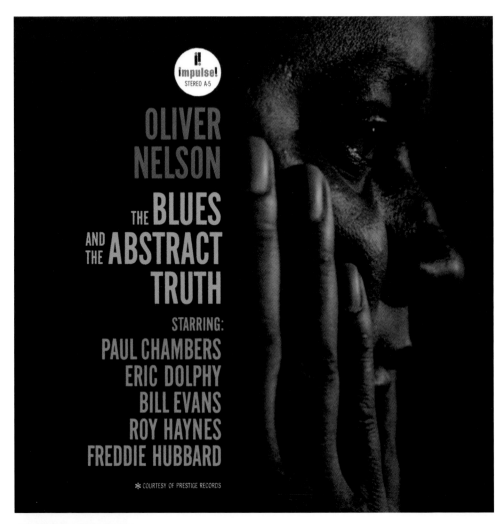

OLIVER NELSON

title THE BLUES AND THE
ABSTRACT TRUTH /
year 1961 / *label* Impulse! /
design Robert Flynn/Viceroy /
photo Pete Turner

OLIVER NELSON

title SKULL SESSION / *year*
1975 / *label* Flying Dutchman /
ad Acy Lehman / *art* Bob Grossé

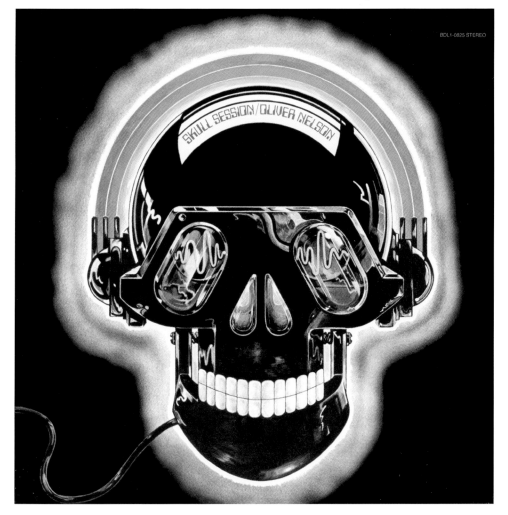

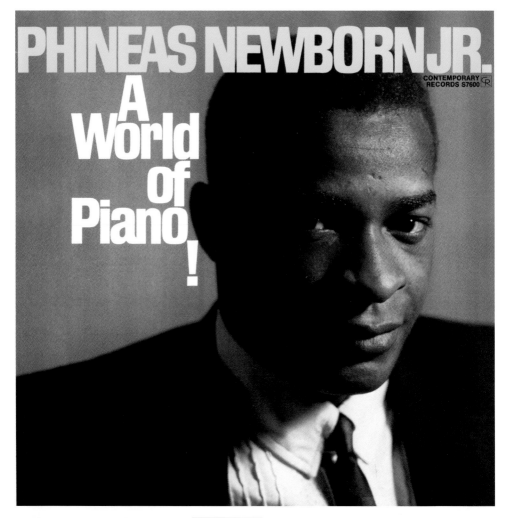

CONTEMPORARY
RECORDS S7600 ℗

PHINEAS NEWBORN JR.

title A WORLD OF PIANO! / *year* 1962 /
label Contemporary / *design* Kershaw, Guidi/
Tri-Arts / *photo* William Claxton

Designers George Kershaw and Roberto Guidi's use
of bold, luminously colored fonts created a distinctive style to the jazz covers of the Los Angeles-based
Contemporary label. What Tri-Arts succeeded in
doing time and time again was to create a distin-
guishable yet highly complementary design to an
often lush photograph, in this case provided by the
inimitable William Claxton. ○
Die Designer George Kershaw und Roberto Guidi
verwendeten Schriften in Fettdruck und Leuchtfar-
be und schufen so einen unverwechselbaren Stil für

die Jazzcover des in Los Angeles sitzenden Labels
Contemporary. Tri-Arts' Erfolgsgeheimnis lag
darin, immer wieder unverwechselbare, auf die
häufig großartigen Fotos abgestimmte Designs zu
kreieren. Dieses Coverfoto stammt von dem einzigartigen William Claxton. ○
Les polices de caractères audacieuses et aux couleurs lumineuses des graphistes George Kershaw et
Roberto Guidi créèrent un style original pour les
pochettes des albums de jazz du label Contemporary
de Los Angeles. Ce que Tri-Arts réussissait à faire
à chaque fois, c'était de créer un style très personnel mais en même temps très complémentaire,
adapté à une photographie souvent magnifique, ici
de l'inimitable William Claxton.

**THE NEW YORK
ART QUARTET**
title MOHAWK / *year* 1965 /
label Fontana / *design* Marte
Röling

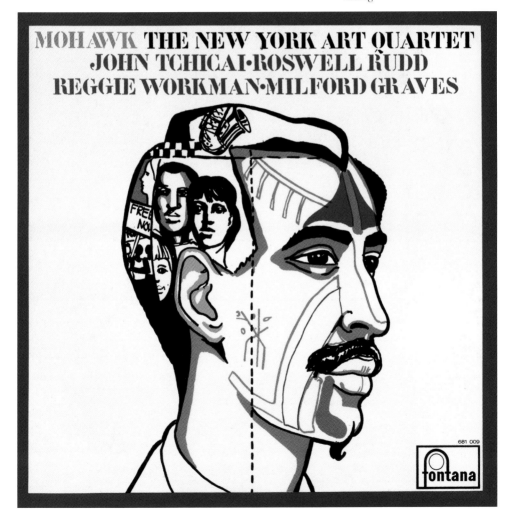

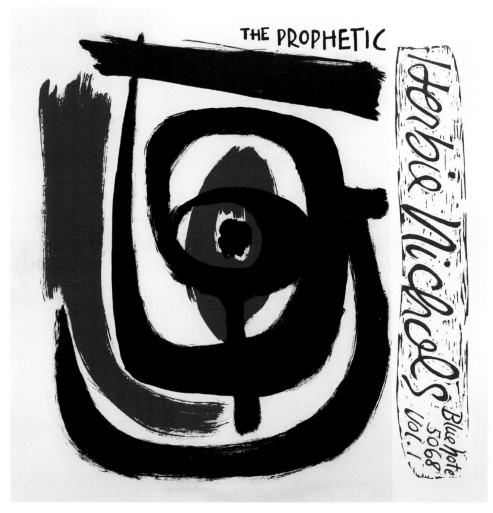

HERBIE NICHOLS

title THE PROPHETIC HERBIE NICHOLS
VOL. 1 / *year* 1955 / *label* Blue Note /
design Martin Craig

New York-School abstract expressionist painter
Martin Craig provides a rare and befitting cover for
the purveyor of art piano music, Herbie Nichols.
From 1947 Nichols spent half a decade trying to
get a contract with Blue Note. His persistence
finally paid off in 1955 when he was finally signed
for three albums. ●
Der abstrakt-expressionistische Maler der New
Yorker Schule Martin Craig gestaltete das mittlerweile selten gewordene, perfekt zur Musik passende
Cover für den Vertreter der Klavierkunst, Herbie
Nichols. Seit 1947 verbrachte Nichols ein halbes
Jahrzehnt damit, sich um einen Vertrag mit Blue
Note zu bemühen. Seine Hartnäckigkeit wurde
1955 belohnt, als er einen Vertrag für drei Alben
unterschrieb. ●
Martin Craig, peintre abstrait expressionniste de
l'école de New York, fournit ici une image de couverture qui convient à merveille à Herbie Nichols,
l'artiste du piano. À partir de 1947, il passa une
demi-douzaine d'années à essayer de décrocher un
contrat avec Blue Note. Son obstination fut récom-
pensée en 1955, lorsqu'il signa enfin un contrat
pour trois albums.

LENNIE NIEHAUS

title VOL.1 "THE
QUINTETS" / *year* 1954 /
label Contemporary /
design William Claxton /
photo William Claxton

"*What's fascinating is
the way they look
when they're not
playing, in other
aspects of their lives
— practicing,
rehearsing, smoking,
standing around
talking, even eating
and using dope.
I guess you could
say I listen with
my eyes.*"
—William Claxton

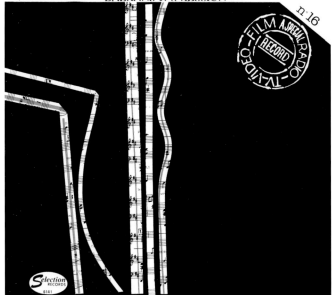

JANKO NILOVIC

title BALKANS
IMPRESSION / *year* 1979 /
label Selection Records

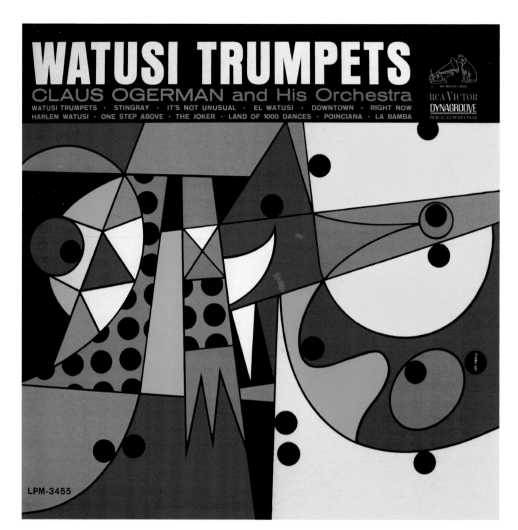

WATUSI TRUMPETS

CLAUS OGERMAN and His Orchestra

WATUSI TRUMPETS · STINGRAY · IT'S NOT UNUSUAL · EL WATUSI · DOWNTOWN · RIGHT NOW
HARLEM WATUSI · ONE STEP ABOVE · THE JOKER ·· LAND OF 1000 DANCES · POINCIANA · LA BAMBA

RCA VICTOR
DYNAGROOVE
RECORDING

LPM-3455

CLAUS OGERMAN AND HIS ORCHESTRA

title WATUSI TRUMPETS /
year 1965 / *label* RCA Victor

GEORGE OTSUKA TRIO
title PAGE 1 / *year* 1967 / *label* Tact Jazz Series

MIKE PACHECO
title BONGO BOP / *year* 1955 / *label* Tampa Records

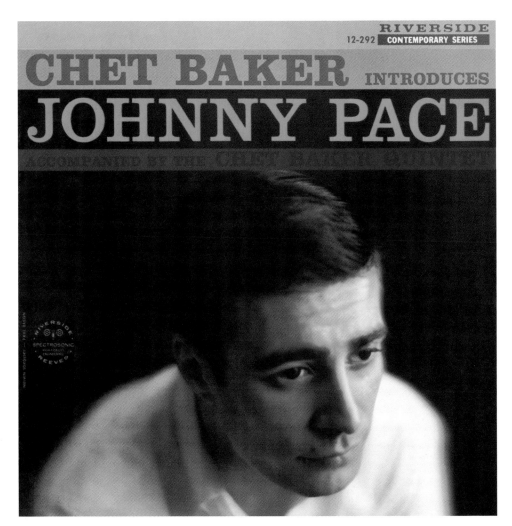

RIVERSIDE
12-292 CONTEMPORARY SERIES

CHET BAKER INTRODUCES
JOHNNY PACE
ACCOMPANIED BY THE CHET BAKER QUINTET

JOHNNY PACE

title CHET BAKER INTRODUCES JOHNNY
PACE / *year* 1959 / *label* Riverside / *design*
Paul Bacon, Ken Braren, Harris Lewine /
photo Melvin Sokolsky

The Riverside design team of Paul Bacon, Harris
Lewine and Ken Braren join forces to create a
richly colorful strip of type that works so perfectly
with the lush cover portrait of the artist. Jazz
crooner Johnny Pace was discovered by Chet Baker
for this rare and only recording of the singer. Pace
is backed here by Baker's quintet. **O**
Das Designteam von Riverside, zu dem Paul Bacon,
Harris Lewine und Ken Braren gehörten, tat sich
hier zusammen, um diesen satten und farbenpräch-

tigen Schriftzug zu gestalten, der wunderbar zu
dem großartigen Coverporträt des Künstlers passt.
Chet Baker entdeckte den Jazzsänger Johnny Pace
und gewann ihn für diese unbekannte und einzige
Albumaufnahme. Pace wird hier von Bakers Quin-
tett unterstützt. **O**
Ce sont les forces réunies de l'équipe de graphisme
de Riverside, composée de Paul Bacon, Harris
Lewine et Ken Braren, qui ont donné ces bandes de
lettres colorées qui fonctionnent si parfaitement
avec le magnifique portrait de l'artiste. C'est Chet
Baker qui découvrit le crooner de jazz Johnny
Pace pour cet enregistrement unique, et rare. Johnny
Pace est ici accompagné par le quintet de Chet
Baker.

CHARLIE PARKER
title NEW SOUNDS IN
MODERN MUSIC / *year* 1950 /
label Savoy

CHARLIE PARKER
title "BIRD" SYMBOLS /
year 1961 / *label* Summit

CHARLIE PARKER
title THE IMMORTAL
CHARLIE PARKER VOL. 1 /
year 1958 / *label* London
Records

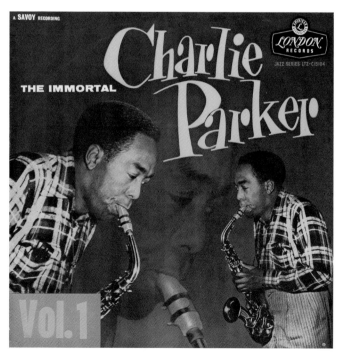

Text in image: BIRD AND DIZ, SUPERVISED BY NORMAN GRANZ, MERCURY, D.S.M.

CHARLIE PARKER
AND DIZZY
GILLESPIE

title BIRD AND DIZ / *year*
1952 / *label* Mercury /
design David Stone Martin

THE FINEST IN JAZZ SINCE 1939

4043 BLUE NOTE

Stanley Turrentine, Tommy Turrentine, George Tucker, Al Harewood

speakin'
my piece
horace parlan quintet

HORACE PARLAN QUINTET

title SPEAKIN' MY PIECE / *year* 1960 /
label Blue Note / *design* Reid Miles / *photo*
Francis Wolff

This rare Blue Note cover shows designer Reid
Miles at his most abstract and inventive. The piano
key motif visually releases the music pressed on the
wax disk within. Miles would repeat this motif on
Freddie Hubbard's 1962 recording *Hub-Tones*.
Horace Parlan was a bop pianist who incorporated
a gospel feel and elements of African roots into his
play. **O**
Dieses seltene Blue-Note-Cover zeigt den Designer
Reid Miles von seiner abstraktesten und innovativsten Seite. Das Motiv mit den Klaviertasten enthält
eindeutige Anspielungen auf die Musik dieser Platte. Miles wiederholte dieses Motiv bei der 1962
entstandenen Aufnahme *Hub-Tones* von Freddie
Hubbard. Der Bop-Pianist Horace Parlan baute
Anklänge an Gospelmusik und afrikanische Elemente in sein Spiel ein. **O**
Pour cette pochette rare de Blue Note, le graphiste
Reid Miles joue à fond la carte de l'abstraction et de
l'inventivité. Le motif des touches de piano laisse
deviner la musique gravée dans la cire. Il allait
reprendre ce motif sur l'album *Hub-Tones* de Freddie Hubbard en 1962. Horace Parlan est un pianiste de bop qui intègre à son jeu une touche de
gospel et des éléments d'inspiration africaine.

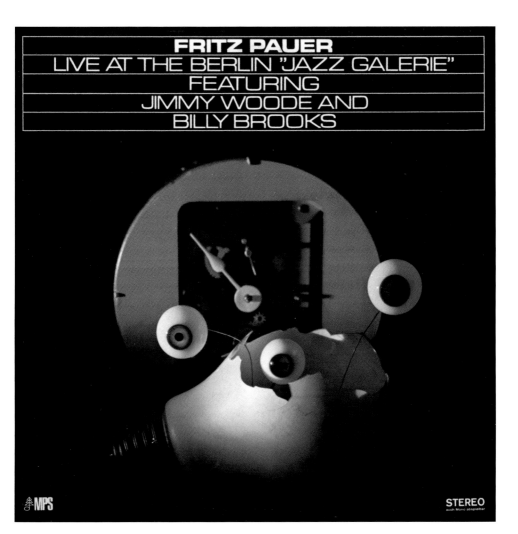

FRITZ PAUER
title LIVE AT THE BERLIN
"JAZZ GALERIE" / *year* 1978 /
label MPS / *art* Masakatsu
Kobayashi / *design* Heyqlow
Kobayashi

CECIL PAYNE

title ZODIAC / *year* 1973 / *label*
Strata-East / *design* Martin
Bough / *photo* Edgar A. Fitt

SES 19734

Zodiac

The music of
Cecil Payne

Dedicated in
memory of:

Wynton Kelly
(December 2, 1932
to April 12, 1971)

Kenny Dorham
(August 30, 1924
to December 5, 1972)

Dolphy Series 3

DUKE PEARSON

title THE PHANTOM / *year* 1968 / *label* Blue Note / *design* Forlenza Venosa Associates / *photo* Francis Wolff

ART PEPPER

title ART PEPPER + ELEVEN: A TREASURY OF MODERN JAZZ CLASSICS / *year* 1959 / *label* Contemporary / *design* Guidi/Tri-Arts / *photo* Roger Marshutz

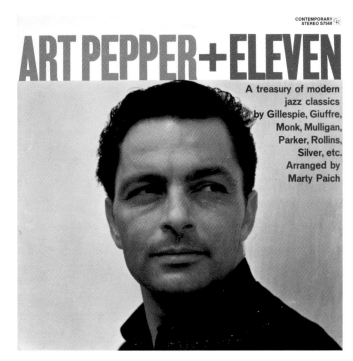

DAVE PELL OCTET
title I HAD THE CRAZIEST
DREAM / *year* 1955 / *label*
Capitol

HOUSTON PERSON

title GOODNESS! / *year* 1969 /
label Prestige / *photo* Al Johnson

OSCAR PETTIFORD

title OSCAR PETTIFORD /
year 1954 / *label* Bethlehem /
design Burt Goldblatt

THE DAVE
PIKE SET

title GOT THE FEELIN' /
year 1969 / *label* Relax /
design J. Peter Vos / *photo*
Marianne

MPS 15014

NOISY SILENCE — GENTLE NOISE

THE DAVE PIKE SET

DELIVER NC!

MPS STEREO
auch mono abspielbar

THE DAVE PIKE SET

title NOISY SILENCE – GENTLE NOISE /
year 1969 / *label* MPS / *design* Heinz Bähr

The German MPS label was founded in 1968. Heinz Bähr produced the graphic assemblage for this 1969 cover, which looks ahead of its time. He has been cited in Germany as the father of modern corporate design. This psychedelic jazz outing from the vastly underrated vibes and marimba specialist Dave Pike became an underground success following its 1969 release. **O**

Das deutsche Label „Musik Produktion Schwarzwald", kurz MPS, wurde 1968 gegründet. Der innovative Designer Heinz Bähr war für die grafische Gestaltung dieses 1969 erschienenen Covers verantwortlich, dessen Design seiner Zeit voraus war. Bähr wurde in Deutschland als der Vater des modernen Corporate Design angesehen. Diese psychedelische Jazzplatte des stark unterschätzten Vibrafon- und Marimbaexperten Dave Pike wurde nach ihrer Veröffentlichung 1969 in der alternativen Musikszene ein Erfolg. **O**

Le label allemand MPS fut fondé en 1968. C'est le graphiste avant-gardiste Heinz Bähr qui créa le montage de cette couverture de 1969, qui a l'air d'être en avance sur son temps. En Allemagne, il est considéré comme le père du graphisme d'entreprise moderne. Cet album de jazz psychédélique de Dave Pike, spécialiste très sous-estimé du vibraphone et du marimba, devint un tube underground dès sa sortie en 1969.

COURTNEY PINE

title DESTINY'S SONG (AND THE IMAGE
OF PURSUANCE) / *year* 1988 / *label* Antilles /
design Island Arts / *photo* Mike Prior

The cover photography is the work of British music
industry photographer Mike Prior, with the Island
Arts creative team, headed by Bruno Tulley, adding
motion to the image with the cool repeat design.
Courtney Pine belongs to the new wave of British
jazz artists. The multi-instrumentalist, specializing
in saxophone, emerged on the UK jazz scene in the
1980s. **O**
Das Foto dieses Covers stammt von dem britischen
Musikfotografen Mike Prior, der zusammen mit
dem Kreativteam von Island Arts unter der Lei-

tung von Bruno Tulley für das coole repetitive
Coverdesign verantwortlich zeichnet. Courtney Pine
gehört zu einer neuen Generation britischer Jazz-
künstler. Der auf das Saxofonspiel spezialisierte
Multi-Instrumentalist tauchte in den 1980ern in
der britischen Jazzszene auf. **O**
Cette photographie est l'œuvre de Mike Prior, un
photographe anglais spécialiste de la musique. C'est
l'équipe créative d'Island Arts, dirigée par Bruno
Tulley, qui a ajouté du mouvement à l'image avec ce
motif de répétition très réussi. Island Records créa
Courtney Pine appartient à la nouvelle vague des
musiciens de jazz britanniques. Ce multi-instrumentaliste spécialisé dans le saxophone apparut
dans les années 1980.

TRUDY PITTS
title INTRODUCING THE
FABULOUS TRUDY PITTS /
year 1967 / *label* Prestige

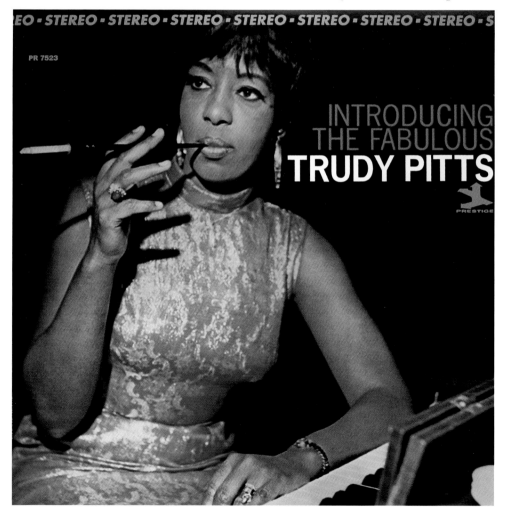

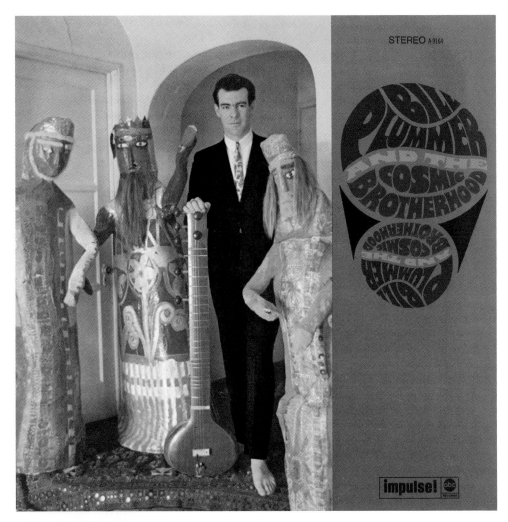

STEREO A-9164

impulse! abc

BILL PLUMMER
AND THE COSMIC
BROTHERHOOD

title BILL PLUMMER AND THE
COSMIC BROTHERHOOD /
year 1968 / *label* Impulse! /
design Robert & Barbara
Flynn/Viceroy / *photo* Irv Glaser

ARGO LP 631
high-fidelity

VITO PRICE

swingin' the LOOP

LOU LEVY
MAX BENNETT
GUS JOHNSON
FREDDIE GREEN

VITO PRICE
title SWINGIN' THE LOOP /
year 1958 / *label* Argo / *design* Don
Bronstein / *photo* Don Bronstein

JOE PUMA
title EAST COAST JAZZ NO. 3 /
year 1954 / *label* Bethlehem /
design Burt Goldblatt

Sun Ra   The Magic City

SUN RA
title THE MAGIC CITY /
year 1973 / *label* Impulse! /
art Don Bied

SUN RA
title THE HELIOCENTRIC
WORLDS OF SUN RA VOL. 2 /
year 1966 / *label* ESP-Disk' /
design Paul Frick / *photo* Al Hicks

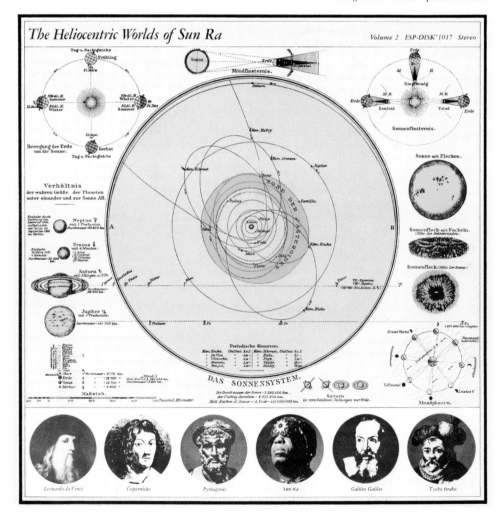

SUN RA
title THE FUTURISTIC
SOUNDS OF SUN RA /
year 1961 / *label* BYG /
photo Charles Stewart

**JOHNNY-CRETU
RADUCANU**
title JAZZ IN TRIO / *year*
1966 / *label* Electrecord /
design Ion Baroi

VI REDD

title BIRD CALL / *year* 1962 /
label United Artists / *design*
Frank Gauna / *photo* Frank
Gauna

DON RENDELL /
IAN CARR QUINTET

title PHASE III / *year* 1968 / *label* EMI /
design Denis Preston / *photo* Stuart McIntyre

Record company executive Denis Preston was a
leading light in the recording of great British jazz
music between the 1950s and 1970s. *The Gramophone* magazine once cited him as 'an impresario of
near-genius'. All rounder, Preston lent his support
to the jazz fraternity by organizing many recordings. He also got involved in the production of the
covers, such as on this EMI/BGO release. **O**
Der Musikmanager Denis Preston war eine führende Persönlichkeit der britischen Jazzmusik von den
1950ern bis in die 70er. Das Magazin *The Gramo-*

phone nannte ihn einen „Musikmanager, dessen
Talent ans Genie grenzt". Als Allroundtalent unterstützte Preston die Jazzgemeinschaft, indem er
viele Aufnahmen organisierte. Er war außerdem an
der Gestaltung der Cover wie bei dieser EMI/BGO-
Veröffentlichung beteiligt. **O**
Denis Preston était un responsable de maison de
disques qui a joué un rôle essentiel dans l'enregistrement du meilleur jazz britannique entre les
années 1950 et 1970. Le magazine *The Gramophone*
l'a qualifié d'«impresario quasiment génial». Véritable homme-orchestre, il a soutenu la fraternité du
jazz en organisant une multitude d'enregistrements.
Il s'est également impliqué dans la création des
couvertures, comme sur cet album sorti chez EMI/
BGO.

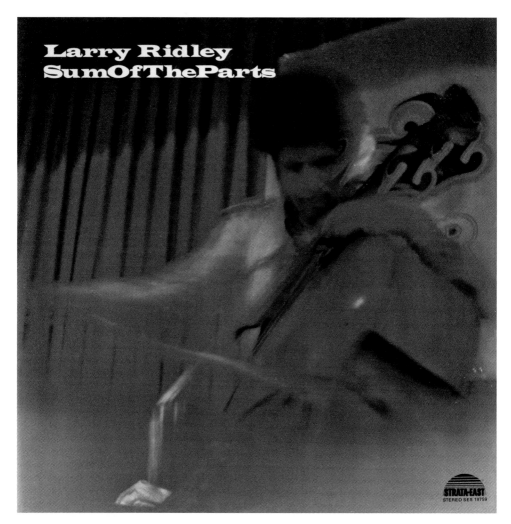

STRATA-EAST
STEREO SES 19759

LARRY RIDLEY

title SUM OF THE PARTS / *year* 1975 /
label Strata-East / *design* Art Krasinky /
photo Art Krasinky

The little-known Art Krasinky photographed and
designed this cover for bass player Larry Ridley.
The former sideman for bandleaders Thelonious
Monk, Lee Morgan and Duke Ellington balanced a
jazz career with lifelong academic achievement.
Ridley gained a doctorate and served as chairman of
the Jazz Panel of the National Endowment for the
Arts and as Professor of Jazz Bass. **o**
Der relativ unbekannte Art Krasinky fotografierte
und designte dieses Cover für den Bassisten Larry
Ridley. Ridley, ehemaliger Sideman für brillante

Bandleader wie Thelonious Monk, Lee Morgan und
Duke Ellington, verband seine Jazzkarriere zeit
seines Lebens mit seiner akademischen Laufbahn.
Er trug einen Doktortitel, war Vorsitzender der
Jazzabteilung des National Endowment for the Arts
und hatte eine Professur für Jazzbass inne. **o**
C'est Art Krasinky, un photographe peu connu, qui
a créé cette couverture pour le bassiste Larry Ridley. Ce dernier a accompagné des étoiles de l'envergure de Thelonious Monk, Lee Morgan et Duke
Ellington, et a mené parallèlement à sa carrière de
musicien une carrière universitaire brillante tout
au long de sa vie. Il est titulaire d'un doctorat et a
été président du Jazz Panel du National Endowment for the Arts. Il a également été professeur de
contrebasse de jazz à la Manhattan School of Music.

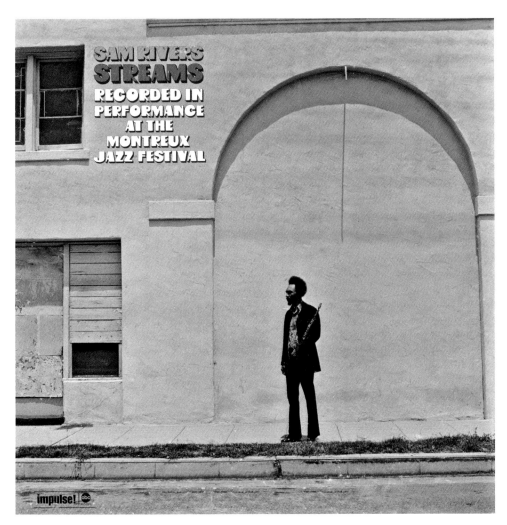

SAM RIVERS

title STREAMS / *year* 1973 / *label* Impulse! /
design Martin Donald / *photo* Philip Melnick

Photographer Philip Melnick has spent much of his
artistic career exploring long-term projects on
themes such as the stylistic aspects of California's
urban landscape. It was his prolific photography of
the Los Angeles music scene that gained him the
attention of various record labels at the end of the
1960s. Multi-instrumentalist Sam Rivers was a
key figure of the New York loft scene during the
1970s. ○

Langzeitprojekte zu verschiedenen Themen, so zum
Beispiel der stilistische Aspekt der städtischen Landschaft Kaliforniens, machten einen großen Teil der
Fotoarbeiten Philip Melnicks aus. Seine schöpferi-
schen Fotografien der Musikszene in Los Angeles
brachten ihm Ende der 1960er Jahre die Aufmerk-
samkeit verschiedener Plattenfirmen ein. Der Multi-Instrumentalist Sam Rivers galt in den 1970ern
als Schlüsselfigur der New Yorker Loftszene. ○

Le photographe Philip Melnick a passé une grande
partie de sa carrière artistique à explorer des projets à long terme sur des sujets tels que les aspects
stylistiques des paysages urbains californiens. C'est
son travail photographique prolifique sur la scène
musicale de Los Angeles qui lui a valu l'attention de
plusieurs maisons de disques vers la fin des années
1960. Multi-instrumentaliste, Sam Rivers était une
personnalité essentielle de la scène loft de New York
dans les années 1970.

SAM RIVERS
title A NEW CONCEPTION /
year 1966 / *label* Blue Note /
design Reid Miles / *photo* Reid
Miles

**THE MAX ROACH
QUARTET WITH
HANK MOBLEY**
title THE MAX ROACH
QUARTET FEATURING HANK
MOBLEY / *year* 1953 /
label Debut

FREDDIE ROACH

title GOOD MOVE! / *year* 1963 / *label* Blue Note / *design* Reid Miles / *photo* Francis Wolff

FREDDY ROBINSON

title BLACK FOX / *year* 1970 / *label* World Pacific Records / *ad* Ron Wolin / *photo* Ron Wolin

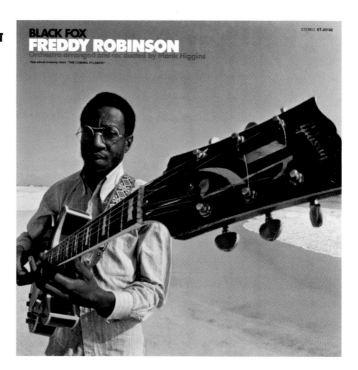

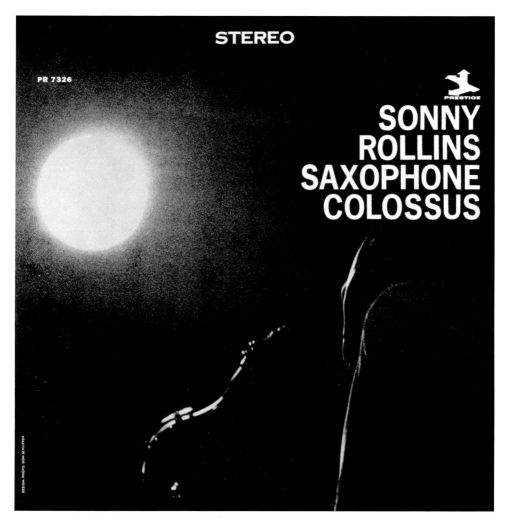

STEREO

PR 7326

PRESTIGE

SONNY
ROLLINS
SAXOPHONE
COLOSSUS

DESIGN · PHOTO DON SCHLITTEN

SONNY ROLLINS

title SAXOPHONE COLOSSUS / *year* 1956 /
label Prestige / *design* Don Schlitten / *photo*
Don Schlitten

During the height of bebop, producer and designer
Don Schlitten recorded several jazz greats. No doubt
his design credit for the cover of this magnum opus
from Sonny Rollins cemented his reputation even
further. Jazz legend Sonny Rollins was already
playing with the great pianist Thelonious Monk by
his late teens. This is often regarded as the most
famous recording of the entire Prestige catalog. **O**
Zur Blütezeit des Bebop machte der Produzent und
Designer Don Schlitten Plattenaufnahmen mit
mehreren Jazzgrößen. Zweifelsohne festigte das

Cover dieses Opus Magnum von Sonny Rollins
Schlittens ohnehin hohes Ansehen weiter. Die
Jazzlegende Sonny Rollins spielte bereits als
Jugendlicher mit dem grandiosen Pianisten The-
lonious Monk. Diese Platte gilt als berühmteste
Aufnahme des gesamten Prestige-Katalogs. **O**
À l'apogée du be-bop, le producteur et graphiste Don
Schlitten fit enregistrer plusieurs grands noms du
jazz. Il ne fait aucun doute que le fait d'avoir créé la
couverture de cet opus majeur de Sonny Rollins ait
encore renforcé sa réputation. La légende du jazz
Sonny Rollins commença à jouer en public dès
l'enfance, et à la fin de son adolescence il jouait
déjà avec le grand pianiste Thelonious Monk. Cet
enregistrement est souvent considéré comme le plus
célèbre de tout le catalogue de Prestige.

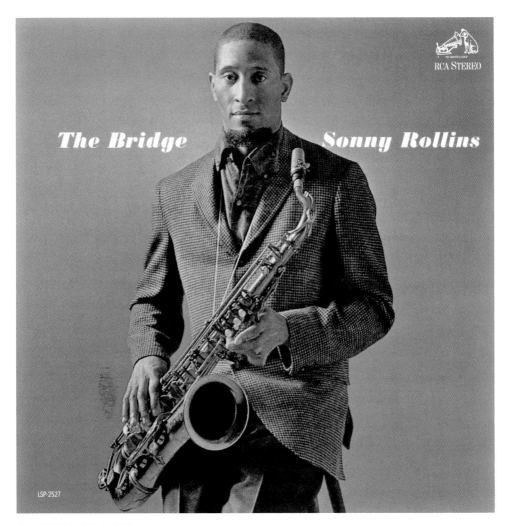

SONNY ROLLINS
title THE BRIDGE / *year*
1962 / *label* RCA / *ad* J.J.
Stelmach / *photo* Charles
Stewart

SONNY ROLLINS

title SONNY ROLLINS AND
THE CONTEMPORARY
LEADERS / *year* 1959 /
label Contemporary /
design Guidi/Tri-Arts / *photo*
William Claxton

CONTEMPORARY S7564
SONNY ROLLINS AND THE
CONTEMPORARY LEADERS:
BARNEY KESSEL
HAMPTON HAWES
LEROY VINNEGAR
SHELLY MANNE

SONNY ROLLINS

title EAST BROADWAY RUN
DOWN / *year* 1966 / *label*
Impulse! / *art* Mel Cherin /
design Robert Flynn/Viceroy /
photo Charles Stewart

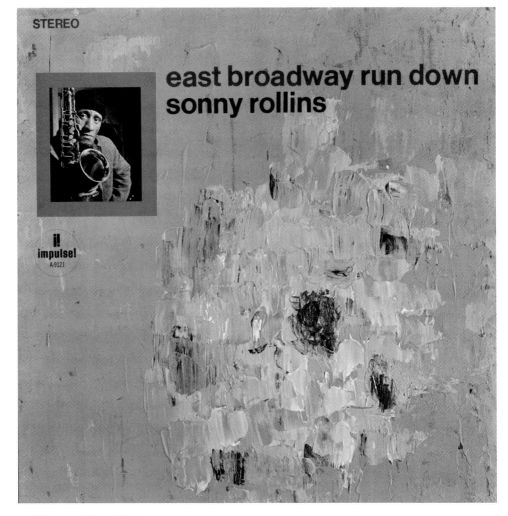

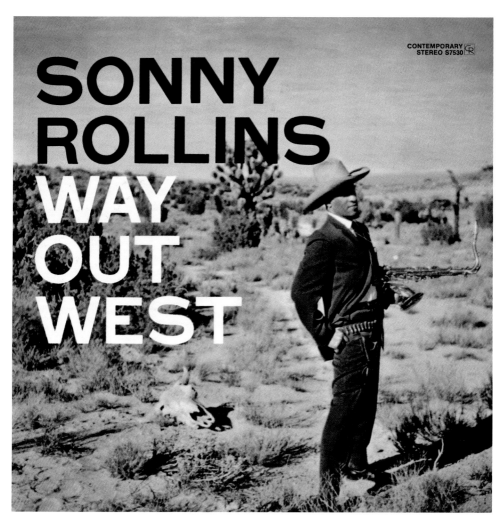

CONTEMPORARY STEREO S7530

SONNY ROLLINS
WAY OUT WEST

SONNY ROLLINS
title WAY OUT WEST / *year*
1957 / *label* Contemporary /
design William Claxton

Fotografía: Godo Romero. Diseño: Gráfico

aldemaro
romero
y su
Onda
Nueva
en el mundo

Incluye: UNA NOCHE UNA CENA
éxito de la película italiana
del mismo nombre

ALDEMARO ROMERO

title ALDEMARO ROMERO
Y SU ONDA NUEVA EN EL
MUNDO / *label* Nova Sonido
Integral / *design* A. Salazar /
photo Godo Romero

"*The New Wave was born in Caracas. This is
a new music that redeems all the airs of
Venezuelan music to become a truly modern
expression capable of competing with the best
popular music of other countries.*"
— Aldemaro Romero

ANNIE ROSS & ZOOT SIMS

title A GASSER! / *year* 1959 /
label World Pacific Records /
design Ted Poyser / *photo* Charles
Stewart

RONNIE ROSS
title CLEOPATRA'S NEEDLE /
year 1968 / *label* Fontana

CHARLES ROUSE

title TWO IS ONE / *year* 1974 /
label Strata-East / *design* Martin
Bough / *photo* Martin Bough

ROSWELL RUDD

title EVERYWHERE / *year* 1966 /
label Impulse! / *design* Robert Flynn/Viceroy /
photo Fred Seligo

Fred Seligo's name is often included among the
ranks of jazz music's top photographers. His images
graced the cover of many jazz releases during the
1960s, including albums by Cal Tjader, Gerry
Mulligan and Gabor Szabo. Free jazz trombonist
Roswell Rudd was a member of the radical
New York Art Quartet. He played extensively with
New York soprano sax player Steve Lacy. **o**
Fred Seligo wird häufig zu den Top-Fotografen der
Jazzmusik gezählt. Seligos Bilder verzieren die

Cover vieler Jazzplatten aus den 1960ern, darunter
Alben von Cal Tjader, Gerry Mulligan und Gabor
Szabo. Der Free-Jazz-Posaunist Roswell Rudd war
Mitglied des radikalen New York Art Quartet.
Er spielte unzählige Male mit dem New Yorker
Sopransaxofonisten Steve Lacy zusammen. **o**
Le nom de Fred Seligo est souvent cité parmi les
plus grands photographes de jazz. Ses images ont
orné les pochettes de nombreux albums de jazz des
années 1960, notamment de Cal Tjader, Gerry
Mulligan et Gabor Szabo. Le tromboniste de free
jazz Roswell Rudd était membre du groupe radical
New York Art Quartet. Il joua beaucoup avec le
joueur de saxo soprano Steve Lacy.

PETE RUGOLO
title MUSIC FOR HI-FI BUGS /
year 1956 / *label* EmArcy

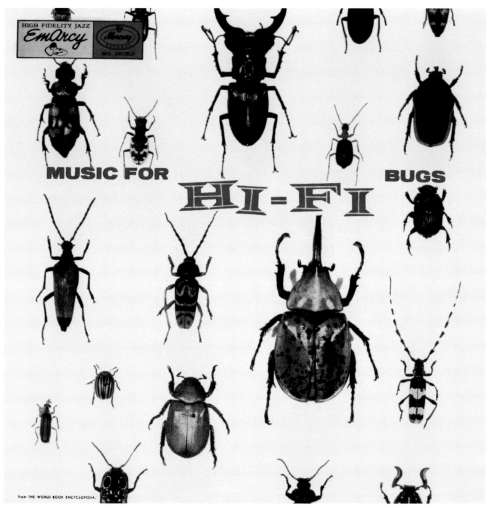

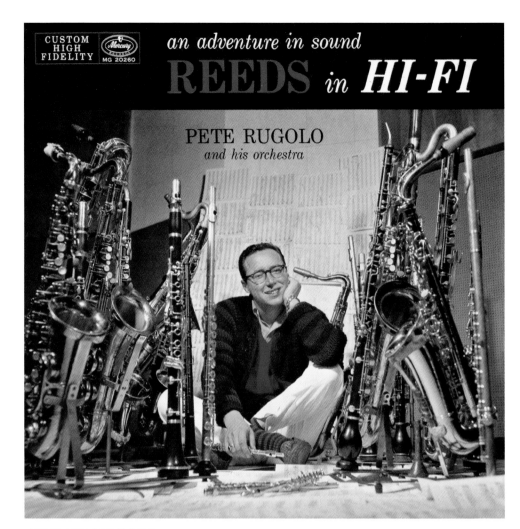

an adventure in sound

REEDS in HI-FI

CUSTOM HIGH FIDELITY — Mercury — MG 20260

PETE RUGOLO
and his orchestra

**PETE RUGOLO AND
HIS ORCHESTRA**
title REEDS IN HI-FI /
year 1956 / *label* Mercury

JORGE LOPEZ RUIZ
title EL GRITO / *year* 1967 / *label* CBS

JIMMY RUSHING
title IF THIS AIN'T THE
BLUES / *year* 1958 / *label*
Vanguard / *design* Jules
Halfant / *photo* Burt Owen

Gene Russell
New Direction

BLACK JAZZ RECORDS

BJ/1
STEREO

Players:
Henry Franklin: Bass
Steve Clover: Drums
Tony William: Conga
Gene Russell: Piano
Larry Gales: Bass (Black Orchid:
  Making Bread)

Side One
Black Orchid 3:13
Hitting The Jug 4:42
Willow Weep For Me 4:58
Listen Here 3:15

Side Two
On Green Dolphin Street 5:02
Silver's Serenade 4:54
My Cherie Amour 3:01
Making Bread 3:21

Exclusively Distributed By
OVATION RECORDS
Available On AMPEX Stereo Tapes.

Credits:
Producer: Gene Russell
Recording Engineer: Gene Russell
Cover Design: Ray Lawrence Ltd.
Cover Art and Photo: Dorothy Tanous
Arrangements by Gene Russell

GENE RUSSELL

title NEW DIRECTION / *year* 1971 /
label Black Jazz / *design* Ray Lawrence Ltd. /
photo Dorothy Tanous

Photographer Dorothy Tanous was an occasional
contributor to Black Jazz in its brief reign, creating
some deep monochrome cover portraits. *New Direction* marked the first release on the cult Los
Angeles-based label. Renowned pianist and Black
Jazz founder Gene Russell is in his element, bounc-
ing off bass maestro Henry "The Skipper" Franklin
on this quality set of soul jazz cuts. **O**
Die Fotografin Dorothy Tanous arbeitete während
dessen kurzer Existenz gelegentlich für Black Jazz
und schuf einige tiefgründige monochrome Cover-

porträts. *New Direction* war die erste Veröffentlichung des Kultlabels aus Los Angeles. Gene Russell,
der bekannte Pianist und Gründer von Black Jazz,
ist auf diesem Album voller Soul-Jazz-Stücke in
seinem Element und liefert sich ein Duell mit dem
Bass-Virtuosen Henry „The Skipper" Franklin. **O**
La photographe Dorothy Tanous a collaboré plusieurs fois avec Black Jazz pendant son bref règne
et a créé quelques portraits monochromes très
profonds pour ses pochettes. *New Direction* fut le
premier album de ce label culte basé à Los Angeles.
Le pianiste renommé et cofondateur de Black Jazz,
Gene Russel, est ici dans son élément et en parfaite
synergie avec le maître de la contrebasse Henry
« The Skipper » Franklin sur ces morceaux de soul
jazz de grande qualité.

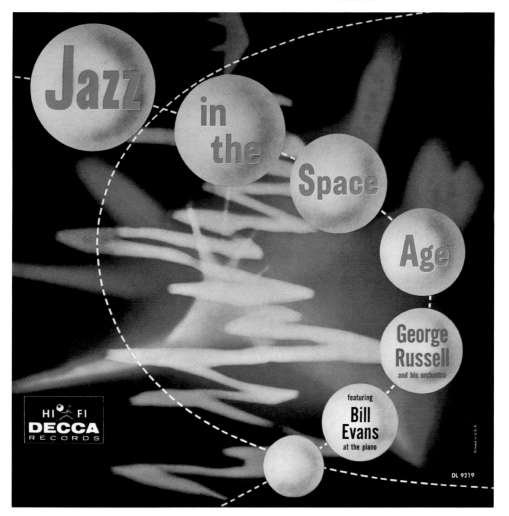

PHAROAH SANDERS
title KARMA / *year* 1969 /
label Impulse! / *design* Robert &
Barbara Flynn / *photo* Charles
Stewart

STEREO AS-9190
impulse! abc
RECORDS

PHAROAH SANDERS
JEWELS OF THOUGHT

PHAROAH SANDERS

title JEWELS OF THOUGHT / *year* 1969 /
label Impulse! / *design* George Whiteman /
photo Charles Stewart

Impulse! designer George Whiteman's treatment
of Charles Stewart's portrait reflects the spiritual
quality of Sanders' blend of Afrocentric jazz.
Following early sessions with the great John
Coltrane, Sanders went on to develop his own
style of overblowing and multiphonic saxophone
techniques. ○
George Whiteman, Designer bei Impulse!, setzt
Charles Stewarts Porträt auf eine Art ein, die die

Spiritualität von Sanders' afrozentrischem Jazz-
Mix widerspiegelt. Nachdem Sanders zu Beginn
seiner Karriere an einer Reihe von Sessions mit
dem großen John Coltrane teilgenommen hatte,
entwickelte er seinen eigenen, von Überblas-
techniken und multiphonem Saxofonspiel geprägten
Stil. ○
La façon dont le graphiste d'Impulse!, George Whiteman, a traité le portrait de Charles Stewart fait
écho aux qualités spirituelles du jazz africain de
Pharoah Sanders. Après quelques sessions avec le
grand John Coltrane, Pharoah Sanders développa
son propre style au saxophone, avec des techniques
telles que l'overblowing et la multiphonie.

ESP-DISK'

pharaoh sanders quintet

PHARAOH
SANDERS QUINTET
title PHARAOH'S FIRST /
year 1964 / *label* ESP-Disk'

MOACIR SANTOS
title 'SAUDADE' / *year* 1974 /
label Blue Note / *ad* Bob Cato /
design Bob Cato

SAUTER-FINEGAN ORCHESTRA

title INSIDE SAUTER-
FINEGAN / *year* 1954 / *label*
RCA Victor / *design* Jim Flora

SAUTER-FINEGAN ORCHESTRA
title THE SONS OF SAUTER-FINEGAN / *year* 1954 / *label* RCA Victor / *design* Jim Flora

The

eddie bert·trombone·ronnie woelmer·trumpet

Compositions

of

hal mckusick·alto·al epstein·baritone

Bobby Scott

milt hinton·bass·ossie johnson·drums

east coast jazz/1

BURT GOLDBLATT

betty·moon tan·aunt sarah·cerebellum·dot

BOBBY SCOTT

title THE COMPOSITIONS OF BOBBY SCOTT –
EAST COAST JAZZ 1 / *year* 1954 / *label*
Bethlehem / *design* Burt Goldblatt / *photo* Burt
Goldblatt

Piano player and vocalist Bobby Scott was most
active in the 1950s, for a while performing with
drummer Gene Krupa. **o**

Der Pianist und Sänger Bobby Scott hatte in den
1950ern seine produktivsten Jahre und trat eine
Zeit lang mit dem Schlagzeuger Gene Krupa auf. **o**
Le pianiste et chanteur Bobby Scott a connu son pic
d'activité dans les années 1950 et a joué pendant
quelque temps avec le batteur Gene Krupa.

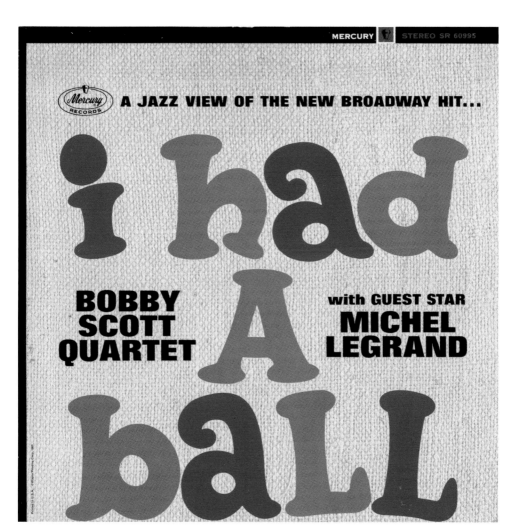

BOBBY SCOTT QUARTET

title I HAD A BALL /
year 1964 / *label* Mercury /
design Wayne Printings Corp.

GIL SCOTT-HERON /
BRIAN JACKSON
title WINTER IN AMERICA /
year 1974 / *label* Strata-East /
art Eugene Coles

GIL SCOTT-HERON/BRIAN JACKSON

Eugene Coles

WINTER IN AMERICA

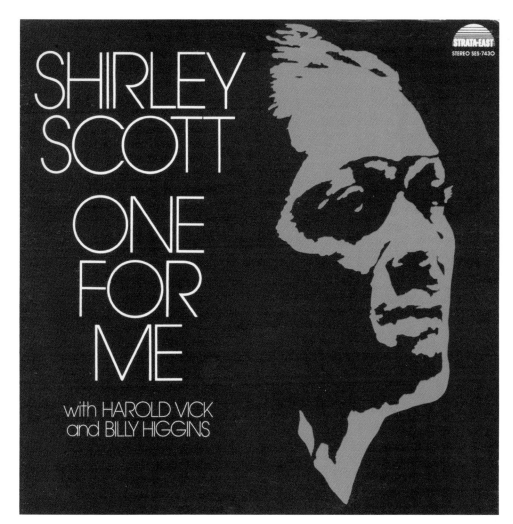

SHIRLEY SCOTT

title ONE FOR ME / *year* 1974 /
label Strata-East

Shirley Scott was one of the few recognized female
musicians to have stamped her mark in jazz history. A hard bop and soul-jazz organist, Scott made
a name for herself while playing with tenorist Eddie
"Lockjaw" Davis in the late 1950s. For this self
produced album, Scott plays organ and mellotron
with the remarkable Harold Vick on tenor, while
legendary drummer Billy Higgins and Jimmy Hopps
on triangle. **O**
Shirley Scott ist eine der wenigen Musikerinnen,
die ihre Spuren in der Geschichte des Jazz hinter-
lassen haben. Sie machte sich Ende der 1950er

einen Namen als Hard-Bop- und Soul-Jazz-Orga-
nistin, als sie mit dem Tenorsaxofonisten Eddie
„Lockjaw" Davis spielte. Auf diesem selbst produzierten Album spielt Scott Orgel und Mellotron,
der bemerkenswerte Harold Vick übernimmt das
Tenorsaxofon, der legendäre Billy Higgins sitzt am
Schlagzeug und Jimmy Hopps an der Triangel. **O**
Shirley Scott fait partie des rares musiciennes qui
ont laissé leur empreinte dans l'histoire du jazz.
Organiste de hard bop et de soul jazz, elle se fit un
nom en jouant avec le joueur de saxo ténor Eddie
« Lockjaw » Davis vers la fin des années 1950. Pour
cet album autoproduit, elle joue de l'orgue et du
mellotron avec le remarquable Harold Vick au saxo
ténor, le légendaire Billy Higgins à la batterie et
Jimmy Hoops au triangle.

SHIRLEY SCOTT
title GIRL TALK / *year* 1967 /
label Impulse! / *design* Robert &
Barbara Flynn / *photo* Charles
Stewart

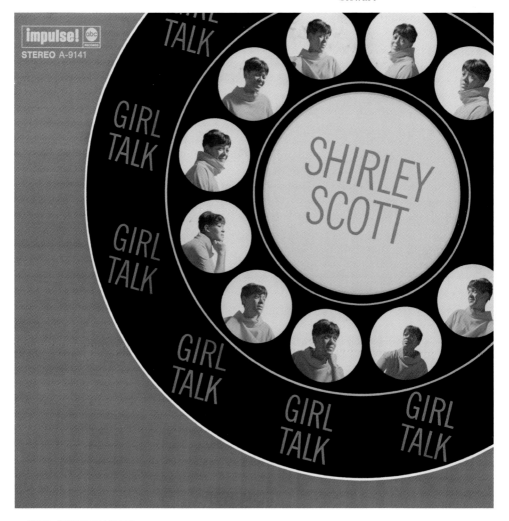

JIMMY SCOTT
title THE SOURCE / *year* 1970 /
label Atlantic / *design* Loring
Eutemey / *photo* Joel Brodsky

TOM SCOTT
title THE HONEYSUCKLE
BREEZE / *year* 1967 / *label*
Impulse! / *design* Robert &
Barbara Flynn / *photo* Irv Glaser

DON SEBESKY
title THE RAPE OF EL
MORRO / *year* 1975 /
label CTI / *design* Bob Ciano /
photo Alan Kaplan

The
Bud Shank
Quartet

featuring

Claude Williamson
Pacific Jazz 1215

BUD SHANK

title THE BUD SHANK QUARTET / *year* 1956 / *label* Pacific Jazz / *art* Pauline Annon / *design* William Claxton

William Claxton was still studying at UCLA when he helped record producer Richard Bock start the Pacific Jazz Records. He also designed most of the label's early covers. Here he uses an artwork by Hollywood sketch artist Pauline Annon based on a photograph by himself. Bud Shank is mainly recognized for his alto sax playing, though he did play flute as a second instrument. ○

William Claxton studierte noch an der UCLA (University of California, Los Angeles), als er zusammen mit dem Plattenproduzenten Richard Bock Pacific Jazz Records gründete. Er designte auch fast alle frühen Cover für das Label. Hier verwendete er ein Kunstwerk der Hollywood-Zeichnerin Pauline Annon, das wiederum auf einem Foto von Claxton basiert. Bud Shank ist hauptsächlich als Altsaxofonist bekannt, obwohl er als zweites Instrument auch Flöte spielte. ○

William Claxton était encore étudiant de l'UCLA lorsqu'il aida le producteur Richard Bock à créer Pacific Jazz Records. Il créa également la plupart des premières pochettes du label. Il utilise ici un dessin de Pauline Annon basé sur une photographie de lui-même. Bud Shank est surtout connu pour son jeu au saxo alto, mais il jouait également de la flûte.

BUD SHANK QUARTET
FEATURING CLAUDE WILLIAMSON
PACIFIC JAZZ 1230

BUD SHANK

title BUD SHANK QUARTET / *year* 1956 /
label Pacific Jazz / *photo* William Claxton

This recording is one of two quartet outings
alto sax player Shank made with pianist Claude
Williamson. **o**
Dies ist eine von zwei Aufnahmen des Quartetts,
bei denen der Altsaxofonist Shank zusammen mit
dem Pianisten Claude Williamson spielte. **o**
Il s'agit de l'un des deux albums en quartet que
le joueur de saxo alto Bud Shank enregistra avec
le pianiste Claude Williamson.

*"Photography is jazz for the
eye. Just as jazz is the music
or art of the moment – it is
spontaneous and just occurs
instantaneously – so is
photography. Like recorded
jazz, photography is a technical
process which tries to capture
and reproduce a feeling or
experience that can be relived
years later."*
—William Claxton

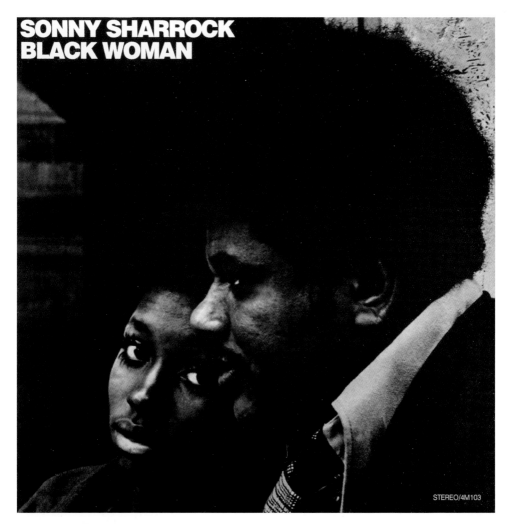

SONNY SHARROCK
BLACK WOMAN

STEREO/4M103

SONNY SHARROCK
title BLACK WOMAN / *year*
1969 / *label* Vortex / *design* Haig
Adishian / *photo* Ray Gibson

ARCHIE SHEPP
title THE MAGIC OF JU-JU /
year 1967 / *label* Impulse! / *design*
Robert & Barbara Flynn / *photo*
William E. Levy

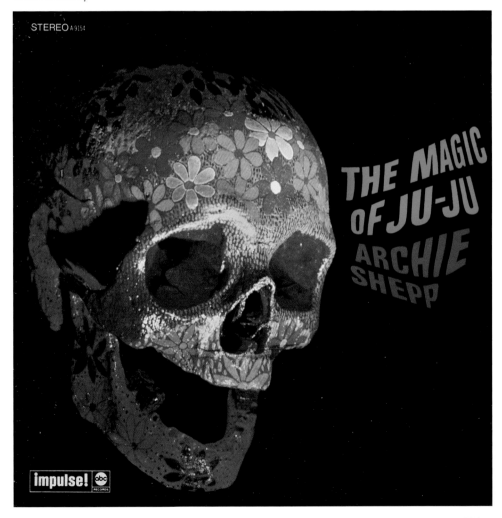

ARCHIE SHEPP
title THE WAY AHEAD /
year 1968 / *label* Impulse! /
design Robert & Barbara Flynn

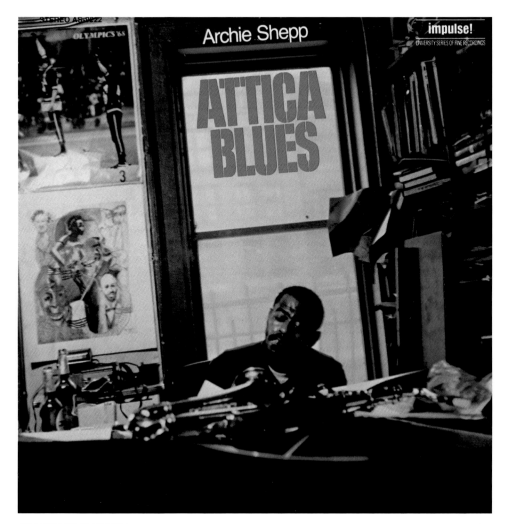

ARCHIE SHEPP

title ATTICA BLUES / *year* 1972 / *label* Impulse! / *design* Clyde Gilliam / *photo* Charles Stewart

Charles Stewart's works reveal the essence and daily life of jazz through his compositions, as exemplified with this photographic portrait of musician Archie Shepp at work. A pianist and sax player, Shepp recorded *Attica Blues* as a direct response to the Attica prison riots of 1971. A key figure in the Afrocentric, avant-garde jazz movement, Shepp worked with icons such as Don Cherry and John Coltrane. ⦾
Charles Stewarts Bilder bringen sowohl die tiefste Seele als auch den Alltag des Jazz an die Oberfläche, wie beispielsweise in diesem Porträt des Musikers Archie Shepp bei der Arbeit. Der Pianist und Saxo-

fonist Shepp nahm *Attica Blues* als Antwort auf den Gefängnisaufstand 1971 in Attica auf. Shepp, der als Schlüsselfigur der afrozentrischen Bewegung und des Avantgarde-Jazz gilt, arbeitete mit Stars wie Don Cherry und John Coltrane zusammen. ⦾
Charles Stewart prit, entre 1950 et 1980, quelques-unes des photographies les plus mémorables du jazz. Ses compositions révèlent l'essence et la vie quotidienne du jazz, comme le montre ce portrait du musicien Archie Shepp en plein travail. Pianiste et saxophoniste, Archie Shepp enregistra *Attica Blues* en réponse directe aux émeutes de 1971 dans la prison d'Attica. Personnage essentiel du mouvement d'avant-jazz afrocentrique, il travailla avec des icônes de l'envergure de Don Cherry et John Coltrane.

ARCHIE SHEPP
title CORAL ROCK / *year* 1973 /
label America Records / *photo*
Gilbert Moreau

OKTAV

OKLP 111

SAHIB SHIHAB and THE DANISH RADIO JAZZ GROUP

SAHIB SHIHAB

title SAHIB SHIHAB AND THE DANISH
RADIO JAZZ GROUP / *year* 1965 / *label* Oktav /
photo Ebbe Wrae

This informal studio photo is credited to Ebbe Wrae
for this rare Danish Oktav release. Edmond Gregory
was one of the first jazz musicians to convert to
Islam in 1947. Over the next decade, sax and flute
player Sahib Shihab played with a host of jazz gi-
ants, including Thelonious Monk and Dizzy Gillespie. **O**
Dieses ungezwungene Studiofoto für die in nur
kleiner Auflage entstandene Veröffentlichung bei
dem dänischen Label Oktav stammt von Ebbe Wrae.
Edmond Gregory war 1947 einer der ersten Jazzmusiker, die zum Islam konvertierten. In den fol-
genden zehn Jahren spielte der Saxofonist und
Flötist Sahib Shihab mit vielen Jazzgiganten, darunter Thelonious Monk und Dizzy Gillespie. **O**
Sur cet album rare sorti chez le label danois Oktav,
cette photo informelle prise en studio est attribuée
à Ebbe Wrae. Edmond Gregory fut l'un des premiers
musiciens de jazz à se convertir à l'islam, en 1947.
Au cours de la décennie suivante, c'est sous le nom
de Sahib Shihab qu'il joua avec une multitude de
géants du jazz, notamment Thelonious Monk et
Dizzy Gillespie.

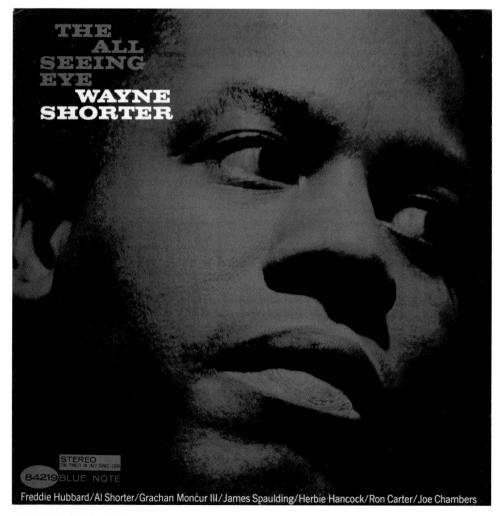

Freddie Hubbard/Al Shorter/Grachan Moncur III/James Spaulding/Herbie Hancock/Ron Carter/Joe Chambers

WAYNE SHORTER

title THE ALL SEEING EYE / *year* 1965 /
label Blue Note / *design* Reid Miles / *photo*
Francis Wolff

Francis Wolff steals the show on this cover image
with a wonderfully expressive portrait of one of the
best tenor and soprano sax artists in the jazz idiom.
At the time of this recording as bandleader, Shorter
had graduated from Art Blakey's Jazz Messengers
and had just been enlisted into Miles Davis' new
quintet. This is Shorter's most dark and avant-
garde work on Blue Note. **O**
Francis Wolff zieht mit dieser Coveraufnahme alle
Register der Fotokunst. Es zeigt ein wunderbar
ausdrucksstarkes Porträt von einem der größten

Tenor- und Sopransaxofonisten des Jazz. Zur Zeit
dieser Aufnahme mit Shorter als Bandleader hatte
dieser gerade seine Reifeprüfung bei Art Blakeys
Jazz Messengers bestanden und war in Miles Davis'
neues Quartett aufgenommen worden. Diese Platte
enthält Shorters düsterste, bei Blue Note herausge-
kommene Avantgarde-Musik. **O**
Francis Wolff ravit la vedette avec ce portrait
merveilleusement expressif de l'un des meilleurs
joueurs de saxo ténor et alto du jazz. À l'époque de
cet enregistrement réalisé sous son nom, Wayne
Shorter avait quitté les Jazz Messengers d'Art
Blakey et venait d'être engagé dans le nouveau
quintet de Miles Davis. C'est son travail le plus
sombre et le plus avant- gardiste chez Blue Note.

**THE HORACE
SILVER QUINTET**
title HORACE-SCOPE /
year 1960 / *label* Blue Note

HOME COOKIN'
4050 BLUE NOTE
THE FINEST IN JAZZ SINCE 1939
THE INCREDIBLE JIMMY SMITH
WITH PERCY FRANCE/KENNY BURRELL/DONALD BAILEY

JIMMY SMITH

title HOME COOKIN' /
year 1958 / *label* Blue Note /
design Reid Miles / *photo* Francis
Wolff

"I have photographed the famous and the not
so famous: business execs and athletes and
especially musicians — jazz, classical and pop.
The resulting pictures have appeared on over
200 LP and CD covers and on promotional
flyers and press kits, in magazines and
company reports and advertising."
— Don Hunstein

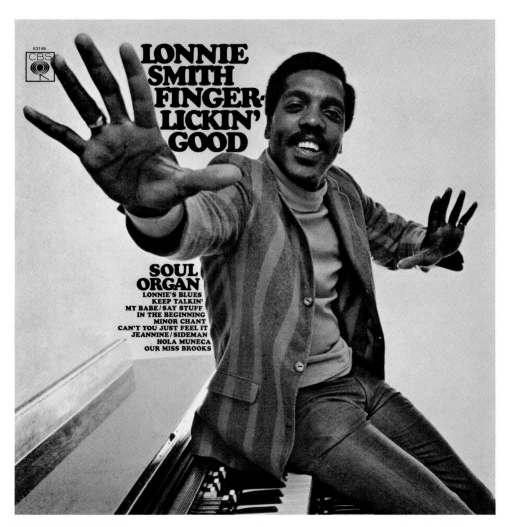

LONNIE SMITH
title FINGER-LICKIN' GOOD / *year* 1966 /
label CBS / *photo* Don Hunstein

Not to be confused with 1970s soul funk keyboard
wizard, the extraordinary organist Dr. Lonnie
Smith's now rare-to-find debut album presents a
forward-sounding groove for its 1966 release. **O**
Das inzwischen schwer aufzutreibende Album des
außergewöhnlichen Organisten Dr. Lonnie Smith

(nicht zu verwechseln mit dem Soul-Funk-Magier
der 1970er Jahre am Keyboard Lonnie Liston
Smith) enthält einen für seine Veröffentlichung im
Jahr 1966 zukunftsweisenden Groove. **O**
Dr Lonnie Smith, à ne pas confondre avec le magi-
cien du clavier soul funk des années 1970 Lonnie
Liston Smith, est un organiste extraordinaire. Sur
son premier album sorti en 1966, aujourd'hui
difficile à trouver, sa musique groovy est en avance
sur son temps.

**LONNIE LISTON
SMITH**

title EXPANSIONS / *year* 1974 /
label Flying Dutchman / *ad*
Acy Lehman / *art* Jack Martin /
design Dick Smith

DLU-75

EXPANSIONS/LONNIE LISTON SMITH & THE COSMIC ECHOES

MARTIAL SOLAL
title LOCOMOTION / *year* 1974 /
label PSI / *art* Mike Carson

Mike Carson is the mystery illustrator of this colorful and funky painting of Martial Solal in racing
helmet. An Algerian-born French jazz pianist, Solal
is most famous for his score to Jean-Luc Godard's
classic film *À bout de souffle* (1960). In Paris during
the early 1950s, Solal played with the great Belgian
gypsy guitarist Django Reinhardt and American
soprano sax master Sidney Bechet. **o**
Mike Carson heißt der geheimnisvolle Illustrator
dieses farbenfrohen, funkigen Gemäldes mit einem
helmtragenden Martial Solal. Der in Algerien geborene französische Jazzpianist Solal wurde bekannt
für seine Filmmusik zu Jean-Luc Godards Klassiker *Außer Atem* (1960). Anfang der 1950er Jahre
spielte er in Paris mit dem Gitarristen Django
Reinhardt und dem amerikanischen Meister am
Sopransaxofon, Sidney Bechet. **o**
Le mystérieux illustrateur auteur de ce tableau
coloré et très funky de Martial Solal en casque de
course est Mike Carson. Martial Solal, pianiste de
jazz français né en Algérie, est surtout connu pour
la musique qu'il a composée pour le grand classique
de Jean-Luc Godard, *À bout de souffle* (1960). Il joua
avec le grand guitariste manouche belge Django
Reinhardt et le maître américain du saxo soprano
Sidney Bechet à Paris au début des années 1950.

MARTIAL SOLAL
title MARTIAL SOLAL /
year 1965 / *label* Columbia

MARTIAL SOLAL
title MARTIAL SOLAL /
year 1953 / *label* Vogue

"Call it what you want: Groove, Soul Jazz, Old-School Acid Jazz, Barbeque Funk, Funk Jazz or whatever. Look up those terms in Webster's and there you'll find a picture of Melvin Sparks, the guitarist credited as the originator of the genre."
— www.melvinsparks.com

MELVIN SPARKS
title AKILAH! / *year* 1972 /
label Fantasy / *design* Tony Lane /
photo Tony Lane

AKILAH!
MELVIN SPARKS

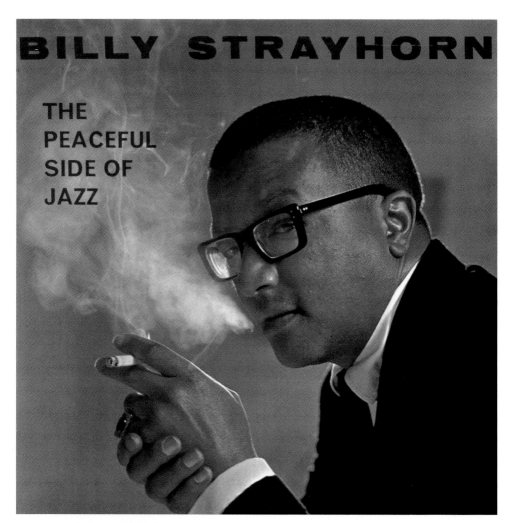

BILLY STRAYHORN

BILLY STRAYHORN
title THE PEACEFUL SIDE OF
JAZZ / *year* 1961 / *label* World
Record Club

JEREMY STEIG
title FIREFLY / *year* 1977 /
label CTI / *design* Sib Chalawick
& Carole Kowalchuk /
photo White Gate

GABOR
SZABO

MACHO

GABOR SZABO

title MACHO / *year* 1975 /
label Salvation / *design* Richard
Mantel / *photo* John Paul
Endress

GABOR SZABO
title DREAMS / *year* 1968 /
label Skye / *design* David
Stahlberg

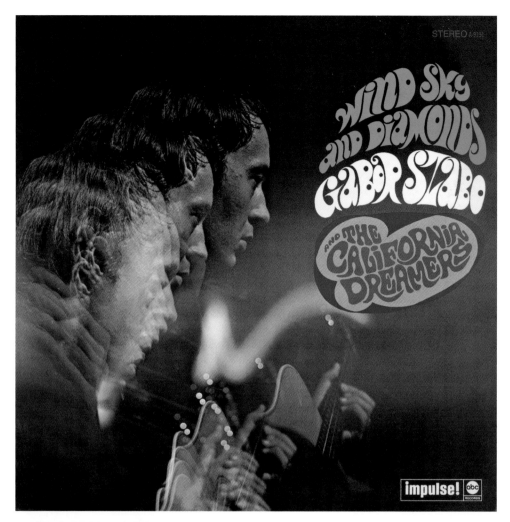

GABOR SZABO AND THE CALIFORNIA DREAMERS

title WIND, SKY AND DIAMONDS / *year* 1967 / *label* Impulse! / *design* Robert & Barbara Flynn/Viceroy / *photo* Jim Marshall

While Bob Venosa was dropping LSD at the Blue Note art department, Robert and Barbara Flynn were also on the pulse at Impulse! Here they give festival photographer Jim Marshall's snap some trippy photo effects with a touch of bubblegum typography. ⊙

Während Bob Venosa im Art Department von Blue Note einen Hauch von LSD verbreitete, gaben Robert und Barbara Flynn bei Impulse! den Ton an. Hier verpassen sie dem Schnappschuss des Festivalfotografen Jim Marshall mit der bunten Bubblegum-Schrift einen psychedelischen Touch. ⊙ Pendant que Bob Venosa saupoudrait de LSD le service artistique de Blue Note, Robert et Barbara Flynn étaient aussi dans la mouvance de l'époque. Ici, ils donnent au cliché du photographe de festival Jim Marshall des effets psychédéliques avec une touche de typographie en bulles de chewing-gum.

ART TATUM
title ART TATUM #3 /
year 1953 / *label* Clef / *design*
David Stone Martin

Art Taylor   Dave Burns
Stanley Turrentine
Wynton Kelly
Paul Chambers
'Potato' Valdez

THE FINEST IN JAZZ SINCE 1939
84047 BLUE NOTE

a.t.'s delight

ART TAYLOR
title A.T.'S DELIGHT /
year 1960 / *label* Blue Note /
design Reid Miles / *photo*
Francis Wolff

CECIL TAYLOR

title UNIT STRUCTURES / *year* 1966 / *label* Blue Note / *design* Reid Miles / *photo* Francis Wolff

Even Reid Miles was inspired by Andy Warhol's repeat image silkscreens. Miles had occasionally hired Warhol when the artist worked in advertising in the 1950s. Andy Warhol's mother, Julia Warhola, even did the lettering for one of Miles' rarer Prestige covers, *The Story of Moondog* (1957). Cecil Taylor is one of the pioneers of free jazz and avantgarde music. **O**

Auch Reid Miles ließ sich von Andy Warhols seriellen Siebdrucken inspirieren. Miles gab Warhol gelegentlich in den 1950er Jahren Aufträge, als dieser noch in der Werbebranche tätig war. Andy Warhols Mutter Julia Warhola gestaltete sogar einmal für eines von Miles' selteneren Prestige-Covern, *The Story of Moondog* (1957), den Schriftzug. Cecil Taylor ist einer der Pioniere der Free-Jazz- und Avantgarde-Musik. **O**

Même Reid Miles s'est inspiré des sérigraphies répétitives d'Andy Warhol. Reid Miles avait occasionnellement eu recours à ses services lorsqu'il travaillait dans la publicité dans les années 1950. C'est même la mère d'Andy Warhol, Julia Warhola, qui a créé les lettres de l'une des pochettes de Reid Miles les plus rares pour le label Prestige, *The Story of Moondog* (1957). Cecil Taylor est l'un des pionniers du free jazz et de la musique d'avant-garde.

NEFERTITI,
The
beautiful
one has
come

fontana

CECIL TAYLOR
JAZZ UNIT

What's New
Nefertiti, The Beautiful One Has Come
(1st variation)
Lena
(2nd variation)
Nefertiti, The Beautiful One Has Come
(2nd variation)

CECIL TAYLOR
title NEFERTITI, THE
BEAUTIFUL ONE HAS COME /
year 1962 / *label* Fontana

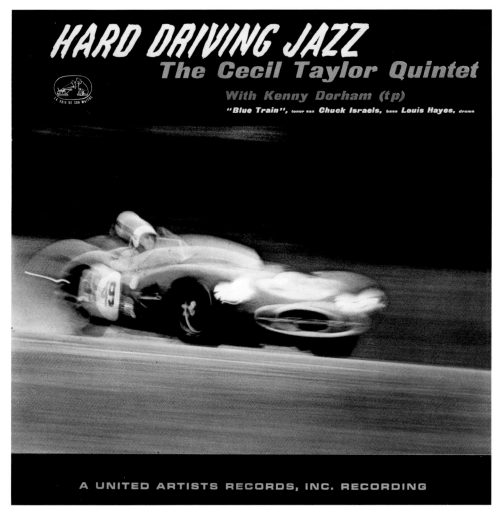

JOHN TCHICAI AND CADENTIA NOVA DANICA

title AFRODISIACA /
year 1969 / *label* MPS /
design Bernard Wetz / *photo*
Steen Kaersgaard

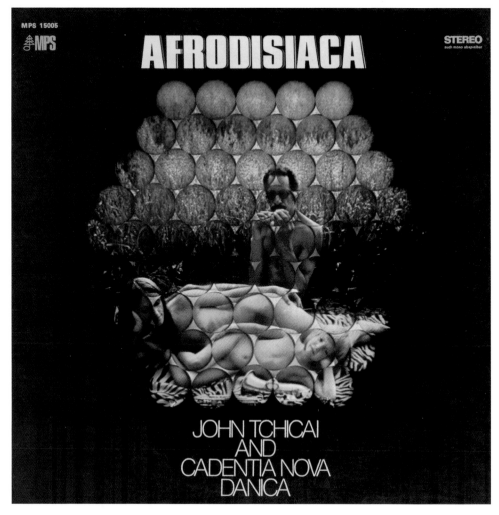

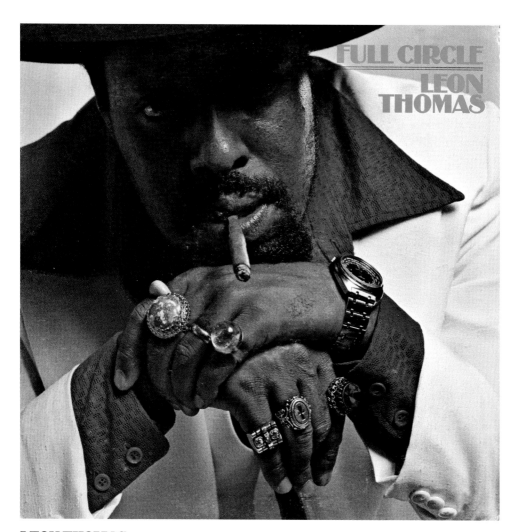

LEON THOMAS

title FULL CIRCLE / *year* 1973 /
label Flying Dutchman /
design Linda Cox / *photo* Charles
Stewart

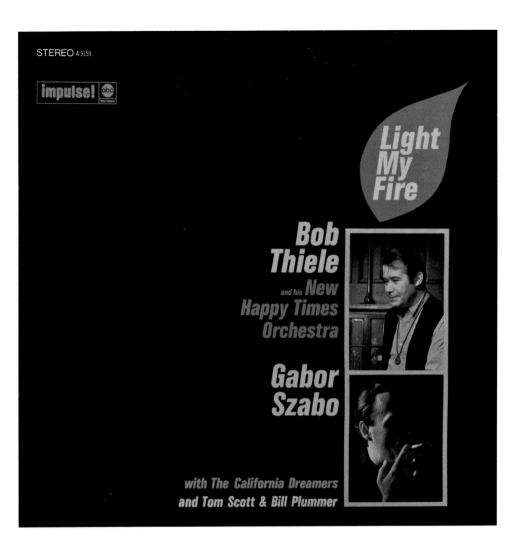

STEREO A 9159

impulse! abc

Light
My
Fire

Bob
Thiele
and his New
Happy Times
Orchestra

Gabor
Szabo

with The California Dreamers
and Tom Scott & Bill Plummer

BOB THIELE

title LIGHT MY FIRE / *year* 1967 / *label* Impulse! /
design Robert & Barbara Flynn / *photo* Charles
Stewart and Fred Seligo

This record contains an Impulse! all-star package.
Legendary jazz lensmen Charles Stewart and Fred
Seligo provide the cover portraits, while design and
layouting is courtesy of Viceroy's Robert and Barbara Flynn. Bob Thiele famously produced John
Coltrane's *A Love Supreme* (1964). On this self-
credited outing, Thiele assembled a host of jazz
talents, including guitar genius Gabor Szabo. **O**
Diese Platte ist ein „Impulse!-All-Star-Paket". Die
Coverporträts stammen von den legendären Jazzfo-
tografen Charles Stewart und Fred Seligo, Design

und Layout von Robert und Barbara Flynn. Bob
Thiele produzierte John Coltranes berühmtes Album *A Love Supreme* (1964). Auf dem unter seinem
Namen erschienenen Album versammelte Thiele
eine Reihe von Jazztalenten, darunter das Gitarren-
genie Gabor Szabo. **O**
Cet album rassemble les grands talents d'Impulse!.
Ce sont les légendaires photographes de jazz Charles
Stewart et Fred Seligo qui ont réalisé les portraits
de la couverture. Le graphisme et la composition
sont l'œuvre de Robert et Barbara Flynn, de Viceroy. Bob Thiele est connu pour avoir produit *A Love
Supreme* de John Coltrane (1964). Sur cet opus, il a
rassemblé une multitude de grands talents du jazz,
notamment le guitariste de génie Gabor Szabo.

**THE LUCKY
THOMPSON
QUARTET**

title LUCKY STRIKES / *year*
1964 / *label* Prestige / *design* Don
Schlitten / *photo* Don Schlitten

THE LUCKY THOMPSON QUARTET

1164 RIVERSIDE STEREO

THIS
HERE
IS
BOBBY
TIMMONS

THE PIANIST-COMPOSER
OF
"THIS HERE"
"MOANIN'"
"DAT DERE"

BOBBY TIMMONS

title THIS HERE IS BOBBY TIMMONS / *year*
1960 / *label* Riverside / *design* Paul Bacon, Ken
Braren, Harris Lewine / *photo* Lawrence Shustak

Paul Bacon is joined by Ken Braren and Harris
Lewine on this 1960 graphic design piece. The style
is beginning to show a more radical interplay between the photographic image, color and graphic
layout. A former member of Art Blakey's Jazz
Messengers, Timmons recorded this Riverside release as the first of only five albums the talented
soul jazz piano player would put on in his career. **O**
Für dieses Grafikdesignwerk hat sich der Designer
Paul Bacon 1960 mit den Fotografen Ken Braren
und Harris Lewine zusammengetan. In dem Stil

zeigen sich bereits die Anfänge eines radikalen Ver-
ständnisses vom Zusammenspiel zwischen Foto,
Farbe und dem grafischen Layout. Timmons war ein
ehemaliges Mitglied von Art Blakeys Jazz Messengers. Diese Aufnahme bei Riverside ist das erste von
nur fünf Alben, die der talentierte Soul-Jazz-Pianist
während seiner Karriere aufgenommen hat. **O**
Pour cette pochette de 1960, Paul Bacon est rejoint
par les photographes Ken Braren et Harris Lewine.
Le style commence à montrer une interaction plus
radicale entre la photographie, la couleur et la
composition graphique. Bobby Timmons était un
ancien membre des Jazz Messengers d'Art Blakey.
Cet album sorti chez Riverside fut son premier. Ce
talentueux pianiste de soul jazz n'allait en enregistrer que cinq dans sa carrière.

CAL TJADER

title CAL TJADER QUINTET /
year 1956 / *label* Fantasy / *design*
Betty Brader

V-8671

CAL TJADER

title ALONG COMES CAL / *year* 1967 / *label* Verve / *art* Jo Grey, Marvin Hayes / *design* Acy Lehman

Grammy Award-winning art director Acy Lehman produced covers for various genres. Among them are Herbie Hancock's movie soundtrack *Blow-Up* (MGM, 1966) and Lonnie Liston Smith's jazz funk classic *Expansions*. Lehman commissioned designers Jo Grey and Marvin Hayes to add a touch of "flower power" with this colorful illustration for Latin jazz champion, Cal Tjader. ⚪

Der Art Director und Grammy-Gewinner Acy Lehman gestaltete die Cover für verschiedene Genres. Darunter befindet sich Herbie Hancocks Soundtrack zu *Blow-Up* (MGM, 1966) und Lonnie Liston Smiths Jazz-Funk-Klassiker *Expansions* (Flying Dutchman, 1974). Lehman beauftragte die Designer Jo Grey und Marvin Hayes, diesem Album, das ein farbenfrohes Porträt des Latin-Jazz-Meisters Cal Tjader zeigt, einen „Flower Power"-Touch hinzuzufügen. ⚪

Acy Lehman est un directeur artistique lauréat d'un prix Grammy. Il a créé des pochettes pour différents styles de musique. Citons notamment *Blow-Up*, la musique du film composée par Herbie Hancock, et *Expansions*, un classique du jazz funk par Lonnie Liston. Acy Lehman avait demandé aux graphistes Jo Grey et Marvin Hayes d'ajouter une touche de flower power avec cette illustration très colorée pour le champion du jazz latin, Cal Tjader.

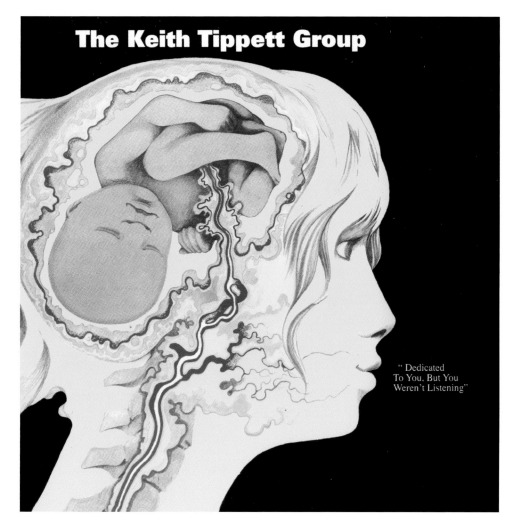

The Keith Tippett Group

" Dedicated
To You, But You
Weren't Listening"

THE KEITH TIPPETT GROUP
title DEDICATED TO YOU, BUT YOU WEREN'T
LISTENING / *year* 1971 / *label* Vertigo / *design*
Roger & Martyn Dean

This beautiful illustrational cover is a very early
collaboration between brothers Roger and Martyn
Dean. Trained in furniture design, Roger is the
more well known of the two. In 1970 he designed
the now world-famous logo for Richard Branson's
Virgin. Keith Tippett was among the new wave of
British free jazz musicians to infuse the genre with
progressive-rock elements. **O**
Dieses wunderbar illustrierte Cover entstammt
einer sehr frühen Zusammenarbeit zwischen den
Brüdern Roger und Martyn Dean. Roger, der ein

Design-Diplom mit Schwerpunkt Möbeldesign be-
saß, ist der bekanntere der Brüder. 1970 gestaltete
er das inzwischen weltberühmte Logo für Richard
Bransons Label Virgin. Keith Tippett gehörte zu
der neuen Generation britischer Free-Jazz-Musiker
und vermischte das Genre mit progressiven Rock-
elementen. **O**
Cette couverture magnifiquement illustrée est le
fruit de l'une des premières collaborations entre les
frères Roger et Martyn Dean. Créateur de meubles
de formation, Roger est le plus connu des deux. En
1970, il créa le logo aujourd'hui célèbre de l'entreprise de Richard Branson, Virgin. Keith Tippett
appartenait à la nouvelle vague de musiciens de free
jazz britanniques qui ont intégré au genre des éléments de rock progressif.

**CHARLES TOLLIVER
MUSIC INC &
ORCHESTRA**

title IMPACT / *year* 1975 /
label Strata-East / *design* Ted
Plair / *photo* Ed Hamilton

BURT GOLDBLATT

MEL TORMÉ
with
the marty paich dek-tette

MEL TORMÉ

title MEL TORMÉ WITH THE
MARTY PAICH DEK-TETTE /
year 1956 / *label* Bethlehem /
design Burt Goldblatt

THE STAN TRACEY
QUARTET

title JAZZ SUITE / *year* 1965 /
label Columbia / *design*
Denis Preston / *photo* Patrick
Gwynn-Jones

"*I'm more mystified than proud.
Mystified by the success it has had.*"
— Stan Tracey on *Jazz Suite*

LENNIE TRISTANO
title THE NEW TRISTANO /
year 1960 / *label* Atlantic /
design Loring Eutemey / *photo*
Lee Friedlander

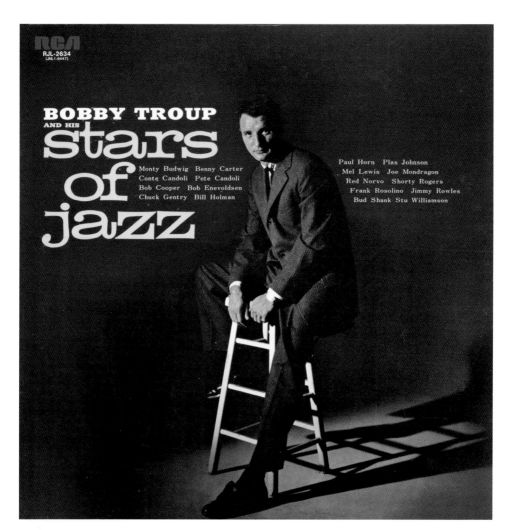

BOBBY TROUP
title BOBBY TROUP AND
HIS STARS OF JAZZ /
year 1958 / *label* RCA

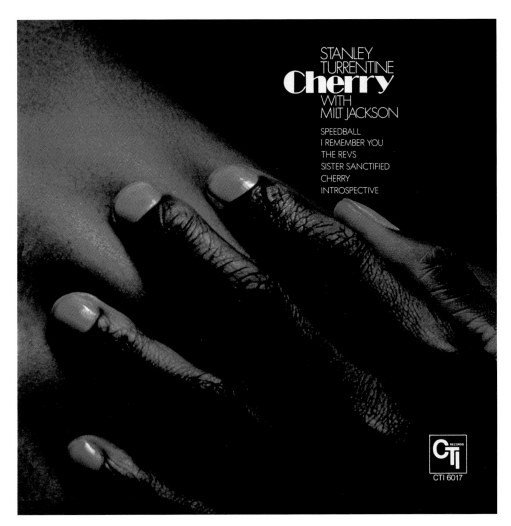

STANLEY
TURRENTINE
Cherry
WITH
MILT JACKSON

SPEEDBALL
I REMEMBER YOU
THE REVS
SISTER SANCTIFIED
CHERRY
INTROSPECTIVE

CTI RECORDS

CTI 6017

STANLEY TURRENTINE
title CHERRY / *year* 1972 / *label* CTI /
design Bob Ciano / *photo* Pete Turner

CTI's art director, Bob Ciano, cropped a close-up image from Pete Turner's photo essay for *Look* magazine entitled "Black Beauty" to create this sensual gatefold sleeve. Stanley Turrentine was a tenor sax player who recorded with the great organist Jimmy Smith for Blue Note. He married another organist, Shirley Scott, with whom he collaborated frequently. *Cherry* is one of CTI's funkiest jazz R&B offerings. **O**

Der Art Director von CTI, Bob Ciano, hat eine Nahaufnahme aus Pete Turners Fotoessay „Black Beauty" für das *Look*-Magazin zurechtgeschnitten, um diese sinnliche Klapphülle zu gestalten. Stanley Turrentine, Tenorsaxofonist, machte mit dem großartigen Organisten Jimmy Smith Aufnahmen für Blue Note. Er heiratete Shirley Scott, mit der er oft zusammenarbeitete. *Cherry* ist eine der funkigsten Jazz-R'n'B-Platten von CTI. **O**

Pour cette pochette à volet sensuelle, le directeur artistique de CTI, Bob Ciano, a recadré une photo que Pete Turner avait réalisée dans le cadre d'un article pour le magazine *Look* intitulé « Black Beauty ». Stanley Turrentine jouait du saxophone ténor et a enregistré avec le grand organiste Jimmy Smith pour Blue Note. Il épousa une autre organiste, Shirley Scott, avec qui il a souvent joué. *Cherry* est l'un des albums de R&B les plus funky de CTI.

STANLEY TURRENTINE

title JOYRIDE / *year* 1965 / *label* Blue Note / *design* Reid Miles / *photo* Reid Miles

MCCOY TYNER

title THE REAL MCCOY / *year* 1967 / *label* Blue Note / *design* Reid Miles / *photo* Francis Wolff

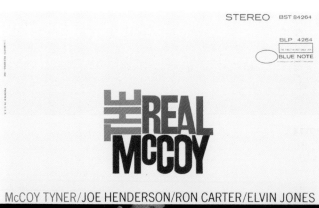

STEREO
SES-1972-4

MTUME UMOJA ENSEMBLE
title ALKEBU-LAN, LAND OF THE BLACKS /
year 1971 / *label* Strata-East / *design* Wabembe

This amazing cover is by an unknown artist called
Wabembe. This double album is a live session re-
corded at The East in New York, featuring Miles
Davis' fusion percussionist James Mtume and Car-
los Garnett on tenor and flute, Gary Bartz on saxes,
Leroy Jenkins on violin, etc. Poetry (Yusef Iman and
Weusi Kuumba) and chanting can be heard through-
out the recording, creating a cacophony of sound. **o**
Dieses fantastische Cover stammt von dem unbe-
kannten Künstler Wabembe. Das Doppelalbum
enthält eine Livesession, die in „The East" in New
York aufgenommen wurde. Zu der Formation ge-

hörten u.a. Miles Davis' Fusion-Perkussionist
James Mtume, Carlos Garnett am Tenorsaxofon
und an der Flöte, Gary Bartz am Alt- und Sopransaxofon sowie Leroy Jenkins an der Geige. Gedichte
(Yusef Iman und Weusi Kuumba) und Gesang be-
gleiten die gesamte Aufnahme und erzeugen eine
gewisse Kakofonie. **o**
Cette pochette magnifique est l'œuvre d'un artiste
inconnu, Wabembe. Ce double album est une séance
enregistrée en public à The East, à New York, avec
le percussionniste fusion de Miles Davis, James
Mtume, Carlos Garnett au saxo ténor et à la flûte,
Gary Bartz aux saxophones, Leroy Jenkins au
violon, etc. On entend de la poésie (Yusef Iman et
Weusi Kuumba) et des chants tout le long du
disque, ce qui crée une véritable cacophonie.

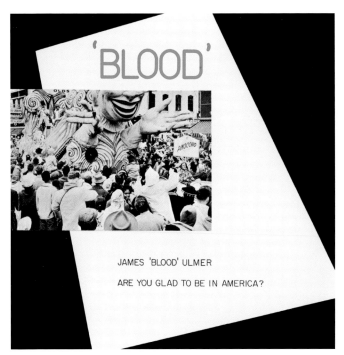

JAMES 'BLOOD' ULMER

title ARE YOU GLAD TO
BE IN AMERICA? / *year*
1980 / *label* Rough Trade

MICHAL URBANIAK CONSTELLATION

title MICHAL URBANIAK
CONSTELLATION – IN
CONCERT / *year* 1973 /
label Muza / *design* Marek
Karewicz / *photo* Marek
Karewicz

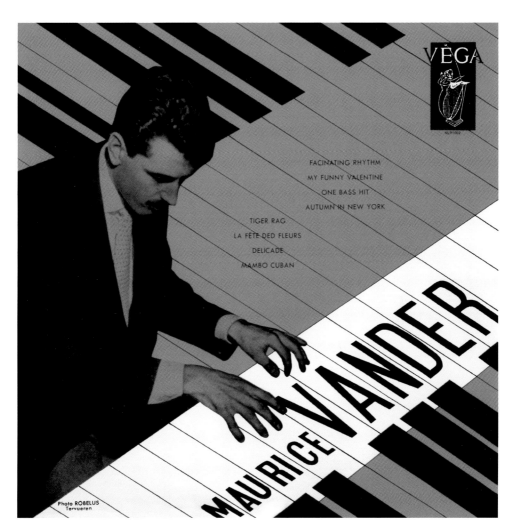

MAURICE VANDER
title MAURICE VANDER /
year 1955 / *label* Disques Vega /
photo Robelus Tervueren

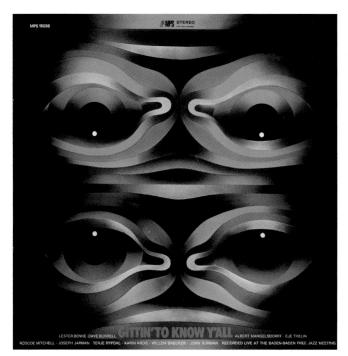

VARIOUS

title GITTIN'TO KNOW
Y'ALL / *year* 1969 / *label*
MPS / *design* Wolfgang
Baumann / *photo* Wolfgang
Baumann

VARIOUS

title BEST COAST JAZZ /
year 1954 / *label* EmArcy

VARIOUS

title I LIKE JAZZ / *year* 1955 /
label Columbia / *photo* Alfred Gescheidt

Born in New York, Alfred Gescheidt enjoyed a long
career as an artist and photographer. He is best
remembered for his satirical photomontages. Gescheidt's work has been widely published, including
in *Esquire*, *Newsweek* and *Life* magazine. For a few
years he also had his own space in *OUI* magazine
called "Gescheidt's World." Over his career he produced over 150 album covers. ○
Der gebürtige New Yorker Alfred Gescheidt genoss
eine lange Karriere als Künstler und Fotograf. Er
ist vor allem für seine satirischen Fotomontagen

bekannt. Gescheidts Arbeiten wurden in vielen
Zeitschriften veröffentlicht, darunter *Esquire*,
Newsweek und das *Life*-Magazin. Einige Jahre lang
hatte er im *OUI*-Magazin seine eigene Rubrik
„Gescheidt's World". Während seiner Schaffens-
phase gestaltete er über 150 Cover. ○
Alfred Gescheidt est né à New York et a connu une
longue carrière en tant qu'artiste et photographe.
On se souvient surtout de lui pour ses photomontages satiriques. Son travail est apparu dans de
nombreuses publications, notamment dans les magazines *Esquire*, *Newsweek* et *Life*. Pendant quelques
années, il a eu un espace réservé dans le magazine
OUI, appelé «Gescheidt's World.» Il a créé plus de
150 pochettes d'album au cours de sa carrière.

GEORGE WEIN PRESENTS

Jazz

at the

Boston

Arts

Festival

featuring

Ruby Braff • trumpet
Samuel Margolis • tenor sax
Buzzy Drootin • drums
Vic Dickinson • trombone
John Field . bass
Al Drootin • clarinet
Dick Lefave • trumpet
George Wein • piano

BURT GOLDBLATT

VARIOUS

title JAZZ AT THE BOSTON ARTS FESTIVAL /
year 1954 / *label* Storyville / *design* Burt Goldblatt

The name Storyville has carried widely in the history of jazz. It was the name of the red light district of New Orleans, frequented by ragtime musicians and Dixieland bands. George Wein can be described as the Godfather of the modern jazz festival. In 1954 he coordinated the very first Newport Jazz Festival in Rhode Island, which became a blueprint for jazz festivals around the world. **o**
Der Name Storyville ist in der Jazzgeschichte weithin bekannt. Es ist der Name eines Rotlichtbezirks in New Orleans, der von Ragtimemusikern und

Dixielandbands besucht wurde. George Wein kann als Erfinder der Modern-Jazz-Festivals bezeichnet werden. 1954 organisierte er das allererste Newport Jazz Festival auf Rhode Island, das als Vorbild für Jazzfestivals in der ganzen Welt diente. **o**
On retrouve souvent le nom de Storyville dans l'histoire du jazz. C'était le quartier chaud de la Nouvelle-Orléans, fréquenté par les musiciens de ragtime et les orchestres de dixieland. On peut qualifier George Wein de parrain du festival de jazz moderne. C'est lui qui a coordonné le tout premier Newport Jazz Festival à Rhode Island en 1954. Les autres festivals de jazz des quatre coins du globe s'en sont inspirés.

VARIOUS

title STAN KENTON
PRESENTS / *year* 1950 /
label Capitol

VARIOUS
title FREEDOM PRINCIPLE –
ACID JAZZ & OTHER ILLICIT
GROOVES VOL. 2 / *year* 1989 /
label Polydor / *design* Andrew
Sutton

VARIOUS

title JAM SESSION #3 /
year 1953 / *label* Clef /
design David Stone Martin

VARIOUS

title JAZZ MADE IN
GERMANY / *year* 1953 /
label Polydor

SARAH VAUGHAN
title THE EXPLOSIVE SIDE
OF SARAH VAUGHAN /
year 1963 / *label* Columbia

SARAH VAUGHAN
AND HER TRIO
title SWINGIN' EASY /
year 1954 / *label* EmArcy

SARAH VAUGHAN

title AFTER HOURS AT THE
LONDON HOUSE / *year* 1958 /
label Mercury / *design* Emmett
McBain / *photo* Don Bronstein

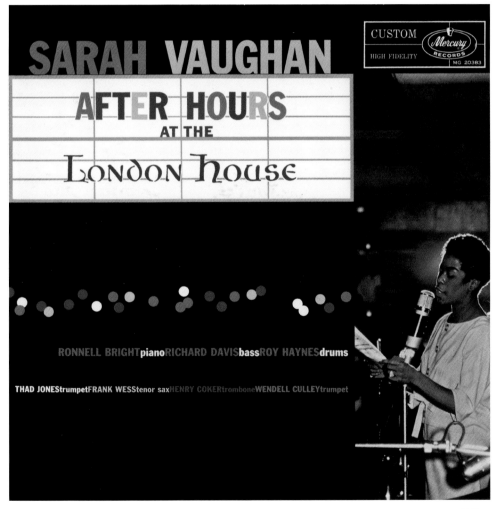

STRATA-EAST
STEREO SES-7431

HAROLD VICK

title DON'T LOOK BACK / *year* 1974 /
label Strata-East / *design* Creative Hands, Inc. /
photo Jim Dun

Designed by the obscure Creative Hands, Inc., with photography credited to Jim Dun, this two-tone cover is reminiscent of many of the early Blue Note 10-inch micro-groove releases. A highly underrated tenorist, noted for his funky soul jazz style of playing, Harold Vick earned his place in jazz history through his work with the likes of organists Brother Jack McDuff and Big John Patton. ○

Von der unbekannten Firma Creative Hands, Inc., aus Fotografien von Jim Dun gestaltet, erinnert dieses zweifarbige Cover an manche der frühen 10-Inch-Mikrorillen-Platten von Blue Note. Der stark unterschätzte Tenorsaxofonist Harold Vick ist bekannt für seinen funkigen Soul-Jazz-Stil und erlangte seinen Platz in der Geschichte des Jazz durch seine Zusammenarbeit mit Künstlern wie den Organisten Brother Jack McDuff und Big John Patton. ○

Créée par une société de graphisme inconnue, Creative Hands, Inc., avec une photographie attribuée à Jim Dun, cette pochette en deux tons évoque les premiers disques 25 cm de la série microgroove de Blue Note. Harold Vick est un joueur de saxo ténor très sous-estimé, avec un jeu soul jazz teinté de funk. Il a gagné sa place dans l'histoire du jazz en travaillant avec des grandes pointures de l'orgue comme Brother Jack McDuff et Big John Patton.

MAL WALDRON
title SWEET LOVE, BITTER /
year 1967 / *label* Impulse! /
design Robert Flynn/Viceroy

STEREO

ORIGINAL SOUND TRACK
COMPOSED AND PLAYED BY MAL WALDRON

GERALD KLEPPEL AND ROBERT FERMAN PRESENT
Don MURRAY • Dick GREGORY • Diane VARSI
SWEET LOVE, BITTER
with ROBERT HOOKS and JERI ARCHER

BASED ON THE NOVEL, "NIGHT SONG" BY JOHN A. WILLIAMS
SCREENPLAY BY HERBERT DANSKA AND LEWIS JACOBS
MUSIC COMPOSED AND PLAYED BY MAL WALDRON
EDITED BY GERALD KLEPPEL
DIRECTOR OF PHOTOGRAPHY: VICTOR SOLOW
PRODUCTION SUPERVISED BY LOUIS KELLMAN
PRODUCED BY LEWIS JACOBS
DIRECTED BY HERBERT DANSKA
EXECUTIVE PRODUCERS: GERALD KLEPPEL AND ROBERT FERMAN
A FILM 2 ASSOCIATES RELEASE

impulse!
A-9142

MAL WALDRON **453**

george
wallington
showcase

arrangements by
QUINCY JONES

FRANK FOSTER *tenor sax*
DAVE BURNS *trumpet*
JAMES CLEVELAND *trombone*
DANNY BANK *baritone sax*
OSCAR PETTIFORD *bass*
KENNY CLARKE *drums*

Hermansader | Wolff

GEORGE WALLINGTON

title GEORGE WALLINGTON SHOWCASE /
year 1954 / *label* Blue Note / *design* John
Hermansader / *photo* Francis Wolff

This fabulous cover design by John Hermansader
shows not only his talent for combining abstract
pictorial elements with photography, provided here
by Francis Wolff, but his clever eye for reprographic
composition. Sicilian pianist George Wallington
(born Giacinto Figlia) was an accomplished bop
pianist and composer. He took early retirement in
1960 and returned to playing in 1984. ○
Das fabelhafte Coverdesign von John Hermansader
zeigt nicht nur sein Talent dafür, abstrakte Bild-
elemente mit der Fotografie von Francis Wolff zu

verbinden, sondern auch sein Talent für reprografi-
sche Zusammenstellungen. Der sizilianische Pianist
George Wallington (geboren als Giacinto Figlia) war
ein begnadeter Bop-Pianist und Komponist. Er zog
sich bereits 1960 aus dem Musikgeschäft zurück,
spielte aber ab 1984 wieder öffentlich. ○
Cette fabuleuse pochette de John Hermansader
montre non seulement son talent pour combiner les
éléments illustratifs abstraits et la photographie, ici
de Francis Wolff, mais également son coup d'œil
pour la composition et la reprographie. Le Sicilien
George Wallington (né Giacinto Figlia) était un
pianiste et compositeur de bop accompli. Il prit une
retraite anticipée en 1960 et recommença à jouer
en 1984.

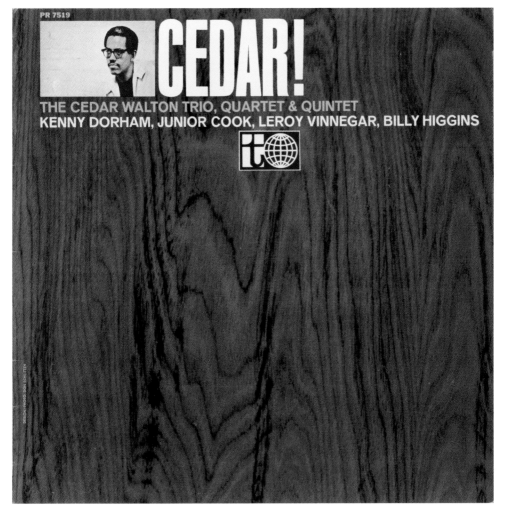

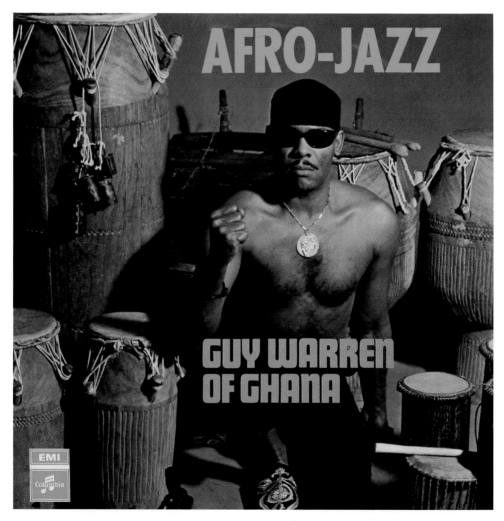

GUY WARREN OF GHANA

title AFRO-JAZZ / *year* 1969 / *label* EMI
Columbia / *design* Denis Preston / *photo*
William Holden

This unusual cover could easily be mistaken for the
latest offering by 50 Cent or Wu Tang Clan, were it
not for its 1969 release – predating gangsta rap
album design by some 30 years. Its designer was
none other than British recording boss and jazz
benefactor Denis Preston. Guy Warren, also known
as Kofi Ghanaba, is often referred to as the father
of Afro-beat jazz. ○
Dieses ungewöhnliche Cover könnte leicht mit einer
der neuesten Veröffentlichungen von 50 Cent oder
dem Wu Tang Clan verwechselt werden, dabei
stammt es aus dem Jahr 1963 und war dem
Gangsta-Rap-Albumdesign um etwa 30 Jahre voraus. Der Designer war niemand anderes als der
britische Plattenboss und Jazzmäzen Denis Preston.
Guy Warren, auch bekannt als Kofi Ghanaba, wird
oft als der Vater des Afrobeat-Jazz bezeichnet. ○
Cette pochette inhabituelle aurait très bien pu
appartenir au dernier album de 50 Cent ou de Wu
Tang Clan, mais ce disque est sorti en 1963, une
trentaine d'années avant l'avènement du gangsta
rap. Son auteur n'est autre que Denis Preston,
grand chef de l'industrie du disque britannique et
mécène du jazz. Guy Warren, également connu sous
le nom de Kofi Ghanaba, est souvent qualifié de père
du jazz afro-beat.

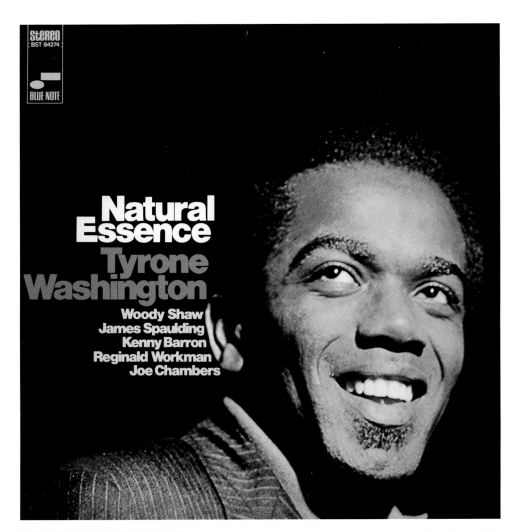

TYRONE WASHINGTON

title NATURAL ESSENCE / *year* 1969 / *label*
Blue Note / *design* Forlenza Venosa Associates /
photo Francis Wolff

"In 1965 I left Columbia to form my own advertising agency in partnership with a friend. Some of
the commercial projects included designing numer-
ous album covers for record companies such as
Motown, Mercury, Decca, and the great jazz label
Blue Note, for whom I personally designed all the
album covers from 1967 to 1970. In the process I
got to shmooze with many jazz greats of that period." — Robert Venosa, designer **O**

„1965 verließ ich Columbia, um zusammen mit
einem Freund meine eigene Werbeagentur zu grün-

den. Zu den Aufträgen gehörte die Gestaltung zahlreicher Cover für Plattenfirmen wie Motown, Mercury, Decca und das großartige Jazzlabel Blue Note,
für welches ich persönlich zwischen 1967 und
1970 alle Cover gestaltete. So konnte ich mit vielen
Jazzgrößen der damaligen Zeit ein Schwätzchen
halten." — Robert Venosa, Designer **O**

« En 1965, j'ai quitté Columbia pour créer ma
propre agence de publicité avec un ami. Parmi nos
projets commerciaux, nous avons créé de nombreuses pochettes pour des maisons de disques
comme Motown, Mercury, Decca et le grand label de
jazz Blue Note, pour qui j'ai personnellement créé
toutes les pochettes de 1967 à 1970. C'est comme
ça que j'ai rencontré de nombreux grands du jazz de
cette époque. » — Robert Venosa, graphiste

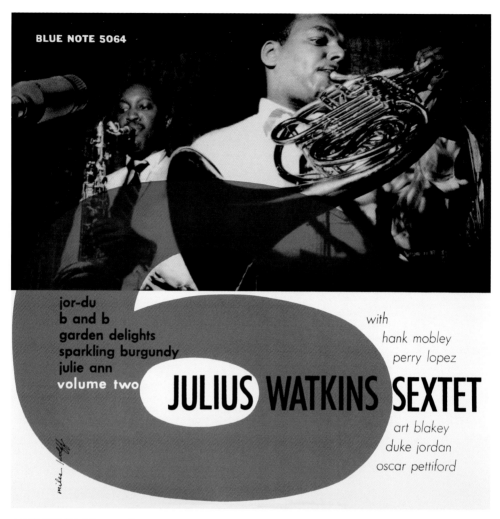

BLUE NOTE 5064

jor-du
b and b
garden delights
sparkling burgundy
julie ann
volume two

with
hank mobley
perry lopez

JULIUS WATKINS SEXTET

art blakey
duke jordan
oscar pettiford

JULIUS WATKINS SEXTET

title JULIUS WATKINS SEXTET VOL. 2 /
year 1955 / *label* Blue Note / *design* Reid Miles /
photo Francis Wolff

It's not that Blue Note was visually a one-man
band, but Reid Miles was the prodigal soloist. He
galvanized the greatness around him to create
legend, transforming the constituent parts into
genre-redefining symphonies of fantastic form and
color. **o**
Blue Note war keine One-Man-Band, aber Reid
Miles war darin der einsame Solist. Er verwandelte

seine großartige Umgebung in eine Legende, indem
er einzelne Teile derselben in Symphonien aus
fantastischen Formen und Farben verwandelte, die
das Genre neu definierten. **o**
La partie visuelle de Blue Note n'était pas vraiment
l'affaire d'un seul homme, mais Reid Miles était le
soliste prodigue. Il a galvanisé la grandeur qui
l'entourait pour créer une légende, en transformant
les différents éléments constitutifs en symphonies
fantastiques qui réinventaient les genres.

WEATHER REPORT
title HEAVY WEATHER / *year*
1977 / *label* CBS / *ad* Lou
Beach / *design* Nancy Donald

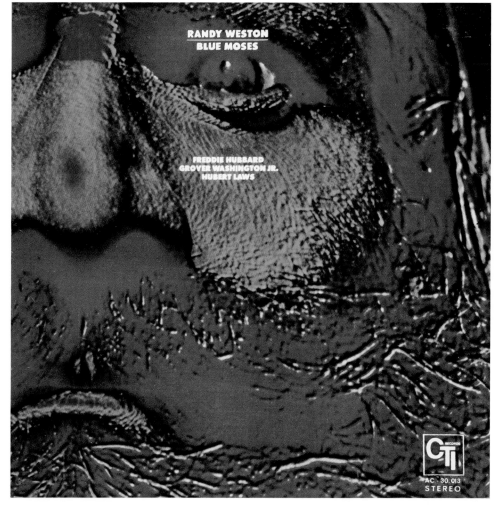

RANDY WESTON

title BLUE MOSES / *year* 1972 / *label* CTI /
design Bob Ciano / *photo* Pete Turner

The psychedelic close-up is that of an Indian holy
man that Pete Turner had taken near the river
Ganges in India. Brooklyn-born pianist, composer
and bandleader Randy Weston infused African
sounds and rhythms into his music, as is evident on
this album, which features other CTI heavyweights,
Freddie Hubbard, Hubert Laws and Grover Washington Jr. ○
Auf dem Cover ist in einer psychedelisch wirkenden
Nahaufnahme ein indischer Heiliger zu sehen, den
Pete Turner in der Nähe des Ganges fotografiert

hatte. Der in Brooklyn geborene Pianist, Komponist
und Bandleader Randy Weston verwendete in seiner
Musik afrikanische Klänge und Rhythmen – auf
diesem Album, auf dem die CTI-Größen Freddie
Hubbard, Hubert Laws und Grover Washington Jr.
mitwirken, tritt dieses Phänomen besonders stark
hervor. ○
C'est Pete Turner qui a pris ce gros plan psychédélique d'un sâdhu près du Gange, en Inde. Originaire
de Brooklyn, le pianiste, compositeur et leader de
groupe Randy Weston introduisait des sons et des
rythmes africains dans sa musique, comme le
montre cet album où l'on retrouve d'autres poids
lourds de CTI, Freddie Hubbard, Hubert Laws et
Grover Washington Jr.

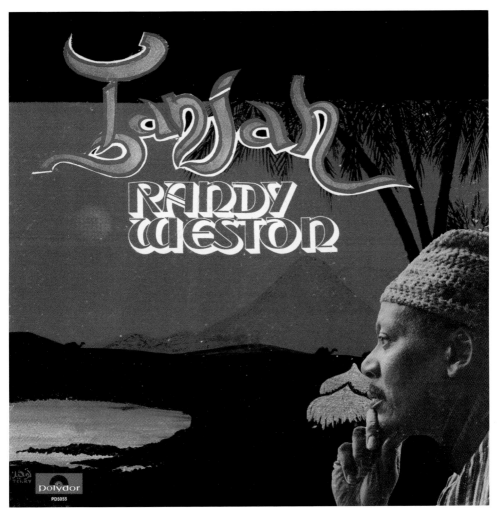

RANDY WESTON

title TANJAH / *year* 1973 /
label Polydor

THE JOE WILDER QUARTET

title JAZZ FROM PETER GUNN /
year 1959 / *label* Columbia

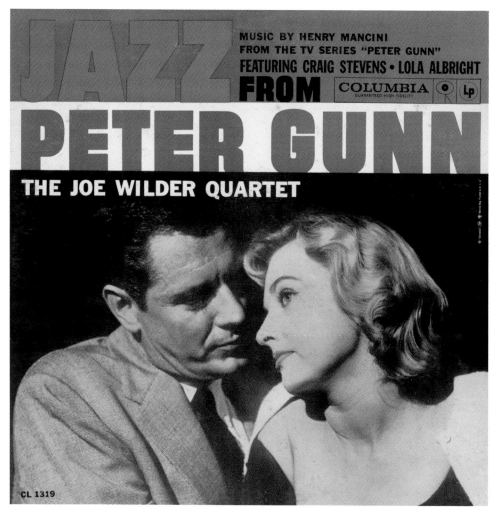

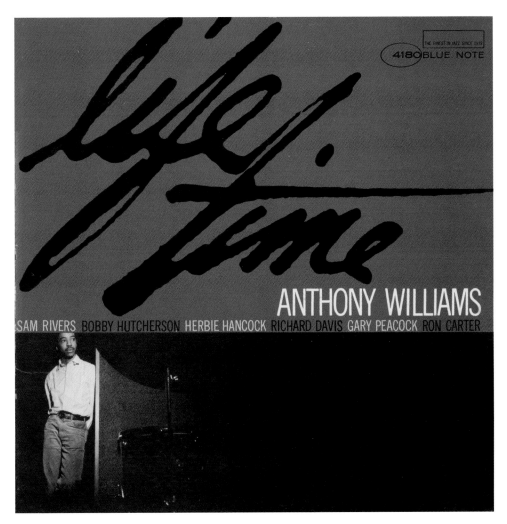

ANTHONY WILLIAMS
title LIFE TIME / *year* 1964 /
label Blue Note / *design* Reid
Miles / *photo* Francis Wolff

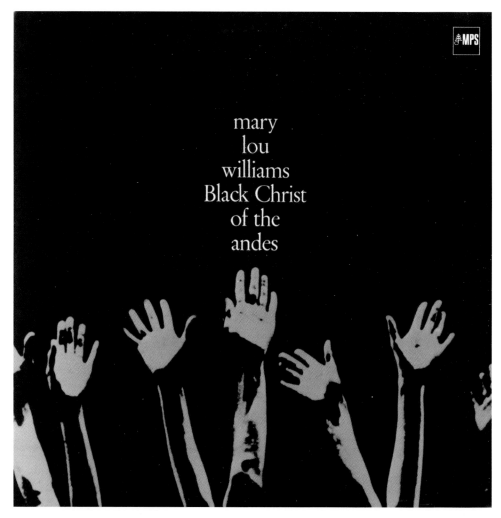

MARY LOU WILLIAMS

title BLACK CHRIST OF THE ANDES /
year 1963 / *label* MPS / *design* Gigi Berendt /
photo Charles Stewart

Photographer Charles Stewart provided the cover image for designer Gigi Berendt. Mary Lou Williams was a leading exponent of stride piano, a difficult style of piano playing similar to ragtime, developed in New York's Harlem during the First World War. One of the most influential women in jazz, Williams was mentor to the likes of Thelonious Monk and Charlie Parker. **O**
Der Fotograf Charles Stewart lieferte das Coverbild für diese von Gigi Berendt designte Platte. Mary Lou Williams gilt als eine der führenden Virtuosin-

nen des „Stride Piano", eines komplexen Solo-Klavierstils, der dem Ragtime ähnelt und während des Ersten Weltkrieges in Harlem entwickelt wurde. Als eine der einflussreichsten Frauen des Jazz beriet und unterstützte sie verschiedene Musiker, darunter Thelonious Monk und Charlie Parker. **O**
C'est le photographe Charles Stewart qui a fourni cette image à Gigi Berendt. Mary Lou Williams était l'une des meilleures représentantes du piano stride, un style de jeu difficile similaire au ragtime, apparu à New York dans le quartier de Harlem pendant la Première Guerre mondiale. Elle fut l'une des femmes les plus influentes dans le monde du jazz, et elle a été le mentor de musiciens de l'envergure de Thelonious Monk et Charlie Parker.

**MARY LOU
WILLIAMS' TRIO**
title ZODIAC SUITE /
year 1945 / *label* Folkways

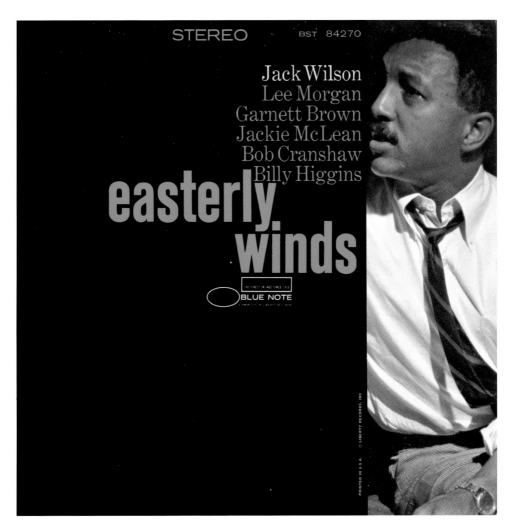

JACK WILSON
title EASTERLY WINDS /
year 1967 / *label* Blue Note /
design Reid Miles / *photo*
Francis Wolff

Nancy Wilson/Cannonball Adderley

41
minutes
59
seconds
of jazz!

Capitol

© CAPITOL RECORDS, INC.

NANCY WILSON WITH CANNONBALL ADDERLEY

title NANCY WILSON/CANNONBALL ADDERLEY / *year* 1962 / *label* Capitol / *design* Franko Caligiuri

Franko Caligiuri's name may not be instantly recognizable, though as a long-serving art director he oversaw the design of several covers for artists such as Nat King Cole and Bobby Hutcherson. ○

Franko Caligiuris Name ist eher unbekannt geblieben, obwohl er lange Jahre als Art Director für zahlreiche Coverdesigns verantwortlich war, darunter für Nat King Cole und Bobby Hutcherson. ○
Le nom de Franko Caligiuri n'est peut-être pas très connu, pourtant il a longtemps été directeur artistique et a supervisé la création de plusieurs pochettes pour des artistes comme Nat King Cole et Bobby Hutcherson.

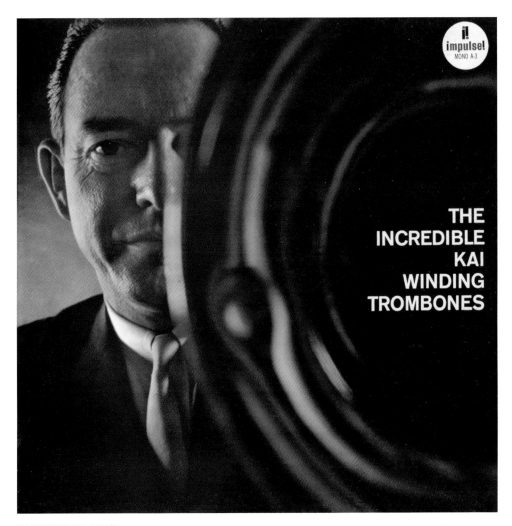

THE
INCREDIBLE
KAI
WINDING
TROMBONES

KAI WINDING

title THE INCREDIBLE KAI WINDING
TROMBONES / *year* 1961 / *label* Impulse! / *design*
Robert Flynn/Viceroy / *photo* Arnold Newman

Arnold Newman is regarded as one of the most
important photographers of the 20th century. During his illustrious career, Newman has photographed world leaders, artists and musicians. One
half of a popular trombone duo with J.J. Johnson,
Danish-born Kai Winding devoted his career to
exploring the broad range of his instrument. **O**
Arnold Newman gilt als einer der wichtigsten Fotografen des 20. Jahrhunderts. Während seiner glän-

zenden Karriere lichtete er führende politische
Persönlichkeiten, Künstler und Musiker ab. Die
Karriere des in Dänemark geborenen Kai Winding,
der mit J.J. Johnson zusammen ein Posaunenduo
bildete, war darauf ausgerichtet, die Möglichkeiten
seines Instrumentes voll auszuschöpfen. **O**
Arnold Newman est considéré comme l'un des
photographes les plus importants du XXe siècle. Au
cours de son illustre carrière, il a photographié des
chefs d'État, des artistes et des musiciens. Le Danois Kai Winding faisait partie d'un duo de trombones populaire avec J.J. Johnson. Il a consacré sa
carrière à l'exploration de son instrument.

MURIEL WINSTON

title "A FRESH VIEWPOINT" AND MURIEL
WINSTON / *year* 1974 / *label* Strata-East / *art*
Jeri Leonard Lambert / *design* Sandy Williams

This richly colored gatefold cover painting is attributed to an unknown artist named Jeri Leonard Lambert, with design by Sandy Williams, who also produced the cover for the 1975 Strata release, *Colors* by The Brass Company. This rare recording by vocalist Muriel Winston is somewhat of an oddity. It features a set of pseudo-children's songs conducted in a classroom style. **o**

Das farbenfrohe Gemälde auf diesem Klappcover wird einem Künstler namens Jeri Leonard Lambert zugeschrieben. Sandy Williams ist auch für das Cover der 1975 herausgekommenen Platte *Colors* der Brass Company verantwortlich. Die Sängerin Muriel Winston schuf mit dieser schwer aufzutreibenden Aufnahme eine wahrhafte Kuriosität. Darauf ist eine Sammlung von Pseudo-Kinderliedern enthalten, die klingen, als wären sie in einem Klassenzimmer aufgenommen worden. **o**

Le tableau paré de riches couleurs de cette pochette à volet est attribué à un artiste inconnu, Jeri Leonard Lambert. Le graphisme est de Sandy Williams, qui a également produit la pochette de *Colors*, un album de The Brass Company sorti chez Strata en 1975. Cet enregistrement rare de la chanteuse Muriel Winston est une vraie petite curiosité. On y trouve des sortes de chansons pour enfants chantées dans un style scolaire. **o**

NORMA WINSTONE
title EDGE OF TIME /
year 1972 / *label* Argo /
design Terry Eden

**JIMMY WOODS
SEXTET**
title CONFLICT / *year* 1963 /
label Contemporary

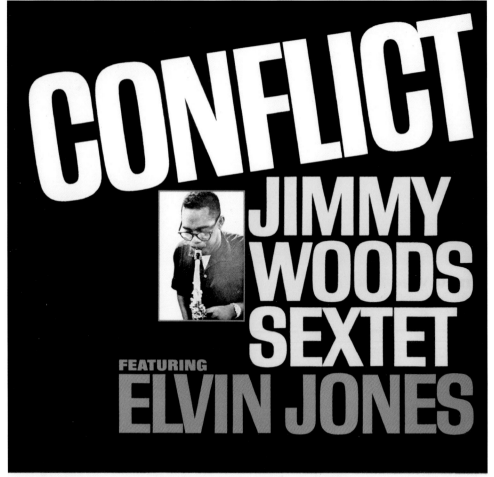

PHIL WOODS

title RIGHTS OF SWING / *year* 1961 / *label* Candid / *design* Frank Gauna / *photo* Frank Gauna

Frank Gauna was the in-house designer for the short-lived Candid Records. The brainchild of Archie Bleyer, boss of the New York-based Cadence label, who hired the renowned critic Nat Hentoff to oversee the label's releases. Hentoff, who was also a civil rights activist, assembled a juxtaposing roster of artists, including Charles Mingus, Lightning Hopkins, and Phil Woods. Because of a lack of financial backing the label closed at the end of 1961. **O**
Frank Gauna arbeitete als fest angestellter Designer für das nur kurz existierende Label Candid Records mit Sitz in New York. Gründer Archie Bleyer stellte den renommierten Kritiker Nat Hentoff ein, um ihn mit den Veröffentlichungen des Labels zu beauftragen. Der als Bürgerrechtler aktive Henthoff holte eine ganze Reihe bekannter Künstler an Bord des Labels, darunter Charles Mingus, Lightning Hopkins und Phil Woods. Aufgrund finanzieller Probleme wurde Candid Ende 1961 aufgelöst. **O**
Frank Gauna était le graphiste du label Candid Records, qui connut une courte existence. Le patron Archie Bleyer engagea le célèbre critique Nat Hentoff pour superviser les albums du label. Ce dernier, défenseur actif de la cause des droits civils, rassembla une équipe d'artistes qui comprenait Charles Mingus, Lightning Hopkins et Phil Woods avec cet album post-bop. Le manque de financement conduisit à la fermeture définitive du label en 1961.

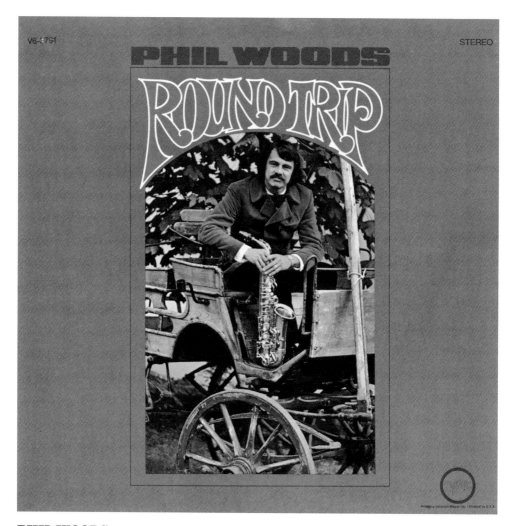

PHIL WOODS

title ROUND TRIP / *year*
1969 /
label Verve / *design* Elaine
Gongora / *photo* Fred Seligo,
Charles Stewart

PHIL WOODS AND HIS EUROPEAN RHYTHM MACHINE

title PHIL WOODS AND
HIS EUROPEAN RHYTHM
MACHINE / *year* 1970 / *label*
Pierre Cardin / *ad* Rowland
Emett / *design* Rowland Emett

PIERRE CARDIN Présente:

PHIL WOODS and his European Rhythm Machine

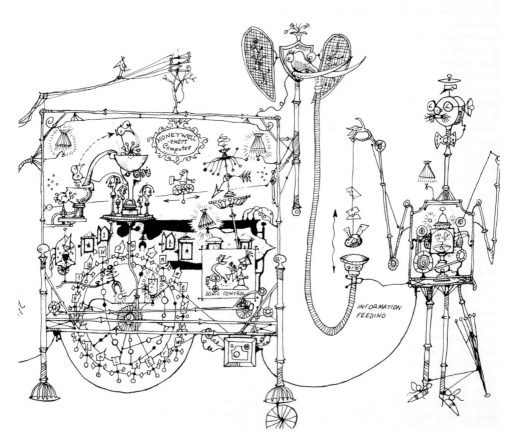

LESTER YOUNG
title COLLATES N° 2 / *year* 1951 / *label* Clef / *design* David Stone Martin

LESTER YOUNG
title TENOR SAX SOLOS / *label* Savoy

SHOICHI YUI
title THE AMAZING
SHOICHI YUI VOL. 2 /
label Blue Note

**ATTILA ZOLLER /
HANS KOLLER /
MARTIAL SOLAL**
title ZOLLER – KOLLER
– SOLAL / *year* 1965 /
label MPS / *photo* Josef
Werkmeister

DJs' TOP-10 LISTS

HAPPENINGS
BOBBY HUTCHERSON
HERBIE HANCOCK/BOB CRANSHAW/JOE CHAMBERS

STEREO
THE FINEST IN JAZZ SINCE 1939
84231 BLUE NOTE

BOBBY
HUTCHERSON
title HAPPENINGS /
year 1966 / *label* Blue Note

AMIR ABDULLAH

THE KINGS OF DIGGIN'

Bitten by the dusty groove bug at the tender age of five in 1986, Brooklyn-based Amir Abdullah is much more than just a crate digger. He is a beat archaeologist, archivist, DJ and mix artist. One half of the internationally renowned beat rescuers and mix-tape artists Kon & Amir, he met his music collaborator Christian "Kon" Taylor in 1996 at a record store in Boston called Biscuit Head Records. Kon & Amir soon joined ranks with the mighty Japanese crate-digging DJ Muro to immortalize their vinyl discoveries in *The Kings of Diggin'* (2006) compilation, part of the BBE/Rapster label's iconic *Kings of...* mix series.

Der in Brooklyn lebende Amir Abdullah ist mehr als nur ein Plattensammler. Er ist Musik-Archäologe, Archivist, DJ und Mix-künstler. Als eine Hälfte des international bekannten Klangbewahrer- und Mixtape-Künstlerduos Kon & Amir lernte er seinen Musikkollegen Christian „Kon" Taylor im Jahre 1996 im Plattenladen Biscuit Head Records in Boston kennen. Kon & Amir schlossen sich bald mit dem berühmten

japanischen „Crate Digger" DJ Muro zu-sammen, um ihre Vinyl-Entdeckungen mit der Compilation *The Kings of Diggin'* (2006), die Teil der Serie *Kings of...* des Labels BBE/Rapster ist, unsterblich zu machen.

Contaminé par le virus du groove à l'âge tendre de cinq ans en 1986, Amir Abdullah vit à Brooklyn et est bien plus qu'un collec-tionneur enthousiaste. C'est un archéologue et archiviste du rythme, un DJ et un artiste du mixage. Il fait partie de Kon & Amir, un duo de sauveteurs de rythmes et de compo-siteurs de compilations remixées à la re-nommée internationale. Amir a rencontré son acolyte Christian « Kon » Taylor en 1996 dans un magasin de disques de Boston, Biscuit Head Records. Kon & Amir n'ont pas tardé à faire équipe avec le grand explo-rateur de bacs à disques japonais DJ Muro pour immortaliser leurs découvertes viny-liques sur la compilation *The Kings of Diggin'* (2006), dans le cadre de la série emblématique de mixtapes *Kings of...* du label BBE/Rapster.

1. GABOR SZABO
JAZZ RAGA Impulse!/1960
2. HORACE SILVER
6 PIECES OF SILVER Blue Note/1950
3. CHARLES MINGUS
MINGUS AH UM Columbia/1959
4. RED GARLAND TRIO
GROOVY Prestige/1957
5. DOROTHY ASHBY
THE JAZZ HARPIST Regent/1957

6. FREDDIE HUBBARD
THE ARTISTRY OF FREDDIE HUBBARD Impulse!/1962
7. ALBERT MANGELSDORFF
NOW, JAZZ RAMWONG Pacific Jazz/1964
8. BOBBY HUTCHERSON
HAPPENINGS Blue Note/1966
9. ART BLAKEY & THE JAZZ MESSENGERS
BUHAINA'S DELIGHT Blue Note/1961
10. JIMMY SMITH
JIMMY SMITH AT THE ORGAN Blue Note/1956

ALICE COLTRANE

JOURNEY IN SATCHIDANANDA

Featuring
PHAROAH SANDERS

STEREO AS 9203

impulse!

ALICE COLTRANE

title JOURNEY IN
SATCHIDANANDA /
year 1970 / *label* Impulse!

PAUL BRADSHAW

STRAIGHT NO CHASER

Publisher and editor Paul Bradshaw is the man behind the groundbreaking British magazine *Straight No Chaser*. From the acid jazz days in 1988 to its final issue in 2007, this magazine, with its cutting-edge graphics and exclusive features, was one of the most influential in the new jazz music scene around the world.

Der Verleger und Redakteur Paul Bradshaw ist der große Name, der sich hinter dem innovativen britischen Magazin *Straight No Chaser* verbirgt. Seit seiner Gründung bis zu seiner letzten Ausgabe im Jahr 2007 war dieses Magazin mit seiner bahnbrechenden Grafik und dem exklusiven Design eine der einflussreichsten Instanzen in der internationalen Jazzmusikszene.

Paul Bradshaw est éditeur et rédacteur en chef du révolutionnaire magazine britannique *Straight No Chaser*. Depuis l'époque de l'acid jazz en 1988 jusqu'à sa dernière édition en 2007, ce magazine au graphisme avant-gardiste et aux articles exclusifs a fait partie des grandes autorités mondiales en matière de nouveau jazz.

1. CHARLIE PARKER
JAZZ AT THE MASSEY HALL Debut/1953
2. SLIM GAILLARD
OPERA IN VOUT Mercury/1946
3. YUSEF LATEEF
LIVE AT THE 20TH MONTREUX DETROIT FESTIVAL Yal/1999
4. THELONIOUS MONK
IN EUROPE Reissue–Charly/1967
5. RAHSAAN ROLAND KIRK
VOLUNTEERED SLAVERY Atlantic/1968

6. VARIOUS ARTISTS
IMPRESSED WITH GILLES PETERSON Universal Jazz/2003
7. SUN RA
LIVE AT THE PIT-INN, TOKYO DIW/1988
8. ALICE COLTRANE
JOURNEY IN SATCHIDANANDA Impulse!/1970
9. CHARLES MINGUS
OH YEAH Atlantic/1961
10. MICHEL LE GRAND
LE GRAND JAZZ Philips/1958

DOUG CARN "REVELATION"

COMPATIBLE STEREO
4 CHANNEL QUADRAPHONIC

BJ/16

featuring the voice of **jean carn**

DOUG CARN
title "REVELATION" /
year 1973 / *label* Black Jazz

KING BRITT

King Britt has been an international ambassador of moody dance music that encompasses funk, soul, jazz, blues, beats and all things electronic since the 1980s. Under the alias of "Silkworm" he toured with hip-hop group Digable Planets before co-founding Ovum Recordings with Josh Wink. Since then he has been releasing records under band projects such as Sylk 130 and Scuba. Following commercial successes, Britt's remixing talents were called upon for a wide variety of artists such as Tori Amos, Jazzanova, and Sister Gertrude Morgan. In 2006, the King produced underscores for Michael Mann's remake of the cult 1980s TV cop drama *Miami Vice*.

King Britt ist seit den 1980ern internationaler Botschafter für Dance Music. Sein Repertoire umfasst Funk, Soul, Jazz, Blues, Beats und elektronische Musik. Bevor er zusammen mit Josh Wink das Label Ovum Recordings gründete, tourte er unter dem Namen „Silkworm" mit der Hip-Hop-Band Digable Planets. Seitdem bringt er mit verschiedenen Projekten, z.B. Sylk 130 und

Scuba, Platten heraus. Nachdem er einigen kommerziellen Erfolg erlangt hatte, weitete Britt seine Aktivitäten auf andere Musiker aus, z.B. Tori Amos, Jazzanova und Sister Gertrude Morgan. 2006 produzierte King Britt den Soundtrack für Michael Manns Remake der 80er-Kult-TV-Serie *Miami Vice*.

King Britt est depuis les années 1980 un ambassadeur international de la musique dance : du funk, soul, jazz, blues, breakbeat et de tout ce qui est électronique. C'est sous le pseudonyme de «Silkworm» qu'il est parti en tournée avec le groupe de hip-hop Digable Planets avant de fonder Ovum Recordings avec Josh Wink. Il a depuis produit Sylk 130 et Scuba. Son succès commercial l'a amené à remixer pour des artistes très différents, notamment Tori Amos, Jazzanova, ainsi que Sister Gertrude Morgan. En 2006, il a composé une partie de la musique d'ambiance de *Deux Flics à Miami*, le remake de Michael Mann de la série policière culte des années 1980.

1. DOUG CARN
"REVELATION" Black Jazz/1973
2. MILES DAVIS AND MARCUS MILLER
SIESTA WEA/1987
3. JOHN COLTRANE
A LOVE SUPREME Impulse!/1964
4. BROTHER AHH
SOUND AWARENESS Strata-East/1973
5. HERBIE HANCOCK
MWANDISHI WEA/1971

6. NANCY WILSON & CANNONBALL ADDERLEY
NANCY WILSON/CANNONBALL ADDERLEY Capitol/1962
7. YESTERDAY'S NEW QUINTET
ANGLES WITHOUT EDGES Stones Throw/2001
8. MURIEL WINSTON
A FRESH VIEWPOINT Strata-East/1974
9. NORMAN CONNORS
LOVE FROM THE SUN Buddah/1974
10. SUN RA
SPACE IS THE PLACE Impulse!/1972

COLTRANE

**JOHN COLTRANE
QUARTET**
title COLTRANE /
year 1962 / *label* Impulse!

MARK DE CLIVE-LOWE

Half-Japanese, half-New Zealander, musician and producer Mark de Clive-Lowe has been on a musical journey since starting to play piano when he was four. Classical piano lessons, jazz for playing pleasure and hip hop and soul on the stereo gave Mark the diverse foundation from which his eclectic style has developed. Performing and recording in different settings, collaborating with DJ/producers, turntablists, acoustic jazz artists, Japanese Kagura, and the world of Latin rhythms, Mark has become a major figure in the nu-jazz movement, blending jazz, ethnic music and urban grooves into a fresh 21st-century flavor.

Der Musiker und Produzent Mark de Clive-Lowe, in dessen Adern neuseeländisches und japanisches Blut fließt, begann seine Karriere mit vier Jahren am Klavier. Seine Klavierstunden, der Jazz, den er außerhalb der Unterrichtsstunden spielte, sowie Hip Hop und Soul sind die Basis für Marks vielseitigen Stil. An den verschiedensten Orten hatte er Auftritte und Aufnahmetermine, er arbeitete mit DJs, Produzenten, akustischen Jazzgitarristen,

japanischen Kagura-Musikern zusammen und lernte die Welt der Latino-Rhythmen kennen. Durch diese Bildung wurde er zu einer Hauptfigur des Nu-Jazz – er erstellt aus Jazz, ethnischer Musik und urbanen Grooves die perfekte Mischung für das 21. Jahrhundert.

Moitié Japonais, moitié Néo-zélandais, Mark de Clive-Lowe est un musicien et producteur qui a entrepris son voyage musical à l'âge de quatre ans, lorsqu'il a commencé à jouer du piano. Les leçons de piano classique, le piano jazz pour le plaisir du jeu ainsi que le hip-hop et la soul qu'il écoutait sur sa chaîne ont jeté les bases de son style éclectique. Il s'est produit et a enregistré dans différents contextes, a travaillé avec des DJ/producteurs, des platinistes, des musiciens de jazz acoustique, des danseurs de Kagura et dans le monde des rythmes latins. Figure importante du mouvement de nu-jazz, et son mélange de jazz, de musiques ethniques et de groove urbain apporte au genre un nouveau parfum très contemporain.

1. AHMAD JAMAL
THE AWAKENING Impulse!/1970
2. CÉSAR CAMARGO MARIANO
SÃO PAULO – BRASIL RCA Brazil/1978
3. MILES DAVIS
NEFERTITI Columbia /Legacy/1968
4. WAYNE SHORTER
NATIVE DANCER Columbia/1974
5. HERBIE HANCOCK
FLOOD Columbia/1975

6. MILES DAVIS
LIVE EVIL Columbia/1970
7. JOHN COLTRANE QUARTET
COLTRANE Impulse!/1962
8. WEATHER REPORT
BLACKMARKET Columbia/1976
9. KEITH JARRETT
THE SURVIVOR'S SUITE ECM/1976
10. MCCOY TYNER
THE REAL MCCOY Blue Note/1967

STRATA-EAST
SES 19737 8
STEREO

THE FIFTH OF THE DOLPHY SERIES

**CLIFFORD JORDAN
QUARTET**
title GLASS BEAD GAMES /
year 1974 / *label* Strata-East

KYOTO JAZZ MASSIVE

Shuya and Yoshihiro Okino began their DJ career in the late '80s in Kyoto. Like so many other Jazz DJs, they were greatly affected by the Rare Groove movement in London. During the peak of Acid Jazz, many international DJs and artists performed in Japan. There they met many influential people including Paul Bradshaw from the magazine *Straight No Chaser* and Gilles Peterson. Their unit name came about when Gilles had mentioned Shuya and Yoshi in the *Chaser* article calling them the Kyoto Jazz Massive. Their sound is often associated with Jazz Fusion. They were certainly influenced by Japanese Jazz musicians, such as Terumasa Hino, Teruo Nakamura, and Ryo Kawasaki.

Die DJ-Karriere von Shuya und Yoshihiro Okino begann im Kyoto der späten 1980er. Zu Beginn wurde das Paar vor allem vom Londoner Rare Groove geprägt. In den besten Zeiten des Acid Jazz, in denen der Einfluss internationaler DJs in Japan stetig wuchs, arbeiteten Shuya und Yoshihiro mit Größen wie Paul Bradshaw vom britischen Magazin *Straight No Chaser* und DJ Gilles Peterson.

Gilles nannte Shuya and Yoshihiro in einem *Chaser*-Artikel einmal „Kyoto Jazz Massive" – somit gab er dem DJ-Paar seinen Namen. Der Sound des Kyoto Jazz Massive wird häufig mit Jazz-Fusion umschrieben. Natürlich ist auch der Einfluss japanischer Jazzmusiker deutlich erkennbar – als wichtigste Namen sind hier Terumasa Hino, Teruo Nakamura und Ryo Kawasaki zu nennen.

Shuya et Yoshihiro Okino ont commencé leur carrière de DJ à Kyoto vers la fin des années 1980. Grâce à l'afflux de DJ et d'artistes internationaux qui sont arrivés au Japon pendant les grandes heures de l'acid jazz, Shuya et Yoshihiro ont rencontré les porte-flambeaux Paul Bradshaw du magazine britannique *Straight No Chaser* et le DJ Gilles Peterson. Ils prirent le nom de Kyoto Jazz Massive à la suite d'un article paru dans *Chaser*, où Gilles s'était référé à Shuya et Yoshihiro dans ces termes. Le son de Kyoto Jazz Massive est souvent associé au jazz fusion. Ils ont certainement été influencés par le jazz japonais, comme Terumasa Hino, Teruo Nakamura et Ryo Kawasaki.

1. FREDDIE HUBBARD
HUB-TONES Blue Note/1962
2. JOE HENDERSON
IN AND OUT Blue Note/1964
3. CLIFFORD JORDAN QUARTET
GLASS BEAD GAMES Strata-East/1974
4. WELDON IRVINE
LIBERATED BROTHER Nodlew Music/1972
5. HERBIE MANN & BOBBY JASPAR
FLUTE FLIGHT Prestige/1957

6. KENNY DORHAM
AFRO CUBAN Blue Note/1955
7. BLACK RENAISSANCE
BODY, MIND AND SPIRIT Baystate/ Luv N' Haight/2002
8. LARRY RIDLEY
SUM OF THE PARTS Strata-East/1975
9. LEE MORGAN
THE SIDEWINDER Blue Note/1963
10. LARRY YOUNG
UNITY Blue Note/1965

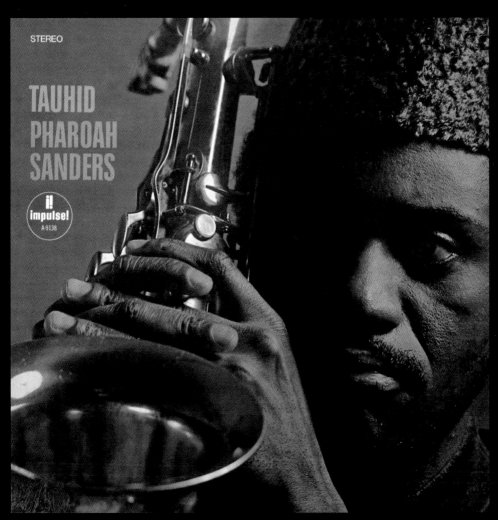

STEREO

TAUHID
PHAROAH
SANDERS

i!
impulse!
A-9138

PHAROAH SANDERS
title TAUHID / *year* 1966 /
label Impulse!

MICHAEL MCFADDEN

UBIQUITY RECORDS

After visiting San Francisco on their honeymoon and falling in love with the city, DJs Jody and Michael McFadden went home to Southern California, sold most of their possessions, and moved to San Francisco with a fuzzy dream of starting a record company. They invested the last of their savings into a business that would combine their passion for music with providing an income to live on, and opened the Groove Merchant record store on Haight Street in early 1990. Within a year the small shop had built a reputation the world over as a place to find rare records and learn about new sounds. In 1993 the company incorporated as Ubiquity Records and has since grown into a company with several imprints and over 100 releases.

Bei ihrer Hochzeitsreise verliebten sich die DJs Jody und Michael McFadden in die Stadt San Francisco. Sie lösten ihren Haushalt in Südkalifornien auf und zogen nach San Francisco, um ihren Traum, die Gründung eines Plattenlabels, zu verwirklichen. Ihre letzten Ersparnisse investierten sie in ein Geschäft, mit dem sie ihrer Musik-

leidenschaft frönen und sich ein regelmäßiges Einkommen sichern konnten, und eröffneten in den frühen 1990ern den Plattenladen Groove Merchant in der Haight Street. Innerhalb eines Jahres hatte der Laden einen weltweiten Ruf erlangt. Er gilt als Ort, an dem man seltene Platten finden und sich über neue Sounds informieren kann. 1993 wurde die Gesellschaft Ubiquity Records ins Leben gerufen.

Les DJ Jody et Michael McFadden ont visité San Francisco pendant leur lune de miel. Tombés amoureux de la ville, ils s'y sont installés en rêvant de créer une maison de disques. Au début des années 1990, ils ont ouvert le magasin de disque Groove Merchant sur Haight Street. En un an, le petit magasin s'était forgé une réputation de classe mondiale pour les disques rares et les nouveaux sons. En 1993, l'entreprise a été constituée sous le nom d'Ubiquity Records et s'est depuis agrandie par le biais de plusieurs filiales et d'un réseau de distribution mondial. Elle a plus de 100 albums à son actif. Au cours de la dernière décennie, Ubiquity est devenue une véritable référence.

1. KOOL & THE GANG
KOOL JAZZ De-Lite/1974
2. IVAN BOOGALOO JOE JONES
SWEETBACK Luv N'Haight/1995
3. CHARLES MINGUS
BLUES AND ROOTS Atlantic/1959
4. YUSEF LATEEF
BEFORE DAWN Verve/1957
5. KENNY DORHAM
AFRO CUBAN Blue Note/1955

6. PHAROAH SANDERS
TAUHID Impulse!/1966
7. GIL SCOTT-HERON
REFLECTIONS Arista/1981
8. DONALD BYRD
PLACES & SPACES Blue Note/1975
9. CAL TJADER & EDDIE PALMIERI
EL SONIDO NUEVO Verve/1966
10. ROY AYERS
MYSTIC VOYAGE Polydor/1975

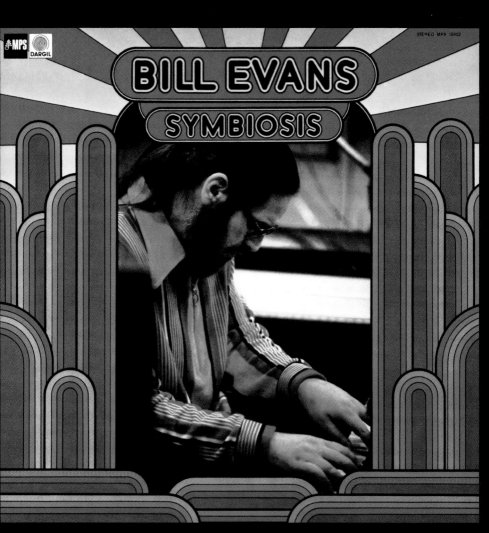

BILL EVANS

title SYMBIOSIS / *year* 1974 /
label MPS

ED MOTTA

Ed Motta is an internationally acclaimed singer, musician, composer, D.J, writer, scholar and prolific record collector. A nephew of Tim Maia, the 'Father of Brazilian Soul' music, Motta grew up listening to soul, funk and disco in his native Rio de Janeiro. After experimenting with various styles, he released the dance music album, *Manual Pratico para Festas, Bailes e Afins, Vol. 1* (Universal, 1997). Motta has performed with such jazz luminaries as Roy Ayers, Eddie Gomez and Bernard Purdie. His 2006 Latin Grammy Award-nominated album *Aystelum* (Beleza/Trama) showcased Motta's incredible ability to blend jazz with Latin sounds and Música Popular Brasileira.

Ed Motta hat sich als Sänger, Musiker, Komponist, D.J, Songwriter, Wissenschaftler und Plattensammler einen internationalen Namen gemacht. Als Neffe von Tim Maia, dem ,Vater des brasilianischen Soul', wuchs Motta in seiner Heimatstadt Rio de Janeiro mit Musik in den Ohren auf. Nachdem er mit verschiedenen Stilen herumexperimentiert hatte, brachte Motta das Dance-Music-Album *Manual Pratico para Festas, Bailes e Afins, Vol. 1* (Universal 1997) heraus. Motta trat mit Jazzgrößen wie Roy Ayers, Eddie Gomez und Bernard Purdie auf. Mit seinem im Jahre 2006 mit dem Latin Grammy Award nominierten Album *Aystelum* (Beleza/Trama) beweist Motta sein Talent, Jazz mit Latin-Sounds und Música Popular Brasileira zu vereinen.

Ed Motta est chanteur applaudi dans le monde entier, musicien, compositeur, D.J, écrivain, chercheur et grand collectionneur de disques. Neveu de Tim Maia, le «père de la soul brésilienne», il a grandi en écoutant de la soul, du funk et de la disco à Rio de Janeiro. Après avoir expérimenté différents styles, il a réalisé son album de dance *Manual Pratico para Festas, Bailes e Afins, Vol. 1* (Universal, 1997). Il s'est produit avec des sommités du jazz de l'envergure de Roy Ayres, Eddie Gomez et Bernard Purdie. Son album *Aystelum* (Beleza/Trama, 2006), nommé aux prix Latin Grammy, montre son talent pour mélanger le jazz, les sons latins et la Música Popular Brasileira.

1. ANDREW HILL
POINT OF DEPARTURE Blue Note/1964
2. MUSIC INC.
MUSIC INC. & BIG BAND Strata-East/1971
3. CHARLES MINGUS
PRE-BIRD Mercury/1960
4. BOBBY HUTCHERSON
NOW! Blue Note/1969
5. WOODY SHAW
ROSEWOOD Columbia/1977
6. STAN KENTON
NEW CONCEPTS OF ARTISTRY IN RHYTHM Capitol/1952
7. JACKIE & ROY
A WILDER ALIAS CTI/1974
8. BILL EVANS
SYMBIOSIS MPS/1974
9. ARCHIE SHEPP
ATTICA BLUES Impulse!/1972
10. SUN RA
SUPER-SONIC JAZZ Saturn/1956

HARLEM BUSH MUSIC UHURU GARY BARTZ NTU TROOP

Milestone
M

Stereo ✛
MX 9032

GARY BARTZ
title HARLEM BUSH MUSIC /
year 1970 / *label* Milestone

NICK THE RECORD

DJ Friendly is the home of Nick Girdwood (aka Nick the Record), legendary record dealer based in Brighton, UK. The label covers hip hop, jazz, soul, funk, breaks, reggae, soundtracks, spoken word, and several other genres. With a staggering collection in excess of 60,000 records, Nick has gained a reputation with DJs, collectors and producers around the world. After hours, Nick is also part of Soul Ascendants, a production duo releasing a blend of nu-jazz, afrobeat deep house on the London-based Nuphonic label.

Nick Girdwood (alias Nick the Record), der in Brighton ansässige legendäre Plattenhändler, wohnt in einer sehr DJ-freundlichen Stadt. Sein Sortiment bietet Hip Hop, Jazz, Soul, Funk, Break, Reggae, Soundtracks, Hörbücher und eine Reihe weiterer Genres. Nicks Plattensammlung, die mehr als 60.000 Exemplare umfasst, ist unter DJs, Sammlern und Produzenten in der ganzen Welt berühmt. Nach Geschäfts-

schluss kümmert sich Nick um seine Produktionsfirma Soul Ascendants, die er zusammen mit einem Partner führt und die eine spannende Mischung aus Nu-Jazz, Afrobeat und Deep auf dem Londoner Label Nuphonic herausgibt.

DJ Friendly est le repaire de Nick Girdwood (également connu sous le nom de Nick the Record), marchand de disques légendaire basé à Brighton, en Angleterre. Hip-hop, jazz, soul, funk, breakbeat, reggae, musiques de film et poésie orale ne sont que quelques-uns des genres que l'on trouve chez lui. Avec une collection stupéfiante de 60 000 disques, Nick s'est imposé auprès des DJ, des collectionneurs et des producteurs du monde entier. Il appartient également à Soul Ascendants, un duo de production qui verse dans un mélange de nu-jazz et de deep house afrobeat et qui opère chez le label londonien Nuphonic.

1. DOUG HAMMOND
REFLECTIONS IN THE SEA OF NURNEN Tribe/1975
2. SUN RA
SLEEPING BEAUTY Saturn/1980
3. LONDON JAZZ FOUR
SONG FOR HILARY Polydor 45/1967
4. MARY LOU WILLIAMS
MARY LOU'S MASS Smithsonian Folkways/1975
5. JAMES TATUM
CONTEMPORARY JAZZ + MASS VOL. 1 JTTP/1987

6. JOKI FREUND SEXTET
YOGI JAZZ CBS/1964
7. GARY BARTZ
HARLEM BUSH MUSIC Milestone/1970
8. MULATU ASTATKE
MULATU OF ETHIOPIA Soundway/2005
9. SHAMEK FARRAH
FIRST IMPRESSIONS Strata-East/1974
10. SAHIB SHIHAB
SAHIB SHIHAB & THE DANISH RADIO JAZZ GROUP Oktav/1965

GILLES PETERSON

Brought up among the South London suburban soul scene in the early '80s, Gilles Peterson's passion for music inspired him to set up his own makeshift radio transmitter – literally an aerial suspended between a tree and a phone box. A quarter of a century later, he is one of the world's most cutting-edge and eclectic club and radio DJs. In the late 1980s, he was instrumental in establishing the acid jazz scene, setting up a label with the same name. Since 1998, Gilles has been "joining the musical dots" with his BBC Radio show Worldwide. Recently, Gilles set up a new record label, Brownswood Recordings, to sign and develop exciting new talent.

Gilles Peterson, der in den frühen 1980ern in die Südlondoner Vorstadt-Soulszene eingeführt wurde, bastelte sich aus Leidenschaft zur Musik seinen eigenen Funksender, dessen Außenantenne zwischen einem Baum und einer Telefonzelle aufgehängt war. Ein Vierteljahrhundert später ist Peterson zu einem der innovativsten und vielseitigsten Club- und Radio-DJs gewor-

den. In den späten 1980ern wirkte er maßgeblich bei der Bildung der Acid-Jazz-Szene mit, indem er ein Plattenlabel mit eben diesem Namen gründete. Seit 1998 hat Gilles seine eigene Radiosendung auf BBC, „Worldwide" unter dem Motto „joining the musical dots". Unlängst gründete er ein neues Label, Brownswood Recordings, das aufregende neue Talente herausbringt.

Gilles Peterson a grandi entouré de soul dans la banlieue de Londres au début des années 1980, et sa passion pour la musique l'a poussé à fabriquer son propre émetteur de radio de fortune, une simple antenne suspendue entre un arbre et une cabine téléphonique. Vingt-cinq ans plus tard, il est l'un des DJ de radio et de club les plus avant-gardistes et les plus éclectiques au monde. Vers la fin des années 1980, il a joué un rôle essentiel dans la consolidation de l'acid jazz en créant un label portant ce même nom. Gilles a récemment créé une nouvelle maison de disques, Brownswood Recordings, pour engager et faire grandir les nouveaux talents intéressants.

1. WAYNE SHORTER
SPEAK NO EVIL Blue Note/1964
2. PAUL HORN
IMPRESSIONS OF CLEOPATRA Columbia/1963
3. MARY LOU WILLIAMS
BLACK CHRIST OF THE ANDES MPS/1963
4. MARK MURPHY
RAH Riverside/1961
5. DEE DEE BRIDGEWATER
AFRO BLUE Trio/1974

6. MOACIR SANTOS
COISAS Forma/1965
7. ART BLAKEY
ANTHENAGIN Prestige/1973
8. HAROLD LAND
THE PEACE MAKER Cadet/1967
9. DONALD BYRD
A NEW PERSPECTIVE Blue Note/1963
10. PHAROAH SANDERS
THEMBI Impulse!/1970

Charles Tolliver/Bobby Hutcherson/Cecil McBee/Billy Higgins

STEREO
THE FINEST IN JAZZ SINCE 1939
84218 BLUE NOTE

Jackie
McLean
ACTION
ACTION
ACTION

JACKIE MCLEAN
title ACTION ACTION ACTION /
year 1964 / *label* Blue Note

GERALD SHORT

JAZZMAN

Gerald Short, aka Jazzman, is one of the foremost tastemakers in the reissue scene today. He was early to the UK funk and soul game in the early 1990s, first as a collector, then dealer, DJ and label head. This was a natural progression for him, which brought him in contact with an immense variety of music. In response to growing demand for rare wax treasures, he founded a variety of sub-labels for different styles. They include Funk45, Jazzman and Stark Reality, named after the infamous album led by Monty Stark on AJP.

Gerald Short alias Jazzman gräbt alte Platten aus und gibt sie neu auf Vinyl heraus – damit hat er die aktuelle DJ- und Sammlerszene maßgeblich geprägt. Er war früh Teil der britischen Soul- und Funkszene der 1990er, zuerst als Sammler, dann als Verkäufer und schließlich als DJ und Label-Chef. Für Short war diese Entwicklung, durch die er seine Musikkenntnisse aufs Unermessliche erweiterte, nur natürlich. Als Reaktion auf die wachsende Nachfrage nach seltenen Wachspressungen gründete er eine Reihe von Sub-Labels für verschiedene Richtungen. Darunter findet man Funk45, Jazzman und Stark Reality. Letzteres wurde nach dem berüchtigten, auf AJP herausgekommenen Album von Monty Stark benannt.

Gerald Short, également connu sous le nom de Jazzman, est l'un des plus grands faiseurs de tendances dans le domaine actuel des rééditions. Il est arrivé au début de l'engouement funk et soul en Grande-Bretagne dans les années 1990, tout d'abord en tant que collectionneur, puis vendeur, DJ et directeur de label. C'était pour lui une progression naturelle, qui l'a mis en contact avec une musique immensément variée. Pour répondre à la demande croissante de trésors rares en vinyle, il a fondé plusieurs sous-labels pour différents styles, notamment Funk45, Jazzman et Stark Reality, baptisé en hommage à l'album que Monty Stark avait sorti chez AJP.

1. PHILIP COHRAN & THE ARTISTIC HERITAGE ENSEMBLE
ON THE BEACH Aestuarium/1968
2. CLARKE-BOLAND SEXTET
MUSIC FOR THE SMALL HOURS EMI/1965
3. DON RENDELL
DUSK FIRE Columbia/1966
4. SAHIB SHIHAB
COMPANIONSHIP Vogue/1965
5. PRISMA MUSIC UNIT
S/T Sono Cairo/1973

6. EAST NEW YORK ENSEMBLE DE MUSIC
AT THE HELM Folkways/1974
7. DUKE ELLINGTON
LATIN AMERICAN SUITE Fantasy/1968
8. MILES DAVIS
KIND OF BLUE Columbia/1959
9. JOHN COLTRANE
GIANT STEPS Atlantic/1959
10. JACKIE MCLEAN
ACTION ACTION ACTION Blue Note/1964

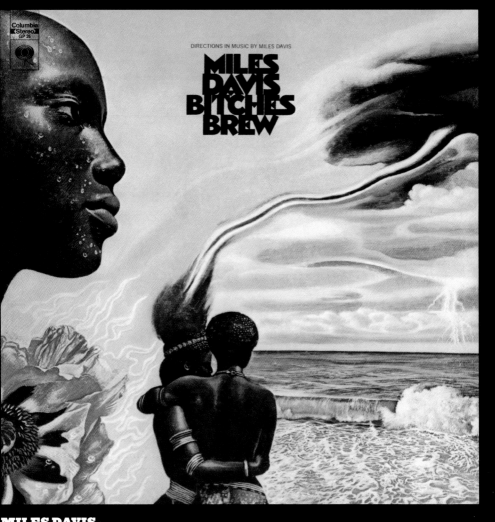

DIRECTIONS IN MUSIC BY MILES DAVIS

MILES
DAVIS
BITCHES
BREW

Columbia
Stereo
GP 26

MILES DAVIS
title BITCHES BREW /
year 1969 / *label* Columbia

ANDRE TORRES

WAX POETICS

Andre Torres is the Editor-in-Chief of *Wax Poetics*, an influential quarterly magazine focusing on hip hop, soul, jazz, and funk records; the technological and innovative aspects of sampling and production and the historical context of DJing. As its name indicates, *Wax Poetics* is all about beat digging: the search for dusty, jazzy and funky vinyl.

Andre Torres ist Chefredakteur von *Wax Poetics*, einem einflussreichen, vierteljährlich erscheinenden Magazin, das sich einerseits mit Hip-Hop-, Soul-, Jazz- und Funk-Platten, andererseits mit den technologischen und innovativen Aspekten des Sampelns, Produzierens sowie den histori-schen Zusammenhängen der DJ-Tätigkeit befasst. Wie der Name schon sagt, geht es in *Wax Poetics* vor allem um das „Digging": die Suche nach staubigen, jazzigen und funkigen Vinylplatten.

Andre Torres est le rédacteur en chef de *Wax Poetics*, un magazine trimestriel qui fait autorité dans les domaines des disques de hip-hop, de soul, de jazz et de funk, les aspects technologiques et innovateurs du sampling et de la production et le contexte historique de l'activité de DJ. Comme son nom l'indique, *Wax Poetics* est avant tout une affaire de fouille des bacs à disques et de quête de vinyles jazzy et funky oubliés.

1. MILES DAVIS
BITCHES BREW Columbia/1969
2. MARC MOULIN
BALL OF EYES CBS/1971
3. DUKE ELLINGTON
SUCH SWEET THUNDER Columbia/1957
4. MUSTAFA OZKENT
GENCLIK ILE ELELE Finders Keepers/2006
5. NATHAN DAVIS
IF Tomorrow International/1976

6. DOUG CARN
ADAMS APPLE Black Jazz/1975
7. LES MCCANN
LAYERS Atlantic/1973
8. EERO KOIVISTOINEN MUSIC SOCIETY
WAHOO Warner Music, Finland/1972
9. ERIC DOLPHY
OUT TO LUNCH! Blue Note/1964
10. MARTIAL SOLAL
LOCOMOTION PSI/1974

SUN RA
LANQUIDITY

SUN RA
title LANQUIDITY /
year 1978 / *label* Philly Jazz

RAINER TRÜBY

Rainer Trüby is a former member of Germany's internationally renowned Compost Records project A Forest Mighty Black from Freiburg in the Black Forest. Digging in the vaults of his huge record collection he compiled the fantastic and still in-demand European fusion compilations *Glücklich (Volumes I–V)*. Following on from A Forest Mighty Black, Trüby created his own project on Compost called Trüby Trio, fusing together jazz, Brazilian, house, boogie and downbeat. Rainer Trüby is also a globally known DJ. When he's not on the road, you can find him at the turntables in his own legendary club-night "Root Down" in Freiburg, crossing the boundaries between retro and future jazz, funky beats, deep house, Brazilian, downtempo beats, drum & bass and contemporary electronic music

Rainer Trüby ist ehemaliges Mitglied des weltweit berühmten Freiburger Compost-Record-Projekts A Forest Mighty Black. Aus den Tiefen seiner riesigen Plattensammlung holte er die schönsten Schätze hervor, um sie auf seinen fantastischen, immer noch gefragten Fusion-Compilations *Glücklich (Volumes I–V)* zu veröffentlichen. Nach A Forest Mighty Black rief Trüby ein eigenes Projekt ins Leben. Trüby Trio veröffentlicht bei Compost einen bestechenden Mix aus Jazz, Brazilian, House, Boogie und Downbeat. Wenn er nicht gerade unterwegs ist, findet man Trüby an den Plattentellern im Freiburger „Waldsee", wo er seine eigene Clubreihe „Root Down" ins Leben gerufen hat.

Rainer Trüby est un ancien membre du projet allemand à la renommée internationale de Compost Records, A Forest Mighty Black, de Fribourg dans la Forêt-Noire. Suite à A Forest Mighty Black, il a créé son propre projet chez Compost, appelé Trüby Trio. Ce groupe opère une fusion entre le jazz, la musique brésilienne, la house, le boogie et le downbeat. Rainer Trüby est également un DJ de niveau international. Lorsqu'il n'est pas sur la route, on peut le trouver derrière les platines dans son club légendaire «Root Down» à Fribourg. Il y traverse les frontières entre le jazz rétro et le nu, les rythmes funky, la deep house, la musique brésilienne, les rythmes downtempo, le drum & bass et la musique électronique contemporaine.

1. DOM UM ROMÃO
SPIRIT OF THE TIMES Muse/1973
2. HAROLD LAND QUINTET
THE PEACE MAKER Cadet/1967
3. MARK MURPHY
MIDNIGHT MOOD Saba/1970
4. MARY LOU WILLIAMS
ZONING Mary Records/1974
5. AHMAD JAMAL
JAMALCA 20th Century/1974

6. NATHAN DAVIS
HAPPY GIRL Saba/1965
7. SUN RA
LANQUIDITY Philly Jazz/1978
8. TUBBY HAYES
DOWN IN THE VILLAGE Fontana/1963
9. HORACE SILVER
TOKYO BLUES Blue Note/1962
10. GEORGE DUKE
THE INNER SOURCE MPS/1971

INDEX

ARTIST, LABEL, DESIGN, ART, AD, PHOTO